# THE 2ND BATTALION ROYAL BERKSHIRE REGIMENT
## IN WORLD WAR ONE

# THE 2ND BATTALION ROYAL BERKSHIRE REGIMENT

## IN WORLD WAR ONE

### The China Dragon's Tales

*With best wishes*
*Ian Cull.*

## IAN CULL

In Association with the Royal Gloucestershire,
Berkshire and Wiltshire Regimental Museum

With contributions from
John Chapman
Martin McIntyre
Len Webb

TEMPUS

First published 2005

Tempus Publishing Limited
The Mill, Brimscombe Port,
Stroud, Gloucestershire, GL5 2QG
www.tempus-publishing.com

British Library Cataloguing in Publication Data.
A catalogue record for this book is available from the British Library.

ISBN 0 7524 3571 X
Typesetting and origination by Tempus Publishing Limited
Printed in Great Britain

# CONTENTS

# LIST OF MAPS

# AUTHOR'S NOTES AND ACKNOWLEDGEMENTS

This book has proved more challenging to produce than our previous books covering the 1st Battalion, and the 5th, 6th and 8th (Service) Battalions of the Royal Berkshire Regiment. Possibly because the battalion had been stationed overseas since before the turn of the century, the 'old sweats' had lost the habit of writing home, for there are comparatively few surviving letters or personal diaries from the 2nd Battalion. Additionally, the official documents – the Battalion War Diary, for example – are terse and laconic. A day of fighting might simply be recorded as 'in action' whereas the other battalions wrote pages of descriptive prose. Furthermore, the 2nd Battalion suffered far higher casualties than the others, and was virtually wiped out on three separate occasions, costing the lives of many potential diarists or correspondents.

For this reason, more reliance has had to be placed on secondary sources. A history of the 8th Division, written by Lieutenant-Colonel Boraston and Captain Bax in 1926, has been particularly useful, as has *The Last of the Ebb* by Captain Rogerson, who witnessed the Aisne débâcle in May 1918. The best source, though, has been *The Land-Locked Lake*, the wartime memoirs of Lieutenant-Colonel Hanbury-Sparrow, who served with the battalion for much of the war, both as a company commander and adjutant, and then went on to command the battalion during most of the third Ypres campaign.

Work on the book would not have been possible without the help and support of David Chilton, the curator, together with his staff and volunteers at the regimental museum in Salisbury. The museum's archives contain many documents and photographs pertaining to the period, and by allowing us unrestricted access to this source, long forgotten incidents have come to light. David has also accompanied us on battlefield visits, where his skills at map-reading and navigation have been invaluable.

Thanks are due to the staff at the National Archives at Kew, who have assisted Len Webb with his extensive trawl through the war diaries of the 8th Division, 25th Brigade, 2nd Royal Berkshires, and numerous other units who fought alongside the Berkshires at various times, together with medal rolls, *London Gazette* citations, and other relevant documents.

Many relatives of men who fought with the Berkshires have generously allowed us access to the fruits of their own research, especially Andy King and Harry Angier.

Special thanks are due to Ian Durham and his wife, who live on the Aisne. Ian is conducting his own research into the May 1918 battle, and freely gave his time to guide us around the area where the Berkshires fought. He also supplied information from German and French sources which we would otherwise have been unaware of, while his wife supplied us with an excellent lunch.

# FOREWORD

Most of the battalions which went out to face the German onslaught in August 1914 were a mixture of regulars on home duty and reservists called back to the Colours. The 8th Division, amongst whose numbers were the 2nd Royal Berkshire Regiment, was quite a different sort of fighting force. These were hardened professionals recalled from guarding the Empire. They found themselves in a kind of war no one could have imagined. Trench warfare was utterly unlike anything they had ever trained for. They faced weather conditions they had grown unaccustomed to and brought back tropical diseases for which there were no cures in France.

The 2nd Royal Berkshires were blooded at Neuve Chapelle and lost nearly a third of their strength in one go. They repeated the exercise on the first day of the Somme at Ovillers, this time losing about half their strength, and were virtually wiped out when the Germans attacked unexpectedly when they were resting near the Aisne in spring 1918.

Despite all these setbacks and many more, the battalion never lost its spirit and never forgot the traditions of the Royal Berkshire Regiment in general and the 66th Foot in particular. They created many of the 'golden threads' which make the regimental spirit such a vital part of the British Army. This book covers a few short years between 1911 and 1919, showing the battalion at its best. It is published at a time when its successor, the Royal Gloucestershire, Berkshire and Wiltshire Regiment, is due to be subsumed into a larger formation within the Light Division. Let us hope this book helps to preserve the memory of a great regiment.

General Sir Kevin O'Donoghue KCB, CBE
Colonel, the Royal Gloucestershire, Berkshire and Wiltshire Regiment

# I

# INDIA

In 1914 Britain had forty-eight infantry battalions stationed in India. Although this was the equivalent of four divisions, the battalions were stationed all over the Indian Empire, which included modern Pakistan and Bangladesh as well as India. The officers and men of the 2nd Battalion, Royal Berkshire Regiment had moved to India in 1909, after transferring from Egypt.

Following the Cardwell army reforms in the 1880s, when the majority of the regiments were restructured into two battalions, it became the practice for one battalion to remain in a home posting, while the other served abroad. After a few years, the foreign service battalion would return home, and it would be the other battalion's turn to serve abroad.

A new recruit would first undergo his basic training at the regimental depot, which in the Royal Berkshire's case was situated at Brock Barracks, Oxford Road, Reading. Once he had taken the oath, he would remain at the depot for two or three months, during which time he would be taught how to take care of his kit, and learn to march and parade in a soldierly fashion. When his sergeant judged that he had reached a standard that would not be an embarrassment to the regiment, he would be sent to join the home service battalion. The Royal Berkshire's 1st Battalion was serving at Aldershot in 1914, and the recruit would expect to spend the next two years with them, gaining his marksman's badge, taking part in manoeuvres, and becoming physically fit and disciplined through regular parades, route marches and sport.

At last, he would be warned for foreign service. Each year, about 150 men in the overseas battalion would be reaching the end of their seven-year period of service. A draft to replace them would be made up from the home service battalion, who, after home leave, would embark on a troopship. The same ship would usually bring home the time-expired men, who would report to the depot. They would then be eligible to join the reserve battalion, and be released to take up a civilian occupation. A reservist could, however, be recalled to the Colours in the event of a national emergency for up to twelve years after first joining. A man who wished to make a career of the army, and had a record of good conduct, could opt to remain on active service, and many signed on for a further period after their twelve years had expired.

Regular soldiers who have left memoirs confessed that their reason for joining the army was to see something of the world, and India was a favourite posting. Unless the whole battalion was ordered elsewhere during his stay with them, the man could expect to spend up to five years in the country. The newly posted man would have noticed a marked contrast to his life in Aldershot. His meagre pay, which put him on the lower rungs of society in Britain, suddenly went a lot further. The troops had sufficient funds for eight or nine of them to club together and employ a servant to look after their kit, do their laundry and keep the barracks swept, relieving them of the more onerous tasks on home service. The men remained responsible for the care and maintenance of their weapons, however, and it was strictly forbidden to delegate this task to a servant. Food was very cheap, and rations could be supplemented by luxuries purchased in the bazaars, or from vendors who traded in the camps.

During the hottest times of the year, the men would rise before dawn so that parades, training sessions or sports could take place before the heat became intolerable, and then they could spend the afternoons on their cots in barracks. The companies would take it in turns to move to the nearest hill station for a couple of weeks, so everybody had a chance to relax in the cooler climate.

Despite these precautions, malaria was rife, together with other tropical diseases such as enteric fever. Deaths from cholera were not unusual, and Private Herbert Garlick, of Kintbury, who recorded his service with the battalion in his memoirs, currently lodged at Newbury museum, describes a curious method of detecting its presence: 'The air was very thick with Choloria [*sic*] we attached pieces of beef to lanterns, which when it goes up in the air is red. If Choloria is in the air the beef when pulled down will be black: if it is black no one should go that direction or they are liable to catch it.' Garlick and his comrades believed that cholera could be caught from invisible clouds. The breakthrough in public health in London during the previous century, when it was established that cholera was spread by contaminated drinking water, did not seem to have penetrated to the outposts of the empire.

Apart from the climate and health, the biggest problem was boredom. British India at the time was generally peaceful, with the exception of the North West Frontier, and in any case the main burden of defence was undertaken by the Indian Army, with the Imperial troops providing back-up during major campaigns, or to assist the civil powers in the event of local unrest. For much of the time there was little to do apart from training, sports, sentry duty and parades.

Lord Kitchener, Commander in Chief, India, instituted an annual competition between all the infantry battalions in India, in which they were awarded points for route-marching, musketry and other military skills. Frank Richards, who was serving in the Royal Welch Fusiliers, describes the exercise in his book, *Old Soldier Sahib*:

> The only men who did not take part were the hospital cases. About 900 of us paraded in fighting order, and each man was issued with so many rounds of ammunition and so many squares of lead that fitted into the pouches. The squares of lead represented more rounds of ammunition, bringing the total weight up to the equivalent of one hundred and fifty rounds. Each man was also issued with iron rations, which was all the food he got that day, consisting of four army biscuits, a tin of compressed soup and three blocks of chocolate. The test consisted of a fifteen mile march followed by an advance for a mile in skirmishing order to targets dotted here and there in the jungle. As soon as the targets were spotted we had to find our own range and open fire. The advance was made by short, sharp rushes, and at a given signal all firing ceased, whether we had expended our ammunition or not. After an imaginary charge at the targets there was a retirement back to the spot where the water carts were, a mile away. We were then given one hour's rest, during which we lit fires and boiled up water for our soup and chocolate. When the hour was up we marched back fifteen miles to the starting point, which was three miles from barracks. Before the battalion arrived back in barracks they had all done thirty-eight miles since morning.

Points were awarded by umpires for marksmanship and for the effectiveness of the mock battle, but deducted for anyone who fell out on the march. Lord Kitchener presented a cup to the winning battalion each year, but there is no mention in the Regimental Journal of the 2nd Royal Berkshires winning it during their stay in India.

When the 2nd Royal Berkshires first arrived in India they were stationed in Meerut, 30 miles north east of Delhi, and as such formed part of the Delhi garrison. They were

Soldiers of the 2nd Battalion practise trench digging during the Kitchener tests.

still there in 1911, the year of the Great Delhi Durbar, which meant that they were to play a major role in the arrangements.

The Durbar was a ceremony to mark the coronation of King George V as Emperor of India. There had been an earlier Durbar, in 1903, for King Edward VII, but on that occasion the monarch had been represented by the Viceroy. In 1911, the King was to attend in person, accompanied by Queen Mary. The rulers of the many Indian states and protectorates attended, and vied with each other to have the most impressive entourage together with magnificent pavilions to house them in.

The royal party spent ten days in Delhi, arriving on 7 December 1911. The Berkshires supplied part of the guard of honour at Delhi station, under Colour Sergeant Farmer, and then mounted guard at the marble throne at Delhi Fort for the next two days while their Imperial Majesties received the Indian dignitaries. The coronation took place on 12 December, with a ceremonial procession which stretched over 6 miles. The next day, the 13th, there was a royal garden party, and the battalion was given the task of erecting the marquees and setting out hundreds of tables and chairs for the occasion.

So far as the army was concerned, the most important event occurred on the following day, with a royal review of the troops. It must have been an impressive sight, for 48,000 men and 12,000 animals marched or trotted past the saluting base. The 2nd Royal Berkshires marched with the 1st Seaforth Highlanders and the 3rd King's Royal Rifle Brigade. After the march-past, the infantry formed up in divisions 400 yards in front of the royal box, with the cavalry on either flank. As the massed bands played *The British Grenadiers*, they advanced 200 yards towards the King, halted, and then the Royal Horse Artillery galloped up from either side, unlimbered, and came into action. The massed ranks then gave three cheers for Their Majesties, and the artillery fired a royal salute of 101 guns as the royal party withdrew.

The march past at the Delhi Durbar 1911, with the 2nd Battalion nearest the camera.

A special medal, the Delhi Durbar Medal 1911, was struck. Over 26,000 were issued, to recognise the enormous efforts of preparation, rehearsals, drills and practices which both military and civilian personnel had undertaken to make it a success. The official distribution was six per battalion, going to the commanding officer, the adjutant, the RSM, senior sergeant, senior corporal and the longest serving private. However, the 2nd Royal Berkshires managed to collect 142 medals, presumably because of the extra work which had fallen to them as part of the Delhi garrison. Their names are listed in Appendix 8; six officers, twelve warrant officers or sergeants, thirty-six junior NCOs, eighty-six privates and six drummers or bandsmen received the medal.

The battalion returned to Meerut, which must have seemed very dull after all the pomp and ceremony, and went back to the routine of training and manoeuvres. They were stationed there for another year before a warning order was received that the Berkshires would henceforth be stationed at Jhansi, some 200 miles to the south of Delhi. A detachment of four officers and 200 other ranks was to be located at Nowgong, some 70 miles away to the east. The battalion arrived at its new home in February 1913.

# II

# THE 8TH DIVISION

In far-away Belgium, on 23 August 1914, the British Expeditionary Force, at that time consisting of only one cavalry and four infantry divisions, clashed with the advancing German First Army at Mons, to the west of Brussels. It was the first occasion in which British soldiers had fought on mainland Europe since the Waterloo campaign, ninety-nine years earlier. Although the superbly trained professionals were more than a match for their opponents, they were vastly outnumbered, and this, combined with the retreat of General Lanrezac's Fifth French Army on their right flank, forced a strategic withdrawal to the south.

Three days later, on 26 August, Colonel Feetham received orders to ensure that his battalion was held in readiness to embark for England at an early date. Field Marshal Kitchener, who had been appointed Minister for War, had ignored the optimists who expected the troops home for Christmas, and had begun to reorganise his forces for a war which would last, in his opinion, at least three years. In 1914 the regular Army had 155 infantry battalions. Of these, eighty-two were based in the British Isles, forty-six were stationed in India, and the balance were scattered between Bermuda to the west and China to the east.

The original expeditionary force comprised one cavalry and six infantry divisions, and the 19th Independent Brigade. The force had been mobilised and transported to France with commendable speed, for war had been declared only three weeks earlier. Four of the divisions fought at Mons, with the others in transit close behind. However, with twelve battalions to each division, this had used up seventy-six of the home-based battalions, and any further expansion meant that the overseas battalions would have to be recalled.

Colonel Feetham's first action was to recall his two companies who were on detachment at Nowgong. Sergeant Hanks recalled that it was a lovely summer evening when the telegram arrived at 5.30 p.m. on 26 August. They were immediately ordered to pack up and the next day they marched the 21 miles to the nearest railway station at Harpalpur, where they embarked for Jhansi by train. The battalion was soon reunited.

A week went by, during which everyone spent the time overhauling their kit, and trying to find out what was happening in Europe. On 6 September the battalion marched out of Jhansi Barracks for the last time, and boarded two trains bound for Deolali, near Bombay. Deolali was familiar to all of them, for it was the large transit camp through which almost every British soldier passed on his way to his new battalion, or on his way home at the end of his service. The place has given its name to 'Deolali Tap', the mild form of madness brought on by the boredom of waiting for the next troopship home, combined with the relaxation of discipline conceded to the time-expired men, which has given English the word 'doolally'. The symptoms reputedly disappeared as soon as the victim embarked on his ship.

However, there was no easing of discipline this time, and the battalion stayed at the camp for only a week before they were taken to Bombay docks by train and boarded His Majesty's Troopship *Dongola* on 14 September. The ship then moved into the outer

The troopship HMT *Dongola* that transported the 2nd Battalion from India to England on the outbreak of war.

harbour to await a convoy. The wait lasted a frustrating six days, swinging at anchor, but the time was used to reorganise the battalion into four companies. Traditionally, an infantry company had comprised about 100 men, and there were eight companies to a battalion, designated by the letters A to H. Army order No.323, issued in 1913, decreed that battalions should reorganise into four companies of 200 men. The 2nd Royal Berkshire Regiment had rather half-heartedly adopted the measure for training purposes in April, but it had not been formally introduced – perhaps the officers and senior NCOs had a somewhat reactionary attitude to decrees from distant Whitehall. Now, however, the return home made it unavoidable, so the old companies were paired off and merged.

The new organisation meant that the battalion now had four companies, lettered from A to D, each commanded by a captain. Each company comprised about 200 men, who were divided into four platoons, commanded by a lieutenant or second lieutenant, assisted by a sergeant. The platoons were numbered from 1 to 16, with 1 to 4 in A Company, 5 to 8 in B Company, and so on. Each platoon contained four sections of eleven men, led by a corporal. The balance of the battalion was organised into a Headquarters Company, which contained the support functions – machine gunners, signallers, stretcher bearers, cooks, transport drivers etc., and brought the total number of officers and men to nearly 1,000. This represents the ideal situation, with the battalion at full strength and with its full complement of officers of the appropriate rank. Once the war zone was reached, a battalion was rarely at full strength, and before long lieutenants were leading companies, and any surviving captains soon found themselves promoted to acting lieutenant-colonels commanding a battalion – and not necessarily one from their own regiment.

The delay in assembling a convoy had been caused by the activities of German cruisers. Admiral von Spee's Far East Squadron had left its base in Tsingtao in China before the outbreak of war, and was somewhere at large. Additionally, SMS *Königsberg* had been stationed in German East Africa, and had sunk the freighter *City of Winchester* with a valuable cargo of tea in the Gulf of Aden on 6 August. Britain could not allow the troop convoys to go unescorted until the enemy cruisers were accounted for.

At last, on 20 September, the huge convoy set out. It consisted of forty-five troopships, escorted by the battleship HMS *Swiftsure* and the cruisers HMS *Fox* and HMS *Dartmouth*, together with three armed merchant cruisers of the Royal Indian Marine. The necessity for the escort became apparent on 22 September, when the German cruiser SMS *Emden*, detached by Admiral von Spee from his squadron to seek targets of opportunity in the Indian Ocean, bombarded the port of Madras on the other side of India. Already *Emden* had captured or sunk eight British transports in the Bay of Bengal.

Hursley Park camp near Winchester, the concentration area for the 8th Division prior to going to France.

Sergeant Hanks recorded a largely uneventful trip:

> The voyage was very pleasant; with the exception of two deaths: one little baby and our big drummer which we buried at sea. We stopped at Gibraltar for two days where we had a little mishap, two Officers Ladies fell in the sea and were nearly drowned but 4 of our men jumped in the sea and rescued them. Nothing more happened until we landed at Liverpool on the 22nd of October 1914.

There was no time to get acclimatised to the English autumn chill. No sooner had the battalion disembarked than they boarded overnight trains to take them to Winchester, where they arrived the next morning, and marched the few miles to Hursley Park. Here they were issued with home service uniforms – up until now they had been shivering in tropical khaki drill.

At the outbreak of war, Sir George Cooper, Bart., placed his country estate, Hursley Park, at the disposal of the government. It had already been used to assemble the 7th Infantry Division, formed from troops recalled from Gibraltar, Malta and South Africa, plus four of the remaining home-based battalions. Soon the beautiful parkland had been transformed by a city of tents and huts, and the grass had been churned to mud by horses, wagons and marching boots. The 7th Division had been sent to protect Antwerp from the invading Germans, but the situation there had deteriorated so quickly that they had diverted to Zeebrugge, and were now fighting desperately to defend Ypres, the last significant town which the Allied forces held in Belgium.

Now Hursley Park was to be the assembly point for the 8th Division, in which the 2nd Royal Berkshires were destined to serve for the next four years. As soon as the kit issue had been completed, everyone was granted 48 hours' leave. Considering that the men had been in India for several years, 48 hours does not seem generous, but they were more fortunate than the six British battalions who formed part of the Indian Corps. Their section of the convoy had landed them at Marseille, and trains had taken them straight into battle on the Western Front – and in many cases to their deaths – without any home leave at all. The same applied to the British officers of the Indian troops in the Corps.

The men spent their leave in a variety of ways. Sergeant Hanks caught a train to Oxford, and proposed to his girlfriend, Esther Hughes. She must have been an optimistic girl, for she accepted. An infantryman on his way to the Western Front in 1914 could hardly offer the prospect of a long and happy marriage. Private Garlick travelled home to Kintbury and

Private Garlick.

went on a heroic two-day pub crawl with his brothers and cousins. At some stage he fell off a bike and injured his elbow, but this did not deter him. At the end of his leave his brothers managed to get him on a Winchester train, and he hitched a lift on an army wagon which was on its way to Hursley. The driver threw him off just before the guardroom, leaving Garlick asleep in a ditch. He woke up at reveille, and managed to stagger onto parade 'with less of my kit missing than some of the others'. Seeing the state of his arm, his Sergeant ordered him to report sick, and he was sent to Haslar Hospital where he was operated on for a fractured elbow. He caught up with the battalion in France a month later.

The Berkshires discovered that they were going to form part of the 25th Infantry Brigade, together with the 1st Royal Irish Rifles, who had come from Aden, the 2nd Lincolnshire Regiment from Bermuda, and the 2nd Battalion, The Rifle Brigade, who had also come from India. The Brigade was to be commanded by Brigadier-General A.W. Lowry-Cole, CB, DSO.

The two other brigades were the 23rd and 24th Infantry Brigades. The 23rd was formed by the 2nd Devonshires from Cairo and the 2nd West Yorkshires, 2nd Cameronians, and 2nd Middlesex Regiment, who had all been based in Malta. The 24th Brigade was made up of two battalions from Egypt, the 2nd Northamptons and 1st Worcestershires, one from South Africa, the 2nd East Lancs, and one from India, the 1st Sherwood Foresters. Thus, the fighting elements of the 8th Division were all regular battalions, and all had been serving overseas. Therefore, their least experienced troops had spent over two years with the colours, and the majority had served for much longer. The only non-regular units were the Northamptonshire Yeomanry, who formed the Divisional Cavalry, the Royal Engineers' Signal Company, and the Wessex Territorial Field Ambulance. The Royal Artillery and Royal Engineers Field Squadrons were all regular troops, and had also returned from overseas postings.

The assembling of the division illustrates just how widely distributed the regular Army was at the height of the Empire, and what an enormous task of logistics it must have been to bring them home. At the same time, battalions from the territorial force were being despatched overseas to take their place as garrisons in the various stations. In addition, three other regular divisions, the 27th, 28th and 29th, were being formed from overseas battalions, and twelve of the new army divisions were also being formed during the first two months of the war.

Whilst the 8th Division was lucky in not needing to train its men from scratch, the divisional commander, Major-General F.J. Davies, CB, still found himself with a significant training problem. Unlike the first six divisions, who had been home-based and had taken part in annual all-arms manoeuvres, his newly formed brigades had never had a chance to work together. The overseas battalions had been so geographically spread out that combined exercises were usually out of the question, and the peacekeeping operations within the Empire could usually be carried out by single battalions, backed up by locally recruited troops. As a result, very few staff officers had practical experience in managing a unit as large as a division or even a brigade. Davies himself had been Director of Staff Duties at the War Office, so he and his staff were all 'new in post' and trying to learn their new tasks while at the same time doing their best to perform them.

Davies' other problem was sickness. Immunisation was still in its infancy, and the troops were carrying a variety of tropical diseases, as well as having to acclimatise themselves to an English autumn. The weather had been fine until the end of October, but heavy rain then set in, turning Hursley Park into a quagmire, and many men succumbed to fever in their sodden tents. The Divisional History records that the sick rate was 'grievously high' during the whole of the first winter as men who had served in the far corners of the world cross-infected each other with different strains of illness.

It would have been nice if the division had remained in England until the problems had been resolved, and it had had time to become a team instead of a collection of different units. However, the situation in Flanders was too serious to allow this, as the BEF was fighting for its very existence at Ypres. After their defeat on the Marne, the enemy had started to consolidate their gains, establishing a defensive line which was steadily extended north towards the coast. This line was duplicated by the Allies, each side attempting to outflank the other, and by the time 8th Division had started its assembly, the two lines had reached the sea at Nieuwpoort. The Germans' next tactic was an attempt to break through the line at Ypres, putting at risk the Channel ports of Calais and Boulogne, which the 7th Infantry Division fought doggedly to protect. The rest of the BEF was hastily brought up from its positions on the River Aisne to reinforce them, and a major battle was now in progress astride the Ypres to Menen road, extending southwards along the Messines Ridge. Heavy casualties had severely impaired the BEF's fighting capabilities: the Royal Berkshires' 1st Battalion, in the 2nd Division, had not suffered as badly as some units, but nevertheless was reduced to fewer than 400 men. The battalion had taken so many officer casualties that senior NCOs were being granted field commissions to second lieutenants.

The Indian Corps had been rushed northwards from Orléans, where it had been assembling, to join in; the Cavalry Division had abandoned its mounts and was fighting as infantry; and two battalions from the territorial force had been sent out as reinforcements. With the exception of the 8th Division, all the available sources of trained men had been used up, and now the decision was made to ship the division to France, whatever its state of readiness. On 4 November, less than two weeks after arriving in Liverpool, the 2nd Royal Berkshires marched to Southampton to embark on SS *Kingstonian*, a converted cattle boat, bound for Le Havre.

# III

# FRANCE

After landing in Le Havre, the 8th Division travelled by trains to Strazeele, the railhead for IV Corps, and then concentrated at Merville, where the Berkshires were billeted. It was 11 November 1914, and the battalion's long journey to the Western Front was over. The war had exactly four years to go.

The struggle for Ypres, some 20 miles to the north east, was drawing to a close, with the enemy exhausted by his failure to break through. However, the cost for the BEF had been high, for few of the experienced officers and other ranks who had come to France in August had survived unscathed, and the reserves were perilously low. The newly arrived 8th Division, even though its component units had hardly had a chance to exercise together, must have been welcomed with open arms by Field Marshal French.

The troops found difficulties in communicating with the natives. The overseas army had developed its own curious *argot*, composed of a mixture of army slang and the several languages used in India, modified by words adopted from the many countries in which the men had served. They regarded themselves as accomplished linguists, and were dismayed when bewildered French shop and café proprietors looked blank when they had made a perfectly reasonable request in 'fluent' Hindustani. 'These people can't even speak their own language,' the men grumbled.

Three days later, the Berkshires left their billets, marched through Estaires, and took up positions in the line, holding trenches at Fauquissart. Soon, they were taking their first casualties, Private Sydney Hawes (7498) from High Wycombe becoming the first man in the battalion to be killed by enemy action. The first tour in the trenches lasted for four days, and cost nine men wounded in addition to the fatality. Sickness was still rife, for during the same period the war diary records that Lieutenant Guest-Williams and twenty other ranks were admitted to hospital.

Soon a routine was established, with the 25th Brigade putting two battalions into the line at Fauquissart. and two in reserve, billeted at Laventie or Estaires, and exchanging every three days. The Berkshires were paired with the 2nd Rifle Brigade, which, despite its name, was a normal infantry battalion. The two battalions established a cemetery at Fauquissart, where thirty-two of the Berkshires' early casualties are buried. Unlike many of the early battlefield cemeteries, it survived the four years of conflict, and was taken over by the Imperial War Graves Commission after the war. The cemetery register acknowledges that it was started by the 2nd Royal Berkshires and the 2nd Rifle Brigade.

The trenches were primitive, uncomfortable and dangerous. The infantry had been trained to use them only as temporary cover during a battle, and the current situation had never been contemplated. The techniques which developed during the war to make them safer and the conditions for their occupants more tolerable had yet to be put in place, and the men found themselves sloshing through mud and water as the winter rains set in. The priority work was filling sandbags and building a breastwork, for most of the casualties were from sniper fire when an unwary head was spotted by the enemy.

The battalion's casualty returns up to the end of December show thirteen men killed and two officers and forty-two other ranks wounded. The enemy, however, was not the main cause of attrition. The same casualty returns show four officers and 261 other ranks admitted to hospital after reporting sick. The miserable conditions in the trenches were taking their toll on the men from India, and no doubt exacerbating the malaria and other tropical diseases which they carried in their bodies. By contrast, the 1st Battalion, Royal Berkshires, who had come to France from Aldershot, recorded seventeen men hospitalised, suffering from rheumatism in the wet trenches, but otherwise their sickness rate was negligible.

An anonymous soldier from the Berkshires was interviewed in the *Berkshire Chronicle*: 'We found the difference in the climate knocked some of us about pretty hard, but we were well looked after in the way of clothes, and although a few had to be nursed up at times in warmer places, we soon got used to it, though we found fighting the Germans a good deal easier than fighting the weather.'

Captain Harris, commanding B Company, wrote home to a brother officer in Reading:

For several days we were halted in billets [i.e. barns and ramshackle farm buildings] and the day we entered the trenches marched about twelve miles. We had not the remotest idea that we were going into the firing line, with the result that several of us were very far from having on the warm clothes we wanted. It seemed like old times to hear the tick-tock of the Mauser – it would have pleased you thoroughly. In the trenches here we never – or rarely – wash or shave, but get covered with mud from head to foot, and are as merry as small boys making mud pies. My particular bit of trench is about 350 yards from our 'friends', but on my right Thornton's commando are within 100 yards or so in one place. We sap up to one another and exchange rifle grenades! Patrolling at night is quite exhilarating and we are all enjoying ourselves immensely. You will feel thoroughly in your element when you arrive.

Harris survived the war, having spent a period in command of the 1st Battalion, Royal Berkshires, and became a temporary brigadier-general in 1917. One can only speculate how long it took his boyish enthusiasm to evaporate. Thornton was the CO of C Company, and Harris is still using the Boer War term 'commando' for his unit.

Ammunition was in short supply, for the British armaments industry was still on a peacetime footing and, to make things worse, had lost many skilled workers who had either been called up as reservists or had volunteered for Kitchener's new army. The enemy seemed to have plenty to spare. 'The church at Laventie was a splendid affair to look at,' a soldier wrote to the *Berkshire Chronicle*, 'but although we did not go inside or have anything to do with it, the enemy was putting about a dozen shells into it every day, instead of looking around for us, and knocking the place to smithereens just to rile the French, who are very proud of their old churches.' In truth, the Germans were probably trying to eliminate an observation post, which was done by both sides, but the press lost no opportunity to record stories which emphasised the beastliness of the enemy.

As 1914 drew to a close, the Berkshires could be forgiven for feeling that they had not done much. They had reached the front too late to participate in the first battle of Ypres, and had merely shivered in the mud with a steady casualty rate from snipers and shelling. On 18 December, the 2nd Devons, supported by the 2nd West Yorkshire Regiment, mounted an attack on Neuve Chapelle. The enemy were taken unawares, and the attackers captured their front line trench, but the raid exposed severe failings in British hand grenades, which were jam tins filled with explosive that had to have their fuses lit by a match before being thrown. The Devons lost nearly a whole platoon to enemy bombers who overwhelmed them while they were still trying to light their grenades. The 2nd Berkshires sent out parties to recover the wounded, but the trench was recaptured by the Germans, who counter-attacked the next day.

# IV

# CHRISTMAS 1914

As Christmas approached, a rumour circulated that the enemy was planning to celebrate the end of the year with a new offensive, and special vigilance was ordered. In fact, the Germans were just as uncomfortable as the BEF, for the hard frosts of November had been followed by a thaw.

The trenches were now in a deplorable condition, and the Divisional History recorded that:

> fighting the water became more difficult than fighting the enemy. The part of the line occupied by the division was so low-lying that it was impossible to carry off the water by drainage. All that could be done was to block off certain sections of the trenches and pump out the water into adjacent portions. This entailed isolating the garrisons of the parts of the trenches so pumped out, for it was impossible to keep the communication trenches from flooding, and the only access to the front line was over the open in full view of the enemy. Mud and water accumulated everywhere, the sides of the trenches fell in, and life became a heart-breaking round of revetting, pumping, draining, wiring, varied though not relieved by the construction of new defences, trench lines and communications.

The enemy lines were in a similar state, for Private Fisher of Maidenhead wrote home: 'We are about 500 yards from the Germans, and we often have a go at one another. Their snipers are very good, but I think we go one better. The German trenches are half-full of water, and we can see them pumping it out.'

Conditions improved on Christmas Eve, when a hard frost solidified the mud. The men were surprised to hear the enemy singing carols in the evening, and joined in. Private Bullock wrote home that 'the enemy sang us a song, and we sang them back a song. Then we cheered each other. We threw some corned beef to the enemy, who seemed to be short of food.'

This was confirmed by Sergeant Powell, from Faringdon, who wrote home that 'I went to the listening post and the sentry told me that the Germans were having a good time singing carols. I was so interested that I stopped up an extra hour on duty to listen to them. At daybreak, when we were able to see the outline of the trenches, we heard the Germans on our left shouting "Happy Christmas Englishmen", which our chaps answered by looking over the top and wishing them the same'.

Then the Germans climbed out of their trenches and advanced into no-man's land. Private Bullock's letter continued: 'They shouted "Don't fire Gentlemen", and we shouted "all right" after getting permission from our officers not to fire.' Lieutenant George Hodgson, from Chertsey, who had been with the battalion since 1910, and was a noted linguist, stepped forward to negotiate the truce with German officers.

Sergeant Higgins of Knowl Hill wrote to his mother:

> In five minutes dozens of men were meeting just half way, shaking hands in the best of style, exchanging cigarettes and tins of bully and even Christmas puddings. Did ever anyone hear of such a proceeding? They said 'Hang it all, we want our holiday.' They looked well, and

Lieutenant George Hodgson.

the four I shook hands with were in their prime. I had one satisfaction in that they were evidently as cold and muddy as I was. On Boxing Day morning one came across and I had to go out and stop him as he was coming too near. He didn't want anything, but simply shook hands. He could say 'yes' and 'no' and made me understand that he would rather have the water than the cold. I think someone must have bet him that he wouldn't go across, or else he wanted to chuck it.

A member of the battalion is quoted anonymously in the *Berkshire Chronicle* of 15 January as saying 'from one source and another we learned that they were tired of the war and they said they would not shoot if we didn't. Not only that, many of them would have given themselves up only they were afraid that some of their men would shoot at them. This state of affairs lasted for several days, but now we are back at the old sniping business again.'

Similar instances of fraternisation occurred at other points along the line, and when news of it filtered up to Corps and Army commands orders were issued for it to cease. The 2nd Royal Berkshires' war diary for Christmas Day records that 'men got up on the parapet and advanced half way towards German trenches and in some cases conversed with them. Orders given at 11 a.m. prohibiting men from going beyond parapet. Much work done improving trenches during the day, the enemy protested about barbed wire being repaired, and we stopped them repairing theirs.'

The informal truce continued on Boxing Day, and that night the Berkshires were relieved by the 2nd Rifle Brigade and went back to billets. Sergeant Powell was pleased to receive a Christmas card from the King and Queen, and Mrs Davies (the divisional commander's wife) had sent enough Christmas puddings, chocolate and butter for the whole division. Princess Mary sent every man serving in the forces a gift of chocolate, cigarettes or tobacco in a decorative brass box, which Powell was so pleased with that he sent it home for safe keeping. 'All the chaps here say how good the people of England are in sending out fags, tobacco and comforts, and I can assure you we appreciate their kindness,' he wrote to the *Faringdon Advertiser*.

The events in this sector were a contrast to the 1st Royal Berkshires' sector near Béthune, where there was no let-up to hostilities. Captain Wyld was killed by a sniper on Christmas Eve, and Private Sear was awarded the DCM for rescuing a wounded man under heavy fire on Christmas Day.

# V

# NEUVE CHAPELLE

When the worst of the winter was over, the attentions of both sides in the conflict turned to resuming their offensives. The establishment of the trench lines presented a new military challenge in 1915, for they could not be outflanked, and were readily defended by barbed wire and machine guns. The General Staffs wrestled with the problem of how they could first break through the trench lines, and when this was achieved, how the attacking force could be sustained and reinforced in order to exploit their success.

In the BEF, there were two other reasons for resuming the offensive. Politically, it was important that the British Army was seen to be 'doing something' by their French and Russian allies. Although no one could deny that they had acquitted themselves well in the fighting, the small size of the British Army compared to those of the other combatants had limited its influence on the outcome of the 1914 battles. Secondly, the morale of the men had been affected by the awful winter months of inactivity in the flooded trenches, and it was important to get them into action again so that they could feel they were achieving something.

The place chosen for the first British attempt to break through was the village of Neuve Chapelle, about 9 miles south west of Armentières. It was the key to an attack on Aubers Ridge, which, although only some 35m high, was the most significant topographical feature in the otherwise flat Artois countryside. German observers on the ridge could overlook the British lines, and it would be a significant achievement to gain possession of the ridge, enabling the British to observe German activity between the ridge and Lille.

Neuve Chapelle village lay between the German first and second lines. It had already changed hands several times, for it had been captured by II Corps on 16 October 1914 and a defensive line named 'Smith Dorrien Trench', after the corps commander, ran behind the remains of the village. The enemy regained the position on 27 October but it was again recaptured by the Indian Corps the following day. However, they were unable to withstand heavy enemy attacks, and were gradually pushed back until the enemy had established a small salient around the village, and it was this salient which would be the first target for the attack.

General Haig, in command of the First Army, delegated the attack to IV Corps, comprising the 7th and 8th Divisions, and the Indian Army Corps, which consisted of the Meerut and Lahore Divisions. The attack on the northern flank of the salient would be made by 23rd and 25th Brigades from the 8th Division, while the Garhwal Brigade of the Meerut Division would simultaneously assault the southern flank. If the attacks were successful, troops from the 25th and Garhwal Brigades would join forces in Neuve Chapelle village, while the 23rd Brigade would attack the enemy positions between the village and the strong point called the Moated Grange.

The 2nd Royal Berkshires moved up to their assault trenches on the evening of 9 March, relieving men of the 24th Brigade, who moved back into reserve. The Berkshires were to form the right battalion for the initial attack, with the 2nd Lincolns on their left. The 2nd Royal Fusiliers and 2nd Royal Irish Rifles would form the second wave, and would leapfrog the two attacking battalions when the edge of the village was reached.

The attack was preceded by a heavy bombardment, with artillery batteries taken from divisions who were not involved in the assault, to form the strongest concentration of guns possible. They included a 15in howitzer called 'Granny' which was manned by a Royal Navy detachment. Although puny by comparison with barrages later in the war, it impressed the waiting troops. Sergeant Hanks, crouching with his platoon behind the sandbagged breastworks, wrote a graphic description in his unpublished memoirs: 'At 7.30 a.m. on the 10th the bombardment opened and oh! I shall never forget. It seemed as if the world was made of glass and had fallen down and broken and all the devils in hell had been let loose. The faces of our men was terrible to look at, their eyes were flaming; Oh! awful was their look, yet they were calm.'

Lieutenant-colonel Feetham had placed the four companies on either side of Chimney-Crescent road leading to the village, the forward company in the old fire trench, and the rear company behind the breastworks. In his report on the action, he recorded that the artillery bombardment opened promptly at 7.30 a.m., but many of the shells fell short among his men. 'During the bombardment, the battalion suffered somewhat heavy casualties from our own artillery fire – some 12 to 15 men were buried by one shell alone. Several of them were not extricated until after the battalion had advanced, some of them being killed and others badly wounded.' At that stage of the war, the poor quality of the ammunition, an acute shortage of shells, and the inexperience of many of the gun crews gave rise to such tragedies.

Sergeant Hanks' platoon was unlucky. 'The shells were dropping so close we were being covered by mud etc. At last one big one dropped right in amongst us it buried me and killed about 6 or 8 men and wounded a lot. I struggled out the best way I could, and when I did get out the sight that met my gaze I shall never forget, there were men cut to pieces dead and wounded all mixed up together, they were covered with blood from head to foot, there was about 4 places like this just by us, before we advanced.'

The barrage lifted promptly at 8.05 a.m., and the Berkshires advanced in four lines on a frontage of about 150 to 200 yards. They encountered little opposition, and in fact the enemy only had two battalions in their line, to oppose an attack being made by eleven battalions. The attackers stormed the German front line trench, shouting 'Maiwand!' and 'Come on the Berkshires!'. Lance-Corporal Collins recalled that they kept very calm under the circumstances: 'It was not a charging, howling mass, but a line of cool-headed Berkshires. Most of us were smoking, and all were out to do or die. We took everything before us, and once again the old regiment has made a name. I never felt more proud as when I looked to left and right and saw them running.'

Private Faulkner wrote home that: 'There was about 300 yards to go, and with the quick fire they kept up our regiment lost heavily. The trenches were like ditches, with the sides broken in, and the whole place was like a shambles, or that the whole lot were camping there and had gone to sleep on the ground.'

The men crossed the German trenches, and passed on to their objective in the centre of the ruined village, where they immediately started to dig themselves in. A detail, commanded by Lieutenant Gordon, established a block in the enemy trenches to the right, but Gordon was badly wounded by an enemy soldier who had previously surrendered.

Exactly as planned, the 2nd Battalion of the Rifle Brigade moved forward to pass through the Berkshire's lines, and establish a line to the east of the village. Meanwhile, the Garhwal Brigade, who had advanced through heavy fire to the right of the 25th Brigade front, entered the village from the south, and men from the 2/3rd Gurkhas and 2/39th Garhwalis started to clear the enemy troops from the ruined houses and trenches. Rifleman Gane Gurung of the Gurkhas rushed into a building from which enemy fire

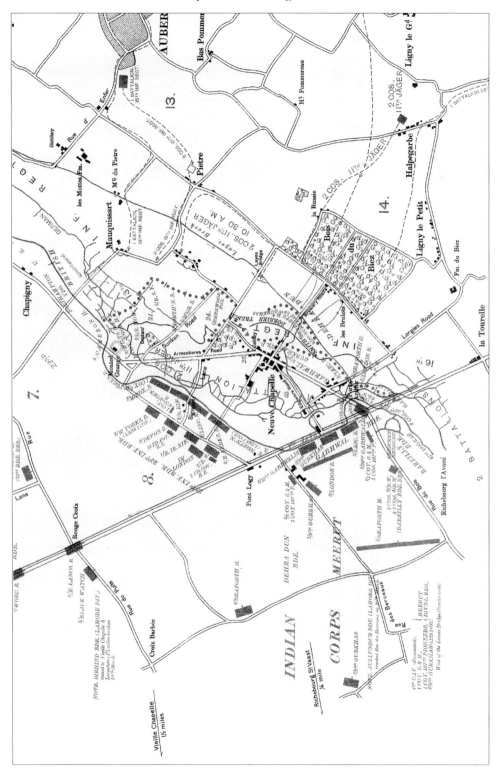

Map of Neuve Chapelle.

An artist's impression showing a sergeant of the Royal Berkshires being dug out by his men after 'an action with the Prussian Guards'. The line was held.

was emerging, to appear a few minutes later prodding eight burly soldiers of the 11th Jaeger Regiment at bayonet point. The men of the 25th Brigade were so impressed that they paused in their fighting to give the diminutive Gurkha three rousing cheers. He was awarded the Indian Order of Merit (Second Class).

Although the 25th Brigade and the Garhwal Brigade had achieved their objectives, the 23rd Brigade to the north of Neuve Chapelle, on the Berkshires' left, had not been so lucky. The batteries of VII Brigade, Royal Artillery, who had been assigned to this sector, had only arrived from England on the afternoon of the day before the assault. There had been no time to set the guns up properly, or fire ranging shots, so their barrage had little effect on the enemy trenches around the Moated Grange. Pinned down by heavy rifle and machine gun fire from these same trenches, the infantry attack had petered out with heavy casualties, leaving the 25th Brigade's left flank exposed. Soon the Berkshires began to suffer casualties, including Captain Aldworth, the adjutant, and Lieutenant Saunders.

Sergeant Hanks had been ordered by Colonel Feetham to take a party of twelve men back to fetch more picks and shovels, and was with Saunders when he was killed:

> I got hold of the men and took them back and brought as many [picks and shovels] as we could carry but by the time we got back I had lost 3 or 4 of my men. My Platoon Officer, Mr Saunders, such a nice gentleman and quite a brave man shouted to me 'Down here, Sgt Hanks'. Knowing what he meant I at once ordered the men to lay down. I asked him if we should dig ourselves in where we were and he said 'No, he would go and find Capt. Harris who was to supervise the digging of the new trenches'. He then turned away and took about 2 paces from me and was instantly killed, with a bullet through his brain.

The shell damaged ruins of Neuve Chapelle.

With his officer dead, Hanks took over command of the platoon. Captain Townsend, the company commander, ordered him to set his men to work digging in. They probably did not need much persuading, for the area was being swept by rifle and machine gun fire from the enemy trenches to the left. Men were falling all around Hanks, and soon Captain Aldworth, the adjutant, was lying beside him, shot through the heart.

Hanks had ignored the injuries which he had suffered when he was buried by a British artillery shell just before the attack, but now they caught up with him. He collapsed into a shell-hole, unable to move, with agonising pains in his back. Men kept asking him where he was hit, including his friend George Smith, the platoon sergeant of No.13 Platoon, who then fell into the shell-hole with Hanks, killed by a bullet in his head.

Once the digging had gone deep enough to provide some cover, the casualties started to diminish, and the battalion settled down to await developments. When dusk fell, it was possible to evacuate the wounded men, including Sergeant Hanks, while the survivors worked hard to improve their breastworks and trenches. Morale was high, for the men felt they had acquitted themselves well in their first real attack, and the battalion had taken the objectives allotted to it. According to Private Faulkner: 'That night we stayed where we were, with one eye open in case of a counter-attack. Our chaps were very jolly, and we sang and smoked and slept as best we could, the night being cold and damp.'

The original plan for the battle now called for IV Corps and the Indian Corps to advance from Neuve Chapelle and assault Aubers Ridge, but now one of the fundamental problems faced by the attacking force manifested itself. As the infantry advanced, communications between themselves and their own artillery support broke down. Reliable portable radios were far into the future, and the officers could neither call down a bombardment on an enemy strong point nor inform the gunners of their own progress to stop the shelling on their own newly won positions. Until telephone cables could be laid across the battlefield, the only way to get a message back was by runner or pigeon. The weather on 11 March did not help, for low clouds prevented aircraft from observing for the guns or reporting progress. The Berkshires spent the day consolidating their position, for so many enemy strong-points were still resisting that the divisional commanders countermanded orders to advance any further.

The next day, 12 March, the Germans launched a counter-attack against all the British gains. The Berkshires moved through the village to the 2nd Rifle Brigade's position, and the two battalions, with the Garhwal Brigade on their right, spent the day repulsing waves of enemy troops. The Germans lost heavily, and failed to dislodge the defenders from their gains. The battle petered out into an impasse, with the British unable to advance across the Layes Brook to the east of Neuve Chapelle, and the Germans unable to recover the village, which remained in Allied hands until the spring of 1918.

The action had cost the lives of four officers, for beside Captain Aldworth and Lieutenant Saunders, Second Lieutenants Raynes and Hogan had also been killed and eleven officers had been wounded. Seventy-five men had died, seventeen were missing and 220 wounded – a total of 312, or nearly one third of the strength.

*Right:* Captain and Adjutant Thomas Aldworth.

*Below:* A contemporary print produced shortly after the battle showing the troops under heavy German shellfire in the trenches at Neuve Chapelle.

# VI

# FROMELLES

A new draft of four officers and 300 other ranks joined the battalion on 21 March to replace the losses of Neuve Chapelle. The officers included Major Richard Harvey, whose brother Russell was chairman of John Harvey & Sons, the well-known Bristol wine merchants. Harvey kept a diary, a transcription of which was lodged with the Regimental museum in 1982 by his daughter, Marjorie Woodward.

Harvey and the draft had a difficult train journey across France from Le Havre to Merville. 'Each RTO [Railway Transport Officer] gives us different instructions, and says the last one was an ass,' Harvey recorded. At last they arrived at La Gorgue, and marched four miles to the battalion's transport lines near Croix Barbée, where they were met by the quartermaster, Captain Lickman.

Lickman took the new officers up to Battalion Headquarters, where they met Colonel Feetham in the cellar of a ruined house in Neuve Chapelle. Major Harvey was invited to return the next day, to have a look round in daylight. He recorded his first trip to the battle front in some detail, and the author makes no excuse for reproducing it in full, for it is so descriptive:

> March 22. Parade at 10.00 until 1.00, attack formation: 'Ground unhealthy' says a French artillery officer. I find the Germans have been shelling that particular area all day. I shove off. Aeroplanes shelled by Germans – a Taube comes over us, but is too high to squirt at. A 'Coal Box' drops 200x away, so we march home in artillery formation. Capital practice for the men.
>
> Stop at an enclosed work originally made by the Germans and lecture to men on different forms of revetments and dugouts. Capital dinners. Parade 3.00–4.00 telling off men to Companies in the battalion. I command A Company. At 4.30 pm start to trenches with guide. Tell the men I am going to engage seats for them and enquire if they want stalls or dress circle. This meets with a general chorus that they would prefer the pit! I carry full load and British Warm in addition. Get on to La Bassee road. House at cross-roads was hit a week ago killing 24 men of East Lancs. Grave outside.
>
> Road being shelled then – my orderly seems to like it, I don't. Men under verandas much appreciate me ducking as shells scream over. One man gets knocked over about 200 yards ahead. Somebody calls out 'Stretcher Bearer'. Everybody laughs. My orderly says this happens every day, as they usually shell Headquarters about this time. 'Where are Headquarters?' 'That house ahead'. Bang! again. 'Thanks, I'm off' and I run like a rabbit under cover. Am met with roars of laughter by a group of officers. Recognise Gardner, and Brodigan of the Glosters, who ask me to tea. They say they are coming up to meet Col. Feetham at 5.30 pm, but propose to postpone till shelling stops.
>
> However I am due at 5 pm so thank them and push on. At a sharp turn where trolley-car starts for the trenches men are sitting pretty close together under cover of the houses.

Major R.P. Harvey, a member of the Harveys Bristol wine merchant dynasty.

However I don't see any use in stopping, so get through houses and feel much relieved at seeing a Sapper, sitting on the exposed side eating bread and cheese and reading the 'Winning Post'. Shove on across country, shells still come over occasionally. As we approach the 1st line of the British old position, a noise like an express train or swarm of bees comes tearing towards me. I saw my orderly for the first time show some consternation and disappear into the ditch. I throw myself flat where I was. Crack! Crack! two shrapnel burst almost on top of us, and the case of one fell close by. A right and left I suppose. A shower of dust, gravel and bricks, but that was all. No use stopping, on we went. At the next line of trenches we meet a big working party coming back. Bang! the same thing again. Two more shells and we bolted into the dugout. We stayed a few minutes, but now keeping away from the road, we struck across some entanglements and pushed on to the ruined house, our headquarters, where I reported to the Colonel that at any rate I had not been bowled out first ball!

There was a good deal to settle regarding our relief tomorrow and shortly before 6 pm the 2nd Glosters officers rolled up, and about 7 pm we all went round the fire trenches. Young Colbourne and 3 men had been hit that morning and they could not be moved till dark. All sniped from one house. They were still where they fell. Everybody was very cheery. The men had all been there without relief since the fight 12 days ago, when we lost 14 officers and 320 men.

Major Harvey had served with the Royal Berkshire Regiment for many years and his return was something of a reunion:

Many old friends came up and shook hands. The breast works were wonderfully made, our men being past-masters at digging. Braziers everywhere, dugouts, blankets, wooden floors, everything very comfy. By now it was dark, except for incessant flares, shot up by both sides. Guns and rifle fire skittered on each flank, occasionally bullets pinged into our breastwork, when Tommy grinned. The German dead lie thick in front of us still. The battalion carried everything before it, whilst those on the left and right were not so successful, and we had to fall back in line, but those bodies are tributes still to the lads from Berkshire, and as one remarked 'we always did like pitching'. No doubt the haymaker's lift stood him in good stead on the 10th. Colbourne had been carried off when I reached his dugout, but a fellow was lying very still behind the parades. I touched his hand and it was quite cold, and I recognised an old Khartoum comrade whom I had last seen at Aldershot, when I recommended him a post in the Great Western Railway. He was quite dead. There was a deep stain on his temple, I said a little prayer, and next moment was joking with the battalion marksman, a man from my Meerut company, who assured me he was using his abilities daily, while half a dozen men were cooking tea and joking a few feet away. It was all very simple and ordinary. At last I got to A Company which I am to take over, and I soon found a lot of old friends and NCOs. whom I had lately trained at Portsmouth. The men were all very busy, filling up sandbags and putting up wire. Most of this work is done in the dark.

Neuve Chapelle is simply blown to pieces, both sides have shelled it from time to time, and our trenches run in front of it. You have no idea what a jumble of roofless houses, smashed transport and wrecked furniture, shell craters everywhere. I had hoped to have remained the night with my company, but my Colonel wanted me to go back to the draft; however a small show had been arranged for 11.30 pm and he told me I could stay for it, and go back afterwards. We all dined in the Headquarters cellar, and at 10 o'clock I went back to my trench. German working parties had been very busy for the last few nights, and we intended to wake them up a bit. At 11.30 pm the guns were to fire a salvo and then every rifle and machine-gun was to give them What-ho! rapid fire. On arrival, I found my company had a party out burying the German dead, who lie very thick there, and are getting a bit unpleasant. I went out with a corporal to bring them in, but met them outside with a few trophies. At 11.20 men's rifles were all ready on the parapet, and I went round depressing the muzzles, and selected one for myself. Two of the burying party had a German rifle each and were sending the German bullets back home!

Then we set our backs against the parapets and waited with the pistol flares at hand. A flicker of light in the sky told us the salvo was fired, three miles behind us. The screams of the shells and the bang as they landed above the German lines was our signal to open fire and I fired my first round against the Kaiser on the 30th anniversary of Tofrek. [Harvey is referring to a battle in the Sudan campaign, where the Berkshires distinguished themselves.] Up went our flares to see the damage; whether the bodies had been added to I could not say, but of course the men claimed a considerable bag. The Germans evidently thought we were attacking, for their flares, (much better than ours) illuminated our lines for hours. By 12.15 am I was back in the cellar. The Colonel had been on his way to another trench, but had run into barbed wire, and lighting his torch to free himself drew considerable fire from the German lines. However he was not touched, thank goodness. He is a fine C.O. It was nearly 2.am before I got back and I was then ready for bed having stood to arms at 4.am. So ended my first day at the Front.

Major Harvey spent only a week in command of A Company before orders arrived for Colonel Feetham. He was to proceed to England to take command of a newly formed brigade, and Harvey found himself in charge of the battalion.

The battalion settled into the routine of trench life, a few days in the line interspersed with a period in billets. The weather was improving, and the water-logged trenches started to dry out. There was a steady toll of casualties, when an unwary man was caught by a sniper, or an enemy shell landed in a trench.

On 14 April, during a spell out of the line, Major Harvey and Captain MacGregor returned to the Neuve Chapelle battlefield:

I collect some evergreens, laurel, yew and bay from a garden and make a cross, in the afternoon MacGregor and I with orderly ride over to Neuve Chapelle to read burial service over Tom

Aldworth and those who fell. We got there without accident, though batteries on both sides were very lively. I was shown the actual positions of our companies and where our officers were killed. All had been buried where they fell, no time for any service, or even looking in their pockets. Our killed totalled nearly 100 in four days. Tom and Saunders lie together side by side. Hogan some 300 yards ahead beside the man who tried to carry him in. Our cross looked quite nice and a doubled postcard tied with royal blue ribbon reads 'In loving memory of Capt. and Adjutant T.R. Aldworth from Major and Mrs. Dick Harvey.' I read the service and we said the hymn 'My God my Father whilst I stray'. As we finished 3 shells screamed overhead from one of our batteries, so he was not without military honours. A good many bullets come flying about, so we did not go up to Hogan's, as it lies almost in the trenches.

We looked into our old headquarters cellar, a bit changed since we left it – it looked as if a high explosive had burst in the room above. The 1/9 Gurkhas were here living in dugouts, and gave us warning regarding certain ground on our way back, and later on a head popped out with a pipe in its mouth and a voice drawled 'I don't want to hurry you chaps but they are pretty busy with their "whizzbangs" just where you are standing'. We moved on.

Two days later, the battalion was inspected by Field Marshal Sir John French, Commander in Chief of the BEF. Major Harvey recorded:

Battalion drawn up in hollow square. We give a splendid General salute, [French] shakes hands with me, glad to meet me again! says 'Is this the battalion that was at Colesburg?' I answer 'Yes, Sir, at McCracken's Hill'. He thanks the battalion for services at Neuve Chapelle and refers to damnable reports spread by liars who should be shot, that the fight was not the success it was, and that many of our men were killed by our artillery. Tells us to deny all such rumours emphatically. He shakes hands again and congratulates me on commanding so fine a battalion. I say 'Thank you very much, Sir'. Then stand easy! Caps off! 3 cheers for the Commander-in-Chief. The men cheer well. Afterwards another short ride and early bed.

The 'rumours' regarding the casualties from our own artillery fire, which Sir John wanted to deny, were already written up as facts in the battalion's digest of service. They appear in the *Berkshire Chronicle*, Sergeant Hanks' unpublished memoirs, and soldiers' letters home. It might have been comforting for the battalion if French had admitted the existence of the problem, and told them of the actions he was putting in place to try to prevent its recurrence.

During the next tour of the trenches, Lieutenant Wright was killed under the enemy wire while on patrol at night. His sergeant reported that Wright had told him he was trying desperately to suppress a coughing fit, but could contain it no longer. When he coughed, about twenty rifles opened up on him, and he was hit in the chest, arm and head. A party went out, managed to recover his body, and Major Harvey conducted a burial service for him the next day.

Meanwhile, Field Marshal French was determined to have another attempt at securing Aubers Ridge, which had been the ultimate objective of the Neuve Chapelle battle. The 8th Division was again to play a major role, but this time they would be further to the north, opposite the village of Fromelles. In preparation, the Berkshires moved back to the trenches at Fauquissart, where they had been stationed during their first few weeks on the Western Front.

A new commander was posted to the battalion. Lieutenant-Colonel Herbert Finch, DSO, had originally come to France in August 1914 with the 1st Battalion, Royal Berkshires, with the rank of major. He had taken part in the retreat from Mons, and the battles of the Marne and Aisne. At the first battle of Ypres, he had briefly assumed command of the battalion when Colonel Graham was seriously wounded, but Finch himself was then wounded in the ankle and invalided home. He recovered from his injuries, and his promotion to lieutenant-colonel was announced in the *London Gazette*, to take effect on 1 May 1915.

Major Harvey reverted to his old position. He sounded rather disappointed, for he wrote in his diary for 2 May that 'I shall enjoy being his 2nd in command, but have held command for over a month.' The next day he seemed to have cheered up, for: 'On arrival at billets, meet old Finch looking so well. I am glad he has come.'

On 8 May, the battalion moved up to a position opposite Fromelles. The front line breastwork was held by the 2nd Rifle Brigade, and the 2nd Royal Berkshires occupied two assembly trenches behind them, C and D Companies in the first, while A and B Companies were in the second. At zero hour, the Rifle Brigade would leave their breastworks and attack across no-man's land, while C and D Companies would move forward and occupy the breastworks. Once A and B had joined them, and the Rifle Brigade had reached their objective, the Berkshires would advance in eight lines at intervals of 30 paces and pass through the Rifle Brigade to continue the attack. There was to be a preliminary artillery bombardment, commencing at 5 a.m. This would stop at 5.40, zero hour.

Major Harvey wrote in his diary: 'Busy learning up orders and writing till evening. mail arrives, get a little sleep and then write home to every-body. Clean up revolver and pistol. Men are singing and very cheery. We parade at 11, and then trust in God.'

All went to plan until the barrage lifted. The men of the Rifle Brigade leapt across the breastwork, and were met by terrific rifle and machine gun fire. D Company of the Berkshires under Captain Nugent advanced to the breastworks and found some of the Rifle Brigade still there. Others were lying flat on the ground a few feet in front, their only protection being vegetation about 9 or 10in high. The old fire trench, out in front

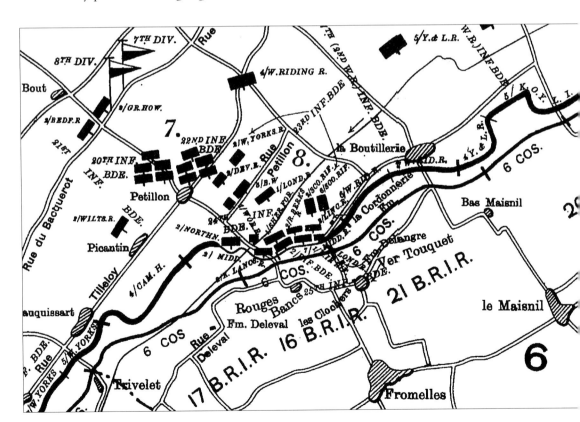

Map of Fromelles.

Lieutenant-Colonel Herbert Marshall Finch, DSO.

of the breastworks, seemed to be full of men. D Company advanced to the fire trench, and found it full of men from 2nd Rifle Brigade and 1st Royal Irish Rifles. They said that an order had been passed along telling them not to advance any further, but no-one could say who had issued it.

Nugent gathered up the stragglers, and with D Company ordered an advance to the German trenches in two rushes, the first rush to cover about half the distance. After the first rush, some men of the Irish Rifles came running back shouting 'retire at the double'. Nugent could not find out who had issued the orders, but, accepting that the attack had failed, ordered his men to crawl back to the breastworks and reorganise, leaving the fire trench empty so that the men still out in front could use it as a refuge.

C Company encountered similar confusion. Once they had cleared the breastworks, an order was passed from the rear 'From the Brigade Commander – no further advance'. Minutes later, a second order arrived to advance to the first German trench. While preparations were being made to carry this out, a group of men came rushing back shouting 'retire at the double'. These men were ordered to halt and lie down with C Company. After the action, no officer could be found who had either originated or passed on these three orders. The survivors of C Company then received genuine orders from Brigade to retire to the breastworks, which they did.

A and B Companies, as planned, arrived at the breastworks after the other two companies. Seeing the situation, B Company's commander ordered his men to remain behind under cover. Two sections (about twenty-two men) did not hear this order, and tried to advance, but retreated to the breastwork when the order to retire was given. B Company, under Captain MacGregor, followed C Company out into no-man's land. MacGregor was wounded and taken prisoner, so it is probable that some of this group reached or at least came close to the German trench.

The situation at 11 a.m. found the survivors of the 2nd Royal Berkshires, 2nd Rifle Brigade and 1st Royal Irish Rifles huddled behind the breastwork or crouching in the

*Above:* An artist's impression of Sergeant B.C. Shea rallying and cheering on the men of the 2nd Royal Berkshire Regiment after being seriously wounded at Rouges Bancs. He was awarded the DCM.

*Left:* Corporal William G. Tame and Lance Corporal Alfred Tame from Windsor, brothers aged twenty-three and twenty-five respectively. They both fell on 9 May 1915 at the same place.

old fire trench. No-man's land was littered with dead or wounded men. Some men had reached the German breastwork on the other side, and were crouching beneath it. Orders were received from the brigade that they would be reinforced. This was to be accomplished by using a sap which had been dug by the 13th London Regiment (the Kensingtons), from which the men would crawl to a mine crater, and then rush the German lines. This action was started at about 2.30 p.m., but when they were about half-way to the breastwork the 2nd Lincolns and 13th Londons retreated with a rush, after being given an order to retire by an officer of the 2nd Scottish Rifles. Nugent felt that this was a general retirement, and ordered the remaining Berkshires back behind the breastwork. This decision was confirmed by an order from Brigade Headquarters to halt the reinforcing plan.

The Berkshires remained behind the breastwork that night, and on 10 May were ordered back to Croix Blanche. The attack had been a complete failure. Seven officers and fifty-two other ranks had been killed, six officers and thirty-nine other ranks were missing, and six officers and 185 men had been wounded. The dead officers included Lieutenant-Colonel Finch, whose command had lasted less than a week, and Major Harvey, who left a widow and four small daughters. Captain Nugent was the senior surviving officer, and it was from his report of the battle that most of this account is taken.

Although the 2nd Royal Berkshires' losses had been considerable, the 1st Royal Irish Rifles marched back to billets under the command of their sergeant-major. All the officers and 450 men had become casualties. The 2nd Rifle Brigade had lost twenty-one officers and 571 other ranks.

# VII

# BOIS GRENIER

The month of June 1915 was spent near Neuve Chapelle. Spells in the line were of six days, alternating with the 2nd Lincolns. The other two battalions in the 25th Brigade had taken so many casualties at Fromelles that they had a period out of the line to recuperate and absorb new drafts. During the time at Neuve Chapelle, the battlefield graves of the men who had fallen on 10 March were identified and marked.

New drafts of both officers and men joined, together with a new Commanding Officer, Captain Gerald Hunt, who had come out to France in November in command of D Company. Wounded in February, he had now recovered, and returned to command the battalion.

Included amongst the drafts was Lieutenant Hanbury-Sparrow, aged twenty-three. At the outbreak of war, he had been the junior subaltern in the 1st Battalion, and had crossed to France on 12 August 1914. The battalion had been short of a transport officer and, to his dismay, Colonel Graham had given him the task. Transport officers were usually commissioned from senior NCOs with an unblemished record, who had accumulated a vast knowledge of horse management and army logistics. Hanbury-Sparrow had neither, but he succeeded in managing the battalion's transport during the chaos of the retreat from Mons. He was relieved of his responsibilities on the Aisne, where an experienced transport officer joined the battalion, rejoined his company and acquitted himself well, winning a DSO at Ypres in November 1914 before being wounded. He had now recovered, and, after spending a period at Colchester helping to train New Army battalions, had been posted to the 2nd Battalion.

Hanbury-Sparrow was initially unimpressed with the 2nd Battalion. He had gone straight from Sandhurst to the 1st Battalion in Aldershot. If the war had not intervened, he would soon have been posted to the overseas battalion, where the more relaxed attitude might have mellowed the formality and discipline that had been instilled in him.

> All the wisdom that had been collected by the first battalion at the cost of so much suffering,' he wrote, 'had been absolutely thrown away on this lot, who hadn't come out until November. They were still up to their hocks in the easy going tradition of South African war discipline. The men were slovenly; some had even been allowed to grow beards! They were being trusted instead of being dominated. Of course they wouldn't and couldn't fight properly under such a lack of strength-giving discipline.

The quotations from Hanbury-Sparrow come from his autobiographic book, *The Land-Locked Lake*, published in London in 1932.

At the beginning of July, the division was marched north to take over a sector on the Franco-Belgian border near Armentières, south of Ploegsteert Wood. Hanbury-Sparrow despaired of the march discipline, and spent the journey haranguing his subalterns to keep

*Far left:* Lieutenant-Colonel G.P.S. Hunt.

*Left:* Captain Hanbury-Sparrow.

the men in line and looking smart. The CO, Captain Hunt, who had now been promoted to temporary lieutenant-colonel, diplomatically avoided a mutiny in A Company by appointing him adjutant, responsible for the battalion's organisation and administration.

Further south, preparations were in hand for a major offensive at Loos. The 8th Division would not be taking part, but were ordered to mount a simultaneous attack in their sector so as to prevent the enemy from moving reserves down to Loos and jeopardising the expected breakthrough.

The area selected for the feint was near a wood called Bois Grenier. There, the German trenches followed a straight line, but for a length of about 1,200 yards the British front line had a pronounced re-entrant which made no-man's land about 800 yards wide.

According to Hanbury-Sparrow, Lieutenant-Colonel Hunt was already keen to straighten the line, and thus reduce the number of men necessary to defend the sector. There were a number of old drainage ditches in no-man's land, and Hunt proposed to use these to secretly construct a new front line across the chord of the re-entrant, which could then be occupied without alerting the enemy.

However, this plan did not fulfil the division's orders to create a diversion. Instead, a four-day bombardment of the enemy front line was to be followed by an infantry attack on 25 September, which was the day planned for the Loos offensive. The assault would be made by three companies of the 2nd Royal Berkshires in the centre, 1 Company of the 2nd Lincolns on the left, and 1 Company of the 2nd Rifle Brigade on the right. The remaining companies of all three battalions would follow up and exploit any gains. On either side of the sector, neighbouring battalions would provide supporting fire from their positions, the 1st Royal Irish on the left and 2nd East Lancs and 1st Sherwood Foresters of 24th Brigade on the right.

There were three strong points in the German line: Bridoux Fort on the left, Corner Fort on the right, and a feature called 'the Lozenge' in the centre. Two trench mortar batteries and six 18-pounder guns were brought forward to deal with them. In addition, two small mines would be detonated at the two corners of the re-entrant to form the start of the new trench, and smoke generators were to be set off to protect the attacking infantry.

At about 7 p.m. on 24 September, the battalion left its billets in Fleurbaix in marching order, without packs or greatcoats, and proceeded into the trenches. A, B and C Companies were going to carry out the assault, with D Company in reserve, except for a working party of fifty men under Sergeant Harrison, who were detailed to help the

*Right:* Aerial photo of Bois Grenier showing the ground covered by the 2nd Battalion on 25 September.

Royal Engineers. Bursts of machine gun fire were aimed at the enemy's wire at intervals to prevent them repairing the damage caused by the bombardment.

The three attacking companies formed two lines each with two platoons in the first line and two platoons in the second line, which was to follow about 100 yards behind. The first line's duty was to take and consolidate the German first trench; the second line was to follow bombing parties and hold the German second trench.

Special bombing parties followed immediately behind the first wave. Lieutenant Simmons with twelve men was with A Company, and was to turn right up the enemy trench, bombing as they went, until they met up with the Rifle Brigade, who would be coming in the opposite direction. Lieutenant Gregory with a similar group would attack with C Company, turn left and join up with the Lincolns. Two parties under Sergeants Johnson and Turvey were to attack either side of the Lozenge strong point, and parties under 2nd Lieutenant Russell and Corporals Pearce and Maher were to deal with the communications trenches between the German first and second lines. These were important, for reconnaissance had shown wire entanglements between the first and second lines, so the second line was to be attacked by means of these communication trenches, as soon as the bombardment lifted.

The artillery bombardment started at 4.25 a.m. on 25 September. The first line received a 5-minute bombardment with field guns, the second line 15 minutes with howitzers; it continued on the third line and communication trenches until 5 a.m. to discourage the enemy from reinforcing the front two lines. Captain Sawyer, who was in overall command of the assault, sent the first wave of attackers off at 4.25, and they crept forward under the bombardment. When they reached 100 yards out, as planned, he led the second wave. The attacking companies of the Lincolns and Rifle Brigade also set off to the left and right of the Berkshires.

The German sector, which was manned by the 20th Bavarian Reserve Regiment, put up flares. Then a searchlight swept no-man's land in front of A Company, but a rapid fusillade opened up on it and it was soon extinguished. Despite these setbacks, the first trench was reached at 4.30, just as the barrage ceased.

A Company, on the right, failed to get in the trench. In his report of the action, Lieutenant-Colonel Hunt stated:

> It is not known whether the failure was due to the wire entanglement or other causes. It seems probable that the wire was not so well cut or had been repaired, that the searchlight

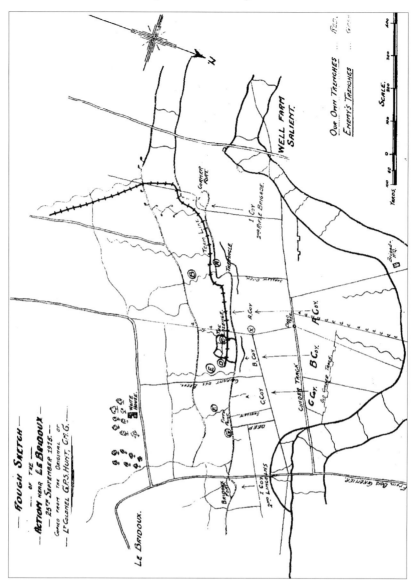

Sketch map of Bois Grenier.

showed up the attackers and that the defenders were more ready in that part. Some survivors state that a platoon under Sergeant Sherwood attempted to crawl along a shallow trench in front of the parapet, to rush from there, but were bombed from the parapet, and taken in the rear when they were crowded up. Some are said to have surrendered. It is probable that a few got into the trench but were too weak to take it. Captain Guest-Williams is said to have been killed on the parapet and Lieutenant Vesey was severely wounded and probably died. Lieutenant Simmons, leading the right bombing party, was killed probably by rifle fire.

In the centre, B Company had better luck. They took the trench with a few casualties, and soon disposed of the defenders, but they found a gap between themselves and A Company. Captain Sawyer immediately began to attack to the right, where A Company should have been. He made some headway but the bombs soon ran out and the enemy held the trench in force. Captain Trotter, commanding the company was killed on the parapet. The two bombing parties made their way along each side of the Lozenge and cleared it.

Second Lieutenant Russell and Corporal Pearce became disoriented in the maze of trenches, and missed the entrance to the communication trench through which they were meant to reach the German second line trench. Russell was killed, and Corporal Pearce found himself in the Lozenge. The second line was not reached.

C Company, on the left, was the most successful. They entered the enemy's trench and either bayoneted the occupants or drove them out. A machine gun caused some casualties to the left platoons, and the company commander, Captain Oke, was killed before reaching the wire. The bombing teams all lost their leaders, Corporal Maher was wounded and Sergeant Matthews, leading the back-up platoon to follow, was blown over and stunned. Lieutenant Gregory led his bombing team into the front line trench and they bombed down it until they met up with men from the Lincolns, but sadly Gregory was killed at the moment of success.

About 5.15 a.m. a party estimated at 200 Germans broke cover and ran back towards their rear trenches. They were heavily fired on by fifty rifles, and many were seen to fall. It was still very dark at the time of the assault, and in the deep and narrow trenches it was difficult to see what was happening. It was even worse in the deep dugouts. Some of the enemy fired from dugouts, but, Colonel Hunt's report continues, 'it does not seem as if they hit many men. Some were killed coming out. The men were little inclined to spare any, and dugouts were cleared by bayonet, revolver or bombs – torches being used in some cases to discover whether they were occupied.'

Colonel Hunt was critical of the hand grenades. 'There was light rain and mist during the night and morning, which made the fuses of some of our bombs damp. Those that required fuses to light became useless, and the Hales hand grenades seldom detonated on falling into the mud. G.S. Grenades, Pitcher and Mills bombs worked well, and the German pattern of time Grenades with a long handle was excellent. About 200 to 300 of these were used in the morning.'

At 5.30 a.m. Captain Sawyer was wounded in several places by a bomb, but was able to go back to the Brigadier to report, before making his way to the dressing station. As the daylight improved, the fight soon became one of bombs and grenades, and it swayed backwards and forwards along the trench according to which side had bombs to throw. Communication by telephone was seldom available owing to wires being cut by shells. During the whole morning there was constant shelling in both directions, some casualties being sustained by D Company, in reserve in the jumping-off trench, but none in the German trench. There was little rifle or machine gun fire.

The enemy were still holding about 300 yards of their front line trench between the Berkshires and the Rifle Brigade. This should have been taken by A Company. Hunt ordered a bombardment on the sector at about 10 a.m., but reported that the enemy was too well supplied with grenades, and though he was held, no progress was maintained for long.

At midday, the Lincolns on the left sustained a determined counter-attack, and started to fall back into the section of trench held by the Berkshires. The trench became so crowded that Lieutenant Lindley was obliged to lead a party back to the British front line to ease the congestion. The supply of bombs kept failing, despite constant pleas being sent back for more supplies, and more men to throw them, because the original attackers were exhausted. Another counter-attack on the Berkshires' sector at 2 p.m. with grenades drove the defenders back, and Hunt ordered a withdrawal.

'These assaults were carried out with the utmost dash and gallantry,' wrote Major General Hudson, the divisional Commander. 'No praise is too high for the conduct of all ranks in the assaulting lines; there was no hesitation and no pause. The enemy fought hard and there was continual bombing by both sides. By 8 a.m. the 2nd Royal Berkshires and 2nd Lincolns had got in touch, and the first line trench was held from the west end of the Lozenge to the east end of Bridoux Fort. The Rifle Brigade was holding Corner Fort and the front line for 200 yards to the east of it. The gap between them and the 2nd Royal Berkshire Regiment, about 300 yards, was never captured.'

Lieutenant Hanbury-Sparrow, in *The Land-Locked Lake*, blamed the 300-yard gap on A Company moving too far to the right. The artillery bombardment, he explained, had insufficient guns to completely destroy the enemy's wire, and two portions between the three assaults had been deliberately left intact. According to Hanbury-Sparrow, he considered the unnamed NCO who was leading the right-hand platoon of A Company to be unreliable, and he believed that the company veered to the right under his guidance and became entangled in the uncut barbed wire. Here they came under intense enemy fire. This allegation is not repeated in the official reports, and must be considered Hanbury-Sparrow's personal view, but, whatever the reason, very few men of A Company appear to have reached the enemy line and the company's allotted task of joining up with the 2nd Rifle Brigade was not completed.

Inevitably, the Berkshires had suffered heavy casualties. One of the dead was Lieutenant Guest-Williams. After the Armistice, his father wrote to the 20th Bavarian Reserve Regiment to ask if anyone could give him information regarding his son's fate. He received a reply from Hauptmann (Captain) Wilhelm Lindner, who had been one of the defenders at Bois Grenier, a copy of which is held in the Salisbury Regimental museum. Lindner's account of the action is as follows:

> On Sept. 25 1915, I was in the 20th Reserve Bavarian Regt., and with my company, took part in the attack of the 2nd Royal Berks Regt against our position near Bois-Grenier. After 3 days bombardment of our position, which actually effected very little damage, the English on Sept 25 attacked two points of my Regt's. position. They succeeded in forcing their way into our front line trenches at two points on a width of about 30 metres. They however, did not in consequence succeed in making use of this extend [sic] in the trenches. Our men, even if outfought, held the enemy fast. It was hardly 6 O.C. when the first Infantry attack which had lasted ½ hour was over. The Berkshires entrenched themselves, and we prepared to counter-attack, to recover our trenches. At 4 p.m. the sector occupied by the English was heavily bombarded by our Artillery. At the same time the trenches were heavily raked by machine-gun fire. At 5 p.m. I gave orders to the Infantry to attack with hand grenades and the bayonet. The few surviving Englishmen defended themselves bravely, but were overcome. The effect of Artillery and Machine-Gun was very severe, and except for two desperately wounded all were dead.

Except for some time differences, which were possibly due to the two armies keeping to different time zones, Hauptmann Lindner's account is confirmed by Major-General Hudson's report:

> At about 1 p.m. a determined counter-attack drove the 2nd Lincolns from Bridoux Fort, and recaptured the trench for about 100 yards to the west of the fort. Both flanks of the 2nd Royal Berkshire Regiment then became hard pressed. At 1.55 p.m. Lieutenant-colonel Hunt, finding his position untenable, gave the order for his regiment to withdraw to our trenches by the ditches. The regiment withdrew steadily, Lieutenant-Colonel Hunt distinguishing himself greatly in carrying out this difficult operation.

'The result of the operation,' Lieutenant-Colonel Hunt concluded, 'besides the casualties inflicted on 20th Bavarian Regiment, was that strong reinforcements of guns and infantry were attracted away from the main attack further South. The battalion

*Left:* The Buxcey brothers, both killed in action on 25 September 1915.

*Above:* The research team in front of the Ploegsteert Memorial to the Missing. The photograph was taken from the Royal Berks extension cemetery, started by the 1/4th Battalion in 1915.

Machine Guns, which had been taken into the captured trench, were all withdrawn, but not without some difficulty. A captured machine gun had to be abandoned in a ditch, but the lock had been removed by a machine gunner who was wounded.'

It had been a costly diversion. The Berkshires had lost seven officers and 124 men killed, sixty other ranks missing, five officers and 201 other ranks wounded – a total of 397 casualties. When the missing had been accounted for, the total killed or died of wounds was 154.

The letter from Hauptmann Lindner describes the aftermath:

By the evacuated trench, we found 2 Captains and 1 Lieutenant, the three officers were comparatively young, I surmise between 25 and 30 years old. Their equipment was almost new. The Officers' papers were taken from them and delivered to the Regimental Staff. The names unfortunately I did not identify, only that they were of the Berkshires, brave soldiers already known to me at Ypres, Wytshaete and Messines. No other fallen or captured Officers were identified in the sector, so your Son was probably among those three. Because of the imminent danger of a counter-attack that night, we were unable to undertake the burial of the fallen, the 3 Officers were therefore laid side by side in a trench cutting. The next morning our Lieutenant-General paid a visit to our fallen comrades and specially praised the courage of the Officers. During the next night the three Officers, in full equipment were buried in a separate grave next to their men. I erected over the grave a plain wooden cross which unfortunately was destroyed by English Machine Gun fire the next day. We German Officers buried our English Comrades with full honours.

Despite his father's efforts, Guest-Williams' grave was never found after the war, and his is one of 134 names from the 2nd Royal Berkshire Regiment from this action whose names can be found on the Ploegsteert Memorial to the Missing at Hyde Park Corner Cemetery near Ploegsteert in Belgium. The memorial records a total of 232 names from the battalion; the others are mostly from the Fromelles action in May 1915.

# VIII

# THE BUILD-UP

The winter of 1915 and the first half of 1916 was a quiet period in the British sector of the Western Front. Although some of the New Army divisions raised by Lord Kitchener had fought at Loos, the majority were still in training, and not ready to participate in any significant attacks.

The enemy co-operated by not mounting any offensives, preferring to consolidate the territory which they had gained in 1914 by improving their defences. This strategy could not be copied by the Allies, for they had the war aim of driving the Germans out of occupied France and Belgium, which could only be achieved by a breakthrough. For this reason the British trench lines were never as elaborate as the Germans', for the BEF only considered them as temporary shelters from which to attack the enemy.

After the action at Bois Grenier, the 2nd Royal Berkshires moved into billets at Bac St Maur, and then spent October alternating between holding the line at Bois Grenier and periods in reserve.

After Loos, it became the policy in the BEF to intermix brigades from the newly arrived New Army divisions with the regular divisions, with the intention that the enthusiasm of the amateurs would rejuvenate the professionals, who, in return, would pass on their experience of soldiering. The 8th Division lost the 24th Brigade to the 23rd Division on 4 November, receiving the 70th Brigade in exchange. For a few days, the Berkshires sent eight platoons – half of their fighting strength – to serve with the 8th York and Lancaster Regiment in 70th Brigade, while eight platoons of the Yorks and Lancs spent time with the 2nd Berkshires during a tour in the front line.

On 23 November, the 8th Division went into 1st Army Reserve near Steenbecque, which meant their first spell out of the line for the whole division since arriving at the front. Before leaving the sector, however, a battery of 9.2-inch howitzers delivered a heavy bombardment on the enemy positions to keep them busy while the relief took place. The 2nd Royal Berkshires marched to Sercus, between Hazebrouck and St Omer, some 20 miles behind the line, where intensive training commenced. New drafts of officers and men arrived to replace the losses at Bois Grenier, and on 12 December a new second-in-command, Major Holdsworth, joined the battalion.

On 20 December the whole 8th Division participated in manoeuvres. They lasted for three days and covered a large area of ground but, the Divisional History recorded, were marred by heavy rain, and restricted because most of the land was planted with seed for next year. Nevertheless, it was the first opportunity that the battalions and brigades had had to practise as a composite division since they were first assembled at Winchester thirteen months before. During the exercises, the 2nd Royal Berkshires were commanded by Major Holdsworth, for Lieutenant-Colonel Hunt was promoted to temporary brigadier and posted to command a brigade. Arthur Holdsworth, who was forty, became an acting lieutenant-colonel on assuming command.

Lieutenant-Colonel Arthur Mervyn Holdsworth,
Commanding Officer on 1 July 1916, wounded in action
and later died of wounds.

There were changes at the very top as well. Field Marshal Sir John French, who had been criticised for not committing the reserves in time during the Loos battle, relinquished his command of the BEF, and Sir Douglas Haig, commander of the First Army, was appointed in his place.

Christmas 1915 was observed quietly while in billets at Sercus, a contrast to the informal truce of the previous year. The Digest of Service reported that 'A Dinner was provided for the men from Regimental Funds', but gives no details of the menu. Units who were serving in the front line had been issued with strong warnings against any fraternisation with the enemy, and there are no reports of any taking place.

In early January 1916, rumours circulated that the division was being transferred to Egypt, or Salonika, or anywhere – nobody much cared where, as long as it was warm and dry. Sadly, they came to nothing, and with their hopes dashed the battalion marched back to the Lys Sector, to take over trenches at Fleurbaix, close to the site of the Bois Grenier battlefield.

Newly raised divisions were now arriving from home on a regular basis, making up for their lack of experience with an unbounded enthusiasm to 'have a crack at the enemy'. Before they were given sectors of their own, GHQ had adopted a policy of placing them with a regular division to learn about real war, and during the next three months in the sector, 8th Division played host and instructor to the 34th Division, which arrived in France in January, and part of the 39th Division, which arrived in March minus one of their brigades, which had been judged as insufficiently trained to go to France.

The presence of the new units gave some variety to what would otherwise have been an uneventful three months in a miserable sector of the line. It also allowed the men more time out of the trenches, which was welcome, as both February and March were dreary, with rain and snow making constant pumping necessary to keep the defences from flooding.

In January, a decision had been taken by the War Office to remove the Vickers machine guns from battalion control, and consolidate them into a machine gun company for each infantry brigade. At the outbreak of war, the allotment had been two guns per battalion, but this was increased to four when more weapons and trained crews became available. On 19 January, Second Lieutenants Brown and Batchelor, together with thirty-six men, transferred to the 25th Company of the newly formed Machine Gun Corps.

The establishment of a specialised company reporting to the brigade commander gave him far more flexibility and control over the use of the guns in supporting the infantry. Putting the companies into a corps would also allow good practice and new tactics to be more rapidly circulated to the specialist machine gun officers. Naturally, this decision caused some consternation at battalion level, but this was alleviated by supplies of the Lewis gun, a new light automatic weapon, which required a crew of two and would become a major asset to the infantry in the years to come.

There had been so many changes among the officers, due to casualties, promotions or transfers, that on the departure of Lieutenant-Colonel Hunt, Captain Hanbury-Sparrow, the adjutant, found himself the longest-serving officer with the exception of the quartermaster and the transport officer. He had scornfully dismissed an overture just after Bois Grenier by a divisional commander to become his aide: 'I held that the post of ADC was the most contemptible that a man could take on; the appointment was enough to damn the holder for ever in your eyes.' As the dreary winter wore on, and casualties mounted, he began to regret his haste, and applied for a post as staff officer with the division. He was successful, and left the battalion at the end of March.

The lack of enemy activity on the British sector in early 1916 was mostly due to the Germans concentrating their resources into a massive assault on the French town of Verdun, which commenced on 21 February. No British forces were involved, but its impact on the French army would have severe consequences on the timing and conduct of the Somme battle, then in the planning stages. Part of the planning included the 8th Division, and, at the end of March, the 35th Division took over the Lys sector, and the 2nd Royal Berkshires found themselves on a train moving southwards.

The journey ended at Amiens, and the battalion marched to the nearby town of Flesselles, where Divisional Headquarters was being set up. The 8th Division became a part of II Corps, in General Sir Henry Rawlinson's Fourth Army. After a period in Divisional Reserve, the 2nd Royal Berkshires moved into the line near La Boisselle on 10 April.

The Somme came as a welcome change of scene. The rolling chalk hills, covered in grass and interspersed with copses of trees, reminded the men of the Berkshire Downs, and they felt far more at home than they had in the Lys Sector. To make things even better, the trenches were dry! In the old sector the water table was only just below ground, but here the chalk provided good drainage, and no longer did the miserable sentries have to spend their period of guard duty up to their knees in freezing water while their comrades spent hours in fruitless pumping and bailing.

Four British divisions had taken over the North Somme sector from the French in August 1915. The previous occupants had adopted a 'live and let live' policy, and the front had remained quiet. This was anathema to GHQ and, once the divisions had become familiar with their new sectors, a policy of aggressive patrolling and sniping had been introduced and the enemy were reacting in kind. This was the situation in which the Berkshires found themselves on their first night.

The battalion, who were just south of Aveluy Wood, had the 1st Royal Irish Rifles on their right. On the night of 11 April the enemy carried out a raid on the Irishmen, taking several prisoners. The raid was preceded by a bombardment, which caught the Berkshires' D Company as well, killing Captain Bowles, the company commander, Second Lieutenant Davies, and three other ranks. They are all buried in Bécourt Military Cemetery, the first of the battalion's Somme casualties. There were to be many more.

Captain Hanbury-Sparrow, General Staff Officer Grade 3 (GSO3) on the 8th Division's staff, was missing the battalion. On 5 June he wrote home to his mother:

> I am feeling most frightfully homesick for my regiment and bitterly repent the day when my selfishness urged me to go on the staff. One feels such an utter rotter back here in comparative safety and I would infinitely rather take my chances of being killed with the

Captain Alan Bowles (left) in the trenches.

regiment than being back here doing a job any fool could do. My conscience pricks me most horribly as I know I am far more useful with them than here. The trouble is I can't get back, although I have tried several times. Of course I am very happy here, but I cannot shake off the feeling of having funked it when I applied for a staff billet.

It was becoming increasingly obvious to the Germans that preparations for a major attack were under way, for as they held the high ground, it was impossible to conceal from them the additional activity of building ammunition dumps, Royal Engineers' stores, dressing stations and all the other requirements. The enemy reacted with increased shellfire, and even behind the line the men found themselves having to form artillery order instead of the customary marching in fours. Nevertheless, the precautions were worthwhile, for only three men were killed in May and June.

According to the 8th Divisional History, the 2nd Royal Berkshires carried out a successful raid on the night of 25 June. After dealing with the sentries in the front line, the enemy could be heard singing in their deep dugouts. Their concert came to a premature end when the Berkshires rolled grenades down the entrances. This story was also recorded by Major John Jack, DSO, second-in-command of the 2nd Scottish Rifles in 23rd Brigade. He later became a brigadier-general and kept a detailed diary, which was published in 1962 as *General Jack's Diary*, edited by John Terraine. The incident is also discussed by Martin Middlebrook in *The First Day of the Somme* and by Lyn MacDonald in her book, *Somme*. Curiously, though, the raid is not mentioned in the war diaries of the 2nd Royal Berkshire Battalion, the 25th Brigade or the 8th Division. There should have been at least an operation order, and a report by the officer in command, but nothing has been traced in either the National Archives or the Regimental Museum.

One can presume that Martin Middlebrook and Lyn MacDonald used the 8th Division History as their source for the story, and the writers of that history had access to documents that have subsequently been lost or misfiled. Major Jack would have been informed as part of the normal distribution of intelligence information to the battalions in the division, and, as he considered it worth recording in his diary, one must assume that it took place.

Hanbury-Sparrow visited the 2nd Royal Berkshires on 29 June, under canvas in Long Valley, and found one of the company messes had used their gramophone records to pave the floor of the muddy ground of their tent. He was dismayed to be told 'we won't be needing them any more', which gave him grave misgivings about the state of mind of his old battalion.

# IX

# THE FIRST DAY OF THE SOMME

The Battle of the Somme is probably the best known and most documented of all the Western Front campaigns in the British sector, and much of the literature concentrates on the opening day, 1 July 1916. In fact, the battle did not cease until 22 November, nearly five months later, only to resume in February 1917. This sometimes gives a disproportionate emphasis to the first day of what developed into a long and complex campaign of attrition.

However, the 2nd Royal Berkshires played a leading role on the first day, so it is appropriate to devote a chapter to one day of the battle.

The map of the front line in June 1916 can be compared to a capital L, with the corner of the letter resting on the village of Fricourt, whence it extended some 9 miles northwards to Serre, and 4 miles eastwards to Montauban. At Montauban the right flank of the British Fourth Army joined with the left flank of the French Sixth Army, who were also attacking on 1 July. The French contribution was not as massive as had originally been planned, because the enemy attack on Verdun had caused them so many casualties that they were unable to supply many divisions for the Somme campaign.

The town of Albert was situated some two miles behind the British line, and the straight Roman road from there to Bapaume bisected the battlefield, crossing the respective front lines at La Boisselle. In most sectors, the enemy had the advantage of the higher ground, which they had occupied for nearly two years, developing a complex maze of trenches, deep dugouts and barbed wire entanglements.

General Rawlinson's plan called for twelve infantry divisions to attack, with an additional five in reserve, although in some instances detachments from the reserve divisions were loaned to the attacking divisions. In addition, two divisions from the Third Army would mount a diversionary attack on Gommecourt, some three miles to the north of the Fourth Army's left flank, with the objective of preventing the enemy from moving his reserves southwards. This had also been the thinking behind the 8th Division's attack at Bois Grenier to coincide with the opening of the battle of Loos. No attack was planned on the sector between Gommecourt and Serre.

The attack was to be preceded by an intense bombardment which was confidently expected to destroy the German wire and trenches, and put the few survivors into such a state of shock that their resistance would be minimal.

The 8th Division was allotted the initial objective of Ovillers, just to the north of the Albert to Bapaume road. Once that was achieved, the way would be open to Pozières, the next village on the road, and, incidentally, the high point of the battlefield, where a ruined windmill afforded the Germans an excellent observation post. The road formed the right hand divisional boundary, with the 34th Division to the south tasked to take and hold the village of La Boisselle. The straight road climbs along an embankment between the two villages, with shallow valleys on either side. The southern valley, in the 34th Division's sector, was overlooked by an enemy 'sausage' observation balloon, and so became known as 'Sausage Valley'. Naturally, the Tommies named its northern twin 'Mash Valley', which slopes gently upwards towards Ovillers.

Major-General Hudson, the commander of 8th Division, disposed his forces as follows: the 23rd Brigade was placed on the right. They had the widest part of no-man's land to cross, up Mash Valley towards the enemy lines just west of Ovillers. If the 34th Division on their right failed to take La Boisselle, then the advancing troops would be horribly vulnerable to machine gun fire from that strongpoint.

In the 25th Brigade's sector, there was less distance to cover before reaching the German lines, for they were to advance along the low ridge to the north of the valley and make a frontal attack on heavily fortified Ovillers.

The 70th Brigade were stationed on the division's left flank, with the objective of taking the complex of enemy trenches to the north of Ovillers. The division on their left, the 32nd, was to take Thiepval Ridge, again heavily fortified by the enemy. On this flank, just as on the right, the 8th Division was depending on the success of this attack, for if it failed, they would be in jeopardy from the Thiepval machine gunners. The attacks were all interdependent, for conversely, if Ovillers remained in enemy hands, the 32nd and 34th Divisions would be vulnerable from its defenders.

In the centre, Brigadier Pollard detailed the 2nd Royal Berkshires and 2nd Lincolns to lead the frontal attack on Ovillers, supported by the 1st Royal Irish Rifles. The 2nd Rifle Brigade was kept as a reserve. The Berkshires were to take the right, with the Lincolns on their left. The north edge of Mash Valley marked the right flank of the Berkshires' attack, where they adjoined the 2nd Devons from 23rd Brigade. Zero hour was 7.30 a.m. on 1 July.

The battalion spent the days before the assault camped in Long Valley near Albert. It must have been difficult to sleep, for the barrage would have been deafening. It had initially been planned for five days, but went on for a further two when the attack was postponed due to bad weather. The Berkshires, with the other attacking battalions, moved up into the line on the night of 29 June. The enemy wire, according to the Divisional History, was observed to be well cut, and working parties cut lanes in our own wire for the assaulting troops, which were then blocked by movable barriers. Everything was ready, and there was nothing to do except wait.

The weather on 1 July proved to be fine, with a slight mist, the rising sun putting the attackers at a further disadvantage, for they would be advancing into it. At 6.25 a.m., with just over an hour to go, the artillery barrage rose to a final crescendo, to be joined by the 8th Division's Stokes mortar batteries at 7.22 a.m. At this stage, the Middlesex and Devons of the 23rd Brigade, on the Berkshires' right, started to crawl forward, for they had a lot further to go to reach their objectives. Although the bombardment was still in progress, and was supposedly keeping the enemy's heads down, both battalions started to suffer heavy casualties from rifle and machine gun fire. Also at this time, the Berkshires and Lincolns started to move forward, and they too came under fire.

At zero hour, 7.30 a.m., the barrage lifted to the second objective, the German support lines behind Ovillers. Two minutes before zero, to the south, an enormous mine laid under the enemy lines just south of La Boisselle was detonated. Comprising nearly 28 tons of ammonal explosive, it formed the crater known as Lochnagar, which is still there today. It must have been a spectacular sight, and shaken the ground, but it is not mentioned in the 8th Division account of the action. Presumably this was because it was outside the division's sector, for it is difficult to believe that it would have gone unnoticed, however focused the men were on their own attack.

At 7.30 a.m. the Berkshires' assaulting companies climbed out of the trenches and moved forward across no-man's land, a manoeuvre which was being repeated all along the 16-mile front. What happened next is summed up in two lines of the battalion's report on the action: 'At 7.30 am the three assaulting Companies advanced to attack the German line. They were met by intense rifle and machine gun fire which prevented any of the waves reaching the enemy's lines.'

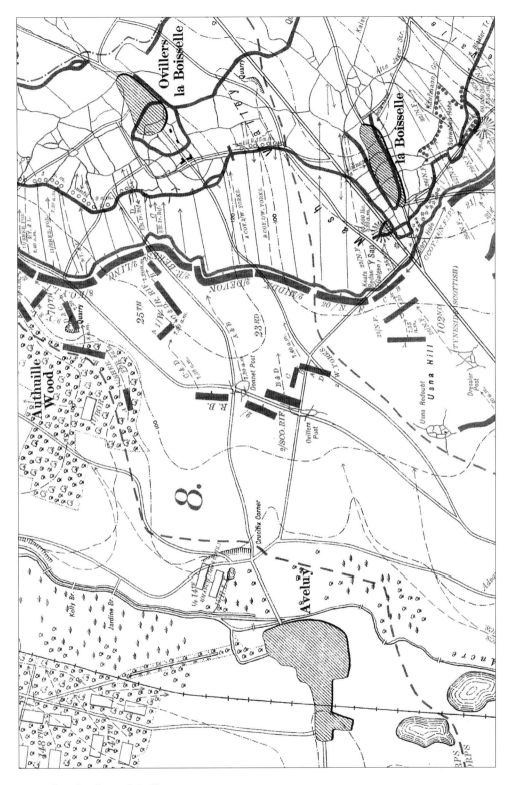

Map of Mash Valley and Ovillers.

There was a similar situation all along the northern section of the front, as the British made the unpleasant discovery that the week-long bombardment had made little impression on the well-constructed German dugouts. At 30ft or more underground, nothing short of a direct hit by a heavy shell would do any damage, and as soon as the barrage ceased the enemy raced up into their battered trenches, brought their machine guns into action, and devastated the attackers. Their task was aided by the fact that the British barrage was now falling harmlessly behind them, pounding the defences in front of Pozières in preparation for the attack on the second objective.

A small group of the Berkshires, on the left, did manage to get into the enemy trench, but were soon bombed out again. The commanding officer, Lieutenant-Colonel Holdsworth, and the second-in-command, Major Sawyer, were both wounded at 7.45 a.m. Command devolved upon the twenty-year-old Second Lieutenant Mollet, who, as acting adjutant, was the senior remaining officer – the company commanders were somewhere out in no-man's land, either dead, wounded, or pinned down in shell-holes by heavy fire.

By now, the parapet of the British front line was being swept by machine gun fire, and was under bombardment from enemy artillery. Mollet was in an unenviable position for his first experience of commanding a battalion. By 9 a.m., the effective strength of the remaining company was down to less than 100 men, and he could not ascertain what was happening on his own front, for it was lethal to look over the parapet. Furthermore, he had received no reports from the adjoining battalions, the 2nd Devons on the right or the 2nd Lincolns on the left. He and the surviving men hung on, hoping for orders or reinforcements.

In fact, the 23rd Brigade's progress up Mash Valley had been a disaster. When the barrage ceased, the two attacking battalions doubled forward, but the machine gun fire increased, and fewer than 200 survived to reach the enemy lines. The support battalion, 2nd West Yorkshires, were sent forward to assist, but they were also cut down before reaching Ovillers. The danger of failing to take La Boisselle became all too apparent, for the 34th Division had also been cut down, failing to take their objective and leaving the German machine guns free to sweep Mash Valley with impunity. By 9 a.m., the only survivors from these three battalions were those who had managed to crouch in shell-holes, where they waited for nightfall. Any movement gave rise to a burst of machine gun fire, and the hot, sunny day added the torment of thirst to the men's misfortunes.

The situation on the Berkshires' left, where the 2nd Lincolns attacked, was initially somewhat better. They suffered fewer casualties crossing no-man's land, and reached the enemy front line, where they encountered troops emerging from the cellars under the ruined buildings of Ovillers. After a fierce struggle, they managed to gain about 200 yards of enemy trench. They succeeded in repulsing a German counter-attack, but intense enfilade machine gun and rifle fire made their position untenable. By 10 a.m. about thirty survivors managed to regain the relative safety of the British front line.

Captain Hanbury-Sparrow had been sent forward with two signallers to act as an observer and report back to Divisional Headquarters. His observation post was probably on the high ground behind the British front line, a position called the Tara Usna line. He wrote to his mother:

> The morning was naturally misty and the smoke and dust made it impossible for me to see what was happening. I could see men going forward and whole lines suddenly lie down, as I thought at the time to let the front line get on further. When the mist rose the lines were still there. They had all been shot down by machine gun or rifle fire. In spite of the furious fire against them the men went awfully well.

Hanbury-Sparrow's uncle was commanding a battalion in the 34th Division, and Hanbury-Sparrow could also see their progress from his observation post. The letter continues: 'Charley's division was on our right. I am afraid they lost rather heavily also,

Private Horace Angier.

but I have never seen anything finer than the way the men went. They were scrapping the whole of the first day and I never saw any hesitation on the part of the men.' Uncle Charlie was probably Lieutenant-Colonel Charles Sillery, of the Northumberland Fusiliers, who was one of five battalion commanders killed in the 34th Division that day.

The letter concludes: 'Whatever is final result of the battle, we have caused very heavy casualties to the Germans, a great deal heavier than at Loos.' But when he had better information, he was very despondent:

> The division met a terrible defeat. Two hundred and eighteen officers out of 300 were lost and 5,274 other ranks out of some 8,500; 65 per cent of the infantry destroyed and not a yard of ground gained. And the enemy, what of him? The whole division had been defeated by two battalions of the 180th Infantry Reserve Regiment at a cost of eight officers and 273 other ranks killed, wounded or missing.'

He blamed the defeat on the hammering which the division had taken at Fromelles, using the argument that the 70th Brigade, which had not joined the 8th Division until afterwards, had made a far more successful attack than the already demoralised 23rd and 25th Brigades.

Hanbury-Sparrow's analysis is, of course, one man's opinion, and his views on morale contradict the official versions. However, he was there, and knew the officers in both the 2nd Royal Berkshires and 8th Division staff.

Few personal accounts have survived, but one that has concerns Private Horace Angier, from Lambeth. He was one of the battalion runners, and had been sent, presumably by Second Lieutenant Mollet, with a message to the brigade's machine gunners. They were positioned on the Albert road, near La Boisselle, in a location called the 'Glory Hole', which was situated on the divisional boundary between the 8th and 34th Divisions. Private Hubert Hemmings of the 2nd Royal Berkshires gave an account of Angier's death to the British Red Cross from his bed in the Red Cross Hospital at Torquay:

> On July 1st 1916, at Albert, in the Glory Hole, Pte. Angier was killed by a shell which came over and killed all the machine gun team. Pte. Angier had only been there a few minutes, having been a runner with a message to the team. I was doing sentry duty and saw it all happen and afterwards heard enquiries made for the runner. It was in the middle of a summer morning. The 2nd Royal Berks had a terrible time from the Germans and when they were relieved that night, only 36 left the trenches.

Colonel Charles Mollet, OBE MC and Bar.
Taken from a painting later in life.

One can speculate that perhaps Second Lieutenant Mollet or one of the other surviving officers had sent Angier to inform the machine gun company of the failure to take Ovillers, and asking them to redirect their fire into the enemy lines rather than the back area.

At 12.30 p.m. Mollet at last received orders from the 25th Brigade that the remnants of the attacking battalions were to be relieved, and at 3.30 p.m. Major Brand led up the 2nd Rifle Brigade from brigade reserve and took over the defence of the front line. The survivors from the Berkshires and Lincolns withdrew to the support lines, and later that day the whole 8th Division, less the artillery, were replaced by the 12th Division, and marched to camp in Long Valley. The unwounded elements of the attacking companies were able to make their way back after nightfall, and rejoin their units, while stretcher bearers made their way out to recover the injured. Lieutenant-Colonel Holdsworth's wounds proved fatal, and he died in hospital at Etaples a week later.

So ended the first day of the Somme. The 2nd Royal Berkshires had lost twelve officers and 148 men killed or missing, the commanding officer and twelve men dying of wounds later, and six officers and 251 men were wounded, a total of 430 casualties. While these numbers are appalling, the battalion had fared better than many, for Martin Middlebrook's book, *The First Day on the Somme*, lists thirty-two battalions who suffered over 500 casualties each. The total British casualties for the day, as is well known, totalled some 57,000, of which over 19,000 were fatalities. There were some successes, however, for the attacks along the southern side of the Fricourt salient had gone well.

The Divisional History comments:

> Dependent as it was, by the very nature of the terrain, upon the simultaneous success of the divisions on either flank, the task allotted to the 8th Division had indeed been one of the utmost difficulty. The odds against success were yet further weighted, as the event showed, by lack of experience in dealing with the deep German dugouts, with their underground communications and many exits, and in the proper control of the artillery barrage.

The Webb brothers from Blewbury, pictured here in India before the war. Private Edwin A. Webb, Corporal Albert W. Webb and Private Edgar G Webb. Albert and Edgar were both killed in action on 1 July 1916.

Brigadier Pollard, commanding the 25th Infantry Brigade, wrote in his report on the action:

> A bombardment on some given line may be of value in damaging the enemy's defences and preventing supports from being sent up; but if the line in question is 1000 yards behind the line from which our assaulting troops are being held up, as was the case on July 1st, the position is very far from being satisfactory. To prevent reinforcements from reaching the enemy is but of minor value, if we are ourselves unable to maintain our hold on the enemy front line. I consider that, in principle, no barrage should lift until the infantry concerned have notified that they are ready for it to do so.

To complete the story of Ovillers, a second attack was made by the 12th Division in the early morning of 3 July. The division included the 5th Battalion, Royal Berkshire Regiment, who attacked up the left side of Mash Valley, over the ground that the 2nd Devons had covered. Despite commencing the attack in the dark, the men were once again cut down by machine gun fire from La Boisselle and Ovillers, and failed to take the objective, although some men from the 5th Royal Berkshires managed to get into the village, where they were killed or captured. Afterwards, survivors reported that they had been stumbling over the bodies of Berkshire soldiers killed on 1 July. Ovillers was finally taken on 16 July by 25th Division, who were able to approach from the south, avoiding the death trap of Mash Valley.

Private Angier is buried in the Commonwealth War Grave cemetery at Ovillers, which is sited on the Berkshire's line of attack from the British front line towards Ovillers. 46 of Angier's comrades from the 2nd Royal Berkshires are also buried there, but 102 men killed in the attack have no known grave, and are commemorated on the Thiepval Memorial to the Missing.

# X

# REBUILDING AT LOOS

The dreadful losses sustained at Ovillers resulted in the 8th Division being withdrawn from the Somme campaign. The Berkshires spent 2 July in camp back in Long Valley, while roll calls were taken to try to establish the extent of the casualties. Nightfall on 1 July had given the survivors sheltering in no-man's land the opportunity to crawl back to the British lines, and the unwounded men rejoined the battalion, where they were asked if they could supply details of the fate of their missing comrades.

To his delight, Captain Hanbury-Sparrow was released from his post as GSO3 in the 8th Division, and rejoined the battalion, which was just as well for there were very few Royal Berkshire regular officers left. Major R. Haig, DSO, who had been second in command of the 6th Rifle Brigade, joined on 4 July as the new commanding officer, assuming the rank of lieutenant-colonel on his appointment.

New orders arrived, transferring the 8th Division to I Corps, 1st Army. By 8 July the surviving Berkshires had travelled by train and route-marches to billets at Allouagne, out of the line to the west of Béthune, where the next two weeks were spent absorbing drafts to replace the casualties, and reorganising.

The heavy casualties in all units had led to the virtual breakdown of the system in which an officer or private soldier joining a regiment could expect to be drafted to one of its battalions. The situation led to men who had completed training being sent to any unit which needed bringing up to strength, and seventy men arrived from the Worcestershire Regiment, seventy-nine from the Army Cyclist Corps, and an officer, Captain R.J. Tucker, from the Bermuda Rifle Volunteer Corps. The battalion was becoming 'Berkshire' in little but its title.

'The chief activity of Records', Hanbury-Sparrow observed, 'was to send drafts of other regiments to reinforce battalions, thereby doing everything to break down the regimental spirit we were striving day and night to build up. For instance, Records sent us a large draft of Midlanders with whom we had not got the smallest connection, whilst they sent our men off elsewhere. Yet such is the transferable element in man that we were as quickly able to absorb them as they were to give us good and loyal service. It was commonly reported that this mixing up of drafts was a deliberate policy imposed on Records, but if it was true it was making an awful fool of units.' His suspicion that this was a deliberate policy may well have been correct, for the 1 July attrition on certain 'Pals' battalions had had such an impact on some local communities that the Army Council was trying to diversify the battalions as far as possible.

Three weeks after the Somme attack, the battalion was back in the line. Their new sector was on the northern edge of the old Loos battlefield, which, before the war, had been a prosperous coalfield. It was now a wasteland of spoil heaps, wrecked pithead machinery, shell-holes and flooded trench workings. Both sides had indulged in mining since the establishment of the front lines, but instead of an innocent search for coal, the

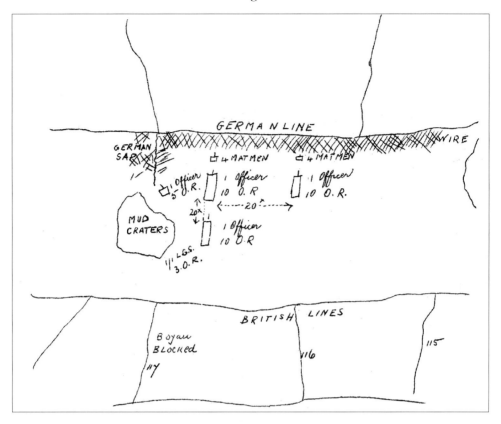

Sketch map of the raid from Captain Ward's report.

excavations were directed to undermining the enemy's trenches and then detonating an explosive charge beneath them. These had left huge craters at various points along the line, and the trench lines snaked around their perimeters.

No-man's land was littered with corpses, mostly from between 25 September and 13 October 1915, the main phase of the battle of Loos. It was too dangerous to attempt to recover them, and they had lain where they had fallen for over nine months, disturbed only by rats, shellfire, mine explosions, or perhaps a horrified soldier from a night patrol who had dived for cover when a flare went up.

The battalion settled back into trench routine, spending four or five days in the line, then in support, then in reserve, while the new men settled down and learned their jobs. There was steady attrition from snipers, shelling and trench mortars, and the ever-present threat that a German mine might explode under one's trench without warning. The men listened anxiously for the sound of picks and shovels underground, for as long as they could hear the enemy at work, they felt safe from instant oblivion.

On the night of 24 September 1916, the Berkshires carried out a strong trench raid under the command of Captain Ward. There were two other officers and forty-nine other ranks, and the objective was to gain information, and, if possible, take prisoners. The men were armed with revolvers and truncheons for close fighting, carried handcuffs for securing prisoners, and had blackened their faces. The enemy wire was to be destroyed by a 'Bangalore Torpedo', a length of drainpipe about 6ft long, packed with explosives and fitted with a fuse. Corporal Taylor had been volunteered to lead a party who would creep up to the enemy wire and poke the pipe into the entanglement, light the fuse and retire immediately.

Private David Byde, MM.

The attackers left the British lines at 9.15 p.m., and carefully got into formation in no-man's land. The men were divided into two attack parties, and silently waited for 10.15 p.m., when the Bangalore Torpedo was due to detonate. After a long wait, Captain Ward decided that the device had failed to explode, and blew his whistle to start the attack just as the artillery barrage opened up on the enemy second line.

When Corporal Taylor heard Ward's signal, he gave up trying to detonate the torpedo, dismantled it, and brought the components back to the British line, where it was discovered that the primer had not been inserted properly.

Captain Ward's whistle took the left hand party by surprise, for they had been waiting for the Bangalore Torpedo to go off. As a consequence, the charge was rather ragged and not all the men reached the enemy trench at the same time. Four of them were carrying mats to throw over the barbed wire, and when this was done a group led by Private Byde managed to enter the trench and turned left. After running down four traverses, three Germans jumped on Byde and tried to strangle him, but, frightened by the rest of the party, they let him go and ran up a communication trench. Byde recovered his wits sufficiently to shoot one of them as they ran. He wanted to recover some identification from the body, but the other two Germans defended it with grenades and Byde was unable to get near. Reinforcements arrived, and a fierce bombing exchange ensued, which lasted about five minutes, by which time the attackers were running short of bombs, and withdrew without loss.

The right hand party had a similar experience. The mat carriers dealt with the barbed wire, and Second Lieutenant Humphreys led a group of bombers into the enemy trench. They encountered numerous defenders, and soon Humphreys was hit in the head and mortally wounded. This group also spent about five minutes in the trench, keeping the enemy occupied while Private Rose carried the dying officer back to a shell-hole. Sergeant Gibson tried to bring him back from there, but was unable to do so on his own. Captain Griffin and Private Tull then went out and recovered him, but he died on the same day.

The covering party, under Ward's direct command, had not entered the enemy trench, but had lain down on the parapet and covered the retreat of the two attack parties. A second covering party, armed with Lewis guns, had been stationed between the mud craters and an enemy sap, but although they made their way down the sap they did not meet any opposition or see any suitable targets. Captain Ward reported that the Germans had been very numerous in this sector, and the sentries were in groups of three or four men, surrounded by barbed wire, and with a passage back to their support line. The shell-holes in front of the front line had been covered in barbed wire, and broken glass was lying in the bottom. The front trench was only about 3ft deep, and very dilapidated. Large sections of it were full of barbed wire. The raiders found no dugouts, and there had been very little hostile artillery, trench mortar, machine gun or rifle fire.

Apart from Second Lieutenant V. Humphreys the casualties were reported to have been light. In fact, the postwar records show that Lance-Corporals Ellis and Hobbs and Private Knight were also killed on 24/25 September, but they may not necessarily have taken part in the raid. All three are buried in Vermelles British Cemetery, together with Second Lieutenant Humphreys. Corporal Taylor, Private Byde and Private Rose were awarded Military Medals for their part in the action.

On 12 October, the Division received orders to return to the Somme sector. The period in the Loos trenches had hardly been a respite, for three officers had been killed, together with thirty-three other ranks. Additionally, 108 had been wounded, and one man was missing.

# XI

# BACK TO THE SOMME

The battalion returned to find a very different battlefield from the Somme that they had known before 1 July. The success of the initial attacks along the southern leg of the British sector had been exploited, and the battle had re-orientated itself to become a push from south to north instead of the advance along the Albert to Bapaume road as originally planned.

Four months of continuous fighting had changed the scenery. The woods and copses had been reduced to a wasteland of shattered branches, the fields and trench lines were pockmarked with shell craters, and the roads had deteriorated into hardly passable rutted tracks.

On the plus side, learning the lessons from 1 July, the Royal Artillery had developed the technique of the 'Creeping Barrage'. Instead of bombarding the enemy front line, and then lifting to the support line when it was hoped that the attackers had reached their first objective, a creeping barrage laid a screen of fire just in front of the jumping off points, which advanced at an agreed distance per minute depending on the condition of the ground the men had to cross. The enemy would be forced to take cover just as the infantry were ready to make the final dash onto their objective. It called for a great degree of trust and confidence between the artillery and the infantry, but it was preventing the dreadful casualties incurred on the first day of the campaign.

The 8th Division had been selected for the next large attack against a strong system of trenches covering the villages of Le Transloy and Beaulencourt, but, records the Divisional History, 'the situation was saved for the Germans by the advance of winter. The weather broke, and broke so badly that it became impossible to exploit the situation with the necessary rapidity.'

Nevertheless, the attack was to go in, and the Berkshires made their way up to the assembly trenches east of Gueudecourt, trudging through knee-deep mud. The rain was unceasing. The Divisional attack would use all three brigades, 25th in the centre, 23rd on the right, and 24th on the left. The objective was a complex of German trenches to the west of Le Transloy centred on Zenith trench, possession of which would bring the Division close enough to Le Transloy to enable a future joint attack from both the west and south of the position.

In the 25th Brigade, Brigadier-General Pollard chose the 2nd Lincolnshires and 2nd Rifle Brigade to be the two assaulting battalions, with the 2nd Royal Berkshires in support. He kept the 1st Royal Irish Rifles in reserve. Zero hour was to be 11.30 a.m. on 23 October. The conditions underfoot were so bad that the creeping barrage was set to advance at 50 yards a minute. The men crouched in their mud holes, wet through from the continual rain.

When daylight came on 23 October, there was a thick fog, and the attack was postponed until 2.30 p.m. By 1.30 p.m., the fog had cleared, and the weather showed considerable improvement, and the attack went in as planned. On the right, the 23rd Brigade were successful, for their assaulting battalions, 2nd Scottish Rifles and 2nd Middlesex, followed the creeping barrage, took their allotted sections of Zenith trench, and started to consolidate some 150 yards beyond it.

In the centre, 25th Brigade were not so lucky. About three quarters of an hour before zero, parties of the enemy were observed moving north along Zenith trench in the sector which was due to be attacked by the Lincolns. It was supposed that they were withdrawing to positions further back in anticipation of the attack on Zenith, but the British bombardment had blocked Eclipse Trench, which would have been their line of retreat. Consequently, the Lincolns' objective was heavily manned when their assault went in. To add to their troubles, they discovered that the ground was so muddy that it was impossible to keep up with the creeping barrage even at only 50 yards per minute.

In the words of the Divisional History, 'The troops had made but little progress across the open when a German officer, with consummate bravery and supreme disregard for death, jumped up and ran along his own parapet ordering up his men. They responded quickly, and standing shoulder high above the parapet, met the advancing Lincolnshires with rapid rifle fire.' The first wave was cut down and similarly the second; only one platoon on the extreme right managed to enter Zenith trench.

The other assaulting battalion in the centre brigade, 2nd Rifle Brigade, had more success, making better progress behind the creeping barrage and reaching Misty trench, their objective, where they consolidated in shell-holes. The attack by the left flank 24th Brigade had also been successful.

While this was going on, the Berkshires had moved up to occupy the Lincolns' trenches as they moved out. C and B Companies went after the first wave, followed by A and D when the second wave left. Heavy casualties were sustained from enemy shellfire while this move was taking place. Soon after 3 p.m., Lieutenant-Colonel Haig ordered B Company to reinforce the Lincolns, and an hour later ordered C Company to join the 2nd Rifle Brigade on the left and if possible attack Zenith trench from the north-west.

As night fell, the situation for the division was that the flank objectives had been gained, but a large portion of Zenith trench in the centre was strongly held by the enemy, and was being reinforced. This sector was now in front of the 2nd Royal Berkshires, and Lieutenant-Colonel Haig informed Brigadier Pollard that it would be impractical to attack it without the aid of an artillery bombardment. Pollard ordered the remnants of the 2nd Lincolns to withdraw, and two companies of 1st Sherwood Foresters were sent up from divisional reserve to be put at Pollard's disposal.

The new attack, to be made by the 2nd Royal Berkshires and the 1st Royal Irish Rifles, was fixed for 3.50 a.m. the next day, with an artillery barrage starting at 1 a.m. During the evening, the weather changed again for the worse, and the rain started to fall in torrents. Hanbury-Sparrow tried to inspire his shivering men with a pep-talk about the importance of the attack. A draft had recently arrived under the Derby Scheme called Group 40 – married men of forty-one years or older. He recorded that their spirit was superb but they just couldn't stand the hardship. One man, shaking with ague, was in tears because he just could not go on. 'It comes a bit hard after only fourteen weeks training,' he confided to Hanbury-Sparrow. 'Hard! It was a soaking hell of misery such as you had never imagined,' the latter wrote in his memoirs.

The attack went in as scheduled, A Company on the right, with A Company of the Royal Irish Rifles on the left. The second wave, following 25 yards behind, consisted of B Company of the respective battalions, with a platoon of the 22nd Durham Light Infantry helping to make up the Berkshires' depleted numbers. The first wave of attackers crawled out of the trenches before the start of the creeping barrage, for the ground was so bad that they preferred to risk being hit by their own artillery than falling behind, but even this tactic failed as the men floundered helplessly in the mud. The enemy opened up with rifle and machine gun fire, and the survivors clawed their way back to the relative safety of the trench.

The battalion remained in the close support trenches for two more days, while orders for new assaults were received, prepared for, and then cancelled due to the incessant rain. The ordeal came to an end when the 2nd Royal Berks were relieved by the 2nd Devonshires and withdrew to brigade support.

Hanbury-Sparrow wrote:

> It rains and rains. Corps Headquarters may storm as much as they like at the end of their telephone and vow to keep the division in the line until Zenith Trench is captured, but it just keeps on raining. In your heart of hearts you believe that the effect of the rain is being over-estimated and that you and your men could capture the trench. But fortunately you are not consulted. The attack is postponed from hour to hour and from day to day, until at last three days later, and very much to your relief, it is cancelled. Corps decides the division is hopeless and order it out of the line.

The attacks on Zenith trench had cost the battalion 203 casualties among the ranks, fifty of them killed or died of wounds, ten missing and 143 wounded. Additionally, five officers had been killed and seven wounded, including the padre, Revd Elwell. The final total of the dead for this period is sixty-five, the majority of whom are commemorated on the Thiepval Memorial to the Missing, for their remains were never identified.

Hanbury-Sparrow is invariably critical of himself and his unit throughout his book, but his view that Corps were not impressed with the 8th Division's performance perhaps has some basis. On 2 November, the division was withdrawn to Méaulte, and placed in reserve. On the same day, albeit in better weather conditions, 17th Division took Zenith trench with the loss of ten men. 'Zenith trench,' Hanbury-Sparrow recorded bitterly, 'was the nadir of 8th Division.'

The Berkshires had two more spells in the line, but the casualties of the past two weeks had brought the strength down to twelve officers and 506 other ranks. Further losses were suffered between 10 and 15 November, when enemy gas attacks and strafing by aircraft cost another ninety-four casualties, nineteen of them fatalities. The surviving 400 received the welcome news on 16 November that the 8th Division was to be withdrawn from the line for at least a month for training, and based at Métigny, some 15 miles to the west of Amiens.

On 9 December, Major-General Hudson, CB, CIE, who had commanded the 8th Division since August 1915, was appointed Adjutant-General to the Indian Army. His place was taken by Major-General William Heneker, DSO.

# XII

# THE NEW BROOM

Major-General William Heneker was well aware that he faced a challenge. The 8th Division, considering that it was composed of regular army units, had hardly covered itself with glory. Although it had done well at Neuve Chapelle, its first serious engagement, the two other attacks in 1915, at Fromelles and Bois Grenier, had failed with heavy casualties. The difficult – or, arguably, impossible – objective for the 1 July Somme attack had not been gained, although over half the division had become casualties in the attempt. The latest assault, on Zenith trench, had once again failed at the cost of more casualties.

The situation is discussed forthrightly in the 8th Divisional History:

> The troops of the Division had suffered as grievously as any in that first day's fighting [1 July 1916]. From it they had gone, with the sense of disappointment and failure still heavy upon them, to a long and anxious tour of duty in the trenches; holding a sector which was over-stretched deliberately, in order that other troops might be set free to carry on the struggle on the Somme. No proper opportunity had been given to train and assimilate the drafts with which their depleted ranks had been filled up. The Division had had no time to find itself when it was hurried back to its share in the last and perhaps most trying phase of the advance. Fate had given the troops no direct part in the victories of the Somme; but had dealt out to them a full measure of its bitterest and darkest hours. It was not to be wondered at that the move out of the line found the morale and temper of the Division at a low ebb.

Hanbury-Sparrow describes Heneker's approach to the challenge. 'He came with the suddenness of a cyclone. One day the old divisional commander called and said good-bye; the next, the CO of the battalion in the next village rang up hurriedly to warn us to look to our guard. The New Man, he said, had just passed and raised hell, had hauled him over the coals and threatened to send the adjutant home in disgrace. "Look out", he reiterated, as he rang off.'

The new General wasted little time. Any officer who did not fit into his scheme of things was posted elsewhere. 'Within a fortnight,' Hanbury-Sparrow recorded, 'the greater part of the big-wigs had disappeared. Never had there been such a fevered replacement and displacement since the massacres of the French revolution. Every day the tumbril carted off some victim, and through it all rode, strode and drove the General, exclaiming: "That guard's a disgrace. Why aren't those buttons cleaner? Get wire put in the men's caps. Those jackets are filthy. Scrap the lot and damn the expense." Like an electric shock, the imperious will jarred through the division.'

The tactics worked. Suddenly so much of the men's day was taken up in caring for their kit, marching smartly, and learning how to salute properly that there was little time to brood on their chances of surviving the next attack, and slowly morale improved. A large exercise area was taped out with imaginary enemy defences, and the troops attacked

Lietenant-General Sir William C.G. Heneker
K.C.B. K.C.M.G. DSO.

in companies, and then in battalions, and then in brigades, and then did it all over again until Heneker was satisfied. Schools were set up to improve marksmanship, to practice with Lewis guns, and to teach fieldcraft, concealment, scouting and sniping skills, restoring the men's confidence in their own and their comrades' abilities.

The next task which the 8th Division was to undertake was to continue the advance beyond Bouchavesnes, by attacking a system of trenches known as Pallas and Fritz. Aerial photographs were taken of the objectives, which were then reproduced on the training ground, and the battalions practised the attack until everyone was familiar with their role, and knew what was expected of them. It was a very different, and rather more confident, 2nd Royal Berkshires who went back into the line on 23 January 1917 near Sailly-Saillisel. The 25th Brigade had a new commander, Brigadier Clifford Coffin, DSO, formerly a lieutenant-colonel in the Royal Engineers, who had taken over from Brigadier Pollard.

The new sector had recently been taken over from the French, and was described as 'fluid' in the war diary:

> The front line of the sector consists of a series of posts not connected up and with only a little wire out. The ground is a swamp of shell-holes and any length of trench at once caves in, in spite of revetment. The support line consists of two bits of trench; Blue Avenue, the only communications trench, is impassable. Reliefs are carried out across the open. There are two main duck-board walks to the front line. The enemy is in very much the same position. He is quite inactive, but carries on intermittent shelling on back areas and roads.

There was much to be done, and the Berkshires, together with the other battalions, spent the first half of February improving the defences, constructing battalion and brigade headquarters, laying wire defences and burying telephone cables. On 11 February, they were relieved by 4th Division, and once again returned to the training area to practise the attack over and over again, before exchanging with 4th Division again on 21 February. The attack had been fixed for 27 February, but the rain, interspersed with periods of hard frost, had so delayed the preparations that General Heneker rescheduled it for 4 March. The attack was intended to gain the enemy

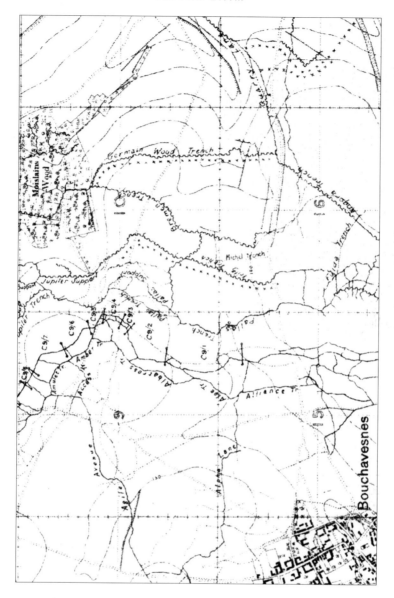

Map of the Pallas trench system.

positions on the saddle of the hill overlooking Bouchavesnes, which would enable the British to dominate the Moislains Valley as far as Nurlu, while at the same time depriving the enemy of his observation posts looking down on Bouchavesnes. Two lines of trenches would have to be taken, on a frontage of about 1,200 yards east and north-east of the village.

The attack was to be made by two brigades, 25th on the right with a frontage of about 300 yards, and 24th on the left with about 900 yards. Brigadier Coffin detailed the 2nd Royal Berkshires to make the attack in his sector. Two battalions, 1st Worcestershires and 2nd Northamptonshires, were attacking in 24th Brigade's sector, while 2nd Lincolnshires and 1st Sherwood Foresters were to follow up the attack with 'mopping-up' parties and to provide ammunition carriers. There was going to be no preliminary artillery bombardment, because Heneker wanted to capture the two trenches intact, so that they could be reused by the British. To compensate, the machine gun support was enhanced by borrowing the 120th Machine Gun Company from 40th Division, bringing the total of companies to four, and enabling a very intense fire to be maintained on the two flanks of the assault.

The Berkshires spent the two days before the attack in rest billets near Bray, and a final practice was made without any officers or sergeant-majors directing it. Lieutenant-Colonel Haig was satisfied that everyone, down to the lowliest private, knew exactly what was expected of them, and that they would perform their tasks even if their officers had become casualties. On 3 March the battalion moved up into the assault positions. It was make or break for the 8th Division and the Berkshires. Hanbury-Sparrow, who was going to lead the battalion's attack, recorded:

> I think we all realised that, cost what it might, this attack must not fail. It became, so to speak, the symbol of our worth, for we knew that we were being given a task well within the capacity of decent men. As far as could be foreseen, we were provided with everything that we might reasonably require. We had artillery and troops in abundance; the operation had been rehearsed over and over again and every man knew exactly what was his task. There could be, and there would be, no excuse for failure. If we failed, we would be disgraced not only in our own eyes, but in the eyes of all who knew.

There had been no time to prepare assembly trenches, and the start lines had been marked with tapes. Two hours before zero the men crawled out to take their places. The Divisional History records that they had been issued with chewing gum, to prevent the enemy from hearing them coughing, and to distract them during the wait. Presumably it was also to take their minds off their desire for a cigarette, for a struck match would have given the whole game away. There was a slight frost, and the waiting men shivered with cold, but at least it would make the going easier when the attack started.

Slightly before 5.15 a.m., the barrage began, and started to lift five minutes later. The attackers followed closely, and captured Pallas trench, the first objective, with little loss. Leaving the surviving occupants to be dealt with by the mopping-up party, they pressed forward and soon gained the second objective, Fritz trench in the Berkshires' sector, and Pallas Support in 24th Brigade's area. In fact, the advance had been so rapid that B Company of the Northamptonshires crossed Pallas Support without realising it, for it was badly damaged, and took a further section of Fritz trench. They killed several of the enemy, captured a machine gun, and bombed a dugout before the British barrage landing nearby made them realise their mistake, and they hastily withdrew to Pallas Support. Similarly, several parties of the Berkshires advanced as far as Bremen Trench, for Fritz Trench had also been badly damaged and they failed to notice it in the dark. Hanbury-Sparrow managed to get them back, and everyone set to work consolidating Fritz Trench to cope with the inevitable counter-attack.

Meanwhile, the 2nd Lincolns' mopping-up party, led by Captain Clifton, were dealing with the enemy in Pallas Trench. They encountered a machine gun team who had emerged from a dugout and were setting their weapon up to fire at the Berkshires who had passed over them. They were speedily dealt with, and the machine gun was handed over to the Berkshires' A Company, who soon set it to work against the German block to the right of Pallas Trench. When it ran out of ammunition a man was detailed to take the trophy back to battalion headquarters, but he never arrived, and the war diary presumes that he was killed by shellfire on the way, and he and the gun buried.

At 6.30 a.m., Hanbury-Sparrow sent a message back to Lieutenant-Colonel Haig reporting 'all objectives gained', and enclosing a sketch map of the positions. Haig forwarded the sketch to Brigade Headquarters at 7.30 a.m. At 8 a.m., Haig received a message from Captain Scobell which said 'Germans sniping only and I think we can hold counter-attack. Trench Mortars have only 6 rounds of ammunition.'

Soon afterwards, Haig's signallers informed him that the line had been cut to brigade headquarters, and at the same time a runner arrived from Lieutenant Prest, commanding A Company in Fritz Trench, to say that he could see the enemy consolidating in Bremen Trench and asking for artillery support. The communication breakdown made it difficult for Haig to contact the artillery, but the Worcesters had spotted a party of the enemy gathering in battalion strength for a counter-attack. They sent up an SOS flare and the resulting bombardment scattered the enemy with heavy casualties.

Haig went forward at about 5.30 p.m. to see for himself what was happening. He found a gap between the Berkshires' A Company and the Worcesters, which he closed up by sending up two platoons of the Royal Irish Rifles. The enemy were still trying to retake the captured trenches, and the bombardment was heavy, but Haig found the men calmly holding them off with rifle and Lewis gun fire, 'never wasting a shot'. Satisfied with the situation, he returned to battalion headquarters, where he was able to brief Brigadier Coffin, who had arrived while he was out in the line.

During the night, the enemy bombardment was unceasing, causing significant casualties, and at 4 a.m. on 5 January it rose to a crescendo while the Germans delivered a powerful infantry assault on the extreme right of the captured Fritz trench. They captured the block, and attacked both along the trench and over the open ground in front of it. Captain Hanbury-Sparrow was wounded, and the enemy recaptured about 300 yards of the trench. Haig learned of this from an officer in the Royal Irish Rifles, and immediately dispatched the battle platoon under Lieutenant Parsons. However, they veered too far to the right in the darkness, and came under heavy fire, losing Parsons and Sergeant Dance, his platoon sergeant.

Meanwhile, Lieutenant Prest, commanding C Company, on his own initiative, launched an immediate counter-attack with bombs and rifles. They succeeded in driving the enemy out of the whole of Fritz trench and regained all the lost ground. They were aided by Captain Cahill's company who provided excellent support with Lewis guns and rifle grenades. 'I should like here to point out the good work the rifle grenadiers did,' Lieutenant-Colonel Haig said in his report. 'It is undoubtedly this co-operation which was the success of our counter-attack.'

That was the last serious attempt made by the enemy to retrieve their trenches, and by 6 March, due to the excellent observation which was now possible from Fritz trench, they could be seen readjusting their lines in the distance towards Nurlu. On that same day, the Berkshires were relieved by the Royal Irish Rifles, and marched to camp in the reserve area.

Two officers had been killed, Lieutenant Parsons and Second Lieutenant Neaton, and six wounded, including Hanbury-Sparrow. Sixty-three other ranks had been killed, sixteen were missing and 170 wounded. Most of the casualties were sustained by the enemy shellfire rather than in the initial assault or whilst repulsing the counter-attacks. Despite the casualties, the Berkshires marched out of the line with their heads held high. The operation had been a complete success, they had taken all their objectives, and held on to their gains despite heavy counter-attacks.

On returning to camp, they were inspected by the XV Corps Commander, who read out a message of congratulations from the Commander in Chief. General Rawlinson, the Army Commander, had added his own words to the message: 'The very careful preparations that were made, and the gallantry of the three battalions engaged, coupled with the effective barrages and counter-battery work, reflect great credit on all concerned in the planning and execution of the enterprise.' The 2nd Royal Berkshires and 8th Division must have felt that they had turned a corner.

Hanbury-Sparrow's wound was not serious, and he returned to the battalion in August. His actions in Fritz trench earned him a bar to the DSO he had won in 1914 with the 1st Royal Berkshires, and the 8th Division History records: 'he had shown conspicuous gallantry throughout the operation until he was wounded and had to withdraw.'

# XIII

# IN PURSUIT

The actions on the Somme, following on from their losses at Verdun in the first half of 1916, had hurt the enemy badly, and the German High Command decided to abandon the battlefield and retreat – or make a strategic withdrawal – to a prepared defensive line some 20 miles in the rear. The Germans had been preparing the line for some time, and had named it the 'Siegfried Stellung'. The British knew it as the Hindenburg Line, and it was a formidable obstacle of deep dugouts, concrete pillboxes, machine gun posts and enormous quantities of barbed wire entanglements.

The German withdrawal commenced soon after the action which had captured Fritz and Pallas trenches, for on 12 March patrols probing the Loupart Line in 5th Army's sector found them unoccupied, and the whole Allied force between Arras in the north and Soissons started to follow up and press the retreating enemy.

In 8th Division's sector, patrols were sent out to reconnoitre the trenches leading eastwards from Fritz trench, and on 15 March Bremen Trench and German Wood Trench were found to be abandoned, and were rapidly occupied. Cautiously, the infantry worked their way through the southern portion of St Pierre Vaast Wood, and by 18 March, having secured the town of Moislains, found themselves on the line of the Canal du Nord. B Company of the 2nd Berkshires were among the units on the canal, while the remainder of the battalion stayed in Fritz Trench, which still formed the division's main defence line.

Events were moving quickly, and by 24 March the main line of defence had moved forward to the area between St Pierre Vaast Wood and Vaux Wood, with the Berkshires relieving the 1st Welch Regiment and 2nd Middlesex in a trench system comprising Vaux Wood Trench, Government Trench and Government farm. Two days later they moved forward to accommodation in tents, shelters and dugouts in Hennois Wood, some 2,000 yards further east.

The first serious action for the 2nd Royal Berkshires since the assault on Fritz Trench came on 30 March 1917. The village of Sorel-le-Grand was being held by an enemy rearguard, mainly consisting of machine guns, and the battalion was ordered to take it. After establishing outposts to the west and south of the village, six strong patrols, each consisting of twelve men under a non-commissioned officer, were formed from A and C Companies. Each company provided three patrols, and an officer to lead them.

The assaulting patrols moved in at 4.45 a.m. They entered the village without encountering any opposition; in fact only four of the enemy were seen. An outpost line was established to the east of the village, whence the enemy could be observed towards the north in the southern part of Dessart Wood. A patrol was sent out to reconnoitre the village of Fins, less than a mile to the north, but it returned with the information that it was occupied by the 2nd Rifle Brigade.

That afternoon, the Berkshires moved up to relieve the 2nd Rifle Brigade, who were to attack Dessart Wood. This they did at 4 p.m., with great success, driving the enemy before them. As soon as they sent up Very lights to indicate that the wood was clear, the 2nd Royal Irish Rifles, who had moved to Sorel-le-Grand as the Berkshires had vacated it, moved forward and occupied the plateau to the south of the wood.

Five days later, on 4 April, the battalion was ordered to mount an attack on Metz-en-Couture in conjunction with the 20th Division, who were operating to the north of the 8th Division. The objective was Gouzeaucourt Wood. The attack was originally scheduled for 7.30 a.m., but was cancelled by Brigadier Coffin due to the heavy snow. This would not only impede the attackers, but make it difficult for the artillery support to see the Very lights. Conditions improved during the morning, and an order arrived from the Brigadier at 11.30 a.m. rescheduling the attack for 12.15 p.m. Because the visibility was still poor, however, the artillery arrangements had been changed to a timed barrage rather than relying on Very light signals.

Haig reported to Brigade at 2.30 p.m. that the assaulting companies had moved off on time, and were conforming to the movements of the 20th Division on their left. Lieutenant-Colonel Haig had sent two patrols out under Second Lieutenants Hinde and Curtis during the night, and they had not yet returned. However, he received a belated message from Hinde at 3 p.m. to the effect that he had sighted a party of about forty of the enemy on the high ground in front of the wood. Shortly afterwards, he received a message from the right-hand assaulting company that they were being held up by rifle fire, and were digging in with entrenching tools. He sent a message back ordering them to work around the enemy's flank.

At 3.50 p.m, a message arrived from the support company that the enemy was being reinforced on their right, and was apparently threatening a counter-attack. Haig informed the brigadier, and was authorised to send his reserve company forward. Their vacated trenches were then occupied by a company of 2nd Lincolns. Another company of the Lincolns was sent forward, and Haig sent them to reinforce his left-hand company, and ordered the Berkshires' A Company to work round the enemy party on the left and try to enter the wood from the west.

Brigadier Coffin then decided to launch the remaining companies of the Lincolns to attack on the right of the Berkshires, but before the assault could start, a British scouting aircraft spotted what were apparently yellow flares in Gouzeaucourt Wood. As 20th Division were using yellow identification flares, it was thought that they had succeeded in entering the wood from the north, so the proposed attack was called off to avoid a 'friendly fire' incident. In fact, the reported yellow flares were burning wooden sheds which the enemy were destroying before abandoning the wood.

Meanwhile, Captain Cahill's A Company had succeeded in outflanking the enemy riflemen, and sent a message back to Haig saying 'Have entered the wood and established a command post. My patrols are searching the wood.'

Haig ordered the other assaulting companies to consolidate in the wood, where they spent the night. At daybreak, he went forward, and established posts along the eastern and northern borders of the wood. Contact was made with the 20th Division on the left flank, and with the 2nd Rifle Brigade on the right, and the operation was successfully completed. Twenty other ranks had been killed and twenty-five wounded, together with three officers wounded. Haig wrote: 'This, in my opinion, is not excessive, considering the difficulty of the attack, the snow, and the amount of ground gained, and I think it shows excellent leadership on the part of my company Commanders, who now hold our objective.'

Haig was also fulsome in his praise of the two patrols. 'I wish to add that good work was done by my patrols sent out the night before, the enemy being much harassed during our attacks by patrols under Second Lieutenants Hinde and Curtis. These officers remained out about 18 hours in close touch with the enemy, and when the enemy did retire, shot down 10 of them.'

The next two weeks were spent in reserve, with working parties clearing the roads of obstacles. The retreating enemy, determined to obstruct the British advance as far as possible, had destroyed as much of the infrastructure as they could. Farms and villages had been burnt, trees had been cut down to block roads, and bridges over every stream and culvert had been blown. It will be recalled that the 'yellow flares' which had delayed the advance into Gouzeaucourt Wood had been burning sheds.

Cheering news was received on 9 April regarding the successful opening of the Arras campaign. The Canadian Corps had captured the strategically important Vimy Ridge, and General Allenby's troops had made impressive advances to the east of Arras, helped by the use of tunnels which concealed their concentration from the enemy observers. However, the French spring offensive, masterminded by General Nivelle, failed. Although planned to coincide with the attack at Arras, it was delayed for four days. The hoped-for breakthrough in Champagne, followed by a thrust northward, incurred heavy losses, and had to be abandoned, with a severe effect on the morale of the French army.

On 16 April, the 2nd Royal Berks moved up to relieve the Devons and Royal Irish Rifles in Gauche Wood, about 1,000 yards west of Villers-Guislain, which was the 8th Division's next objective. The village was to be attacked by the 23rd Infantry Brigade on 18 April, advancing from the south-west under cover of an artillery barrage. The barrage would concentrate on the main east–west road until the southern half of the village was captured, and then lift after 53 minutes to allow the remainder of the village to be secured. While this was taking place, the Berkshires were to co-operate by keeping a strong machine gun barrage on enemy positions to the north of the village, and endeavour to establish a series of outposts when the objective had been taken.

Lieutenant-Colonel Haig detailed D Company to supply four strong patrols, armed with Lewis guns, who were to work their way north of the village and then establish four strongpoints at 200-yard intervals. When the village was captured, A Company would move out to the north and establish touch with the 23rd Brigade, dealing with any occupied dugouts en-route. B Company was to bomb its way down a trench leading from Quentin Mill towards Villers-Guislain, but if they came upon strong opposition, were to establish and hold a double block.

The four patrols from D Company went out at 12.15 a.m. They successfully established the four strong points. At 3.30 a.m. Haig received a message from them that they were in place, so he then sent the bombing party from B Company down the trench from Quentin Mill.

The artillery bombardment started as planned at 4.25 a.m., but at 5 a.m. a message arrived from B Company saying that they could find no trace of the trench. When Haig received a message from Brigade that our troops were entering Villers-Guislain, he ordered B Company to bomb its way down the road from Quentin Mill to Villers-Guislain, for it was this road that had been mistakenly identified as a trench by aerial reconnaissance.

At 5.30 am A Company advanced as arranged, but soon after they had left, Haig received information that the enemy had begun shelling Villers-Guislain. He hurried after them, and caught up with them on the western edge of the village. He ordered them to dig in instead of entering the village, and then moved up to the road from Quentin Mill, where he made contact with the bombing party from B Company, together with the Stokes Mortar section. He directed them to move north-east, where they dug in on the ridge overlooking the village.

At 7.30 a.m. Haig was able to report to the 25th Brigade headquarters that all objectives had been gained, and that he was in touch with 2nd Devons and 1st Royal Irish Rifles on the right and left. Casualties had been light, for the whole operation had only cost three men wounded. That afternoon, the battalion was relieved by the 2nd Lincolns, and returned to billets in Heudicourt.

By now, the enemy were ensconced behind their new and formidable defence line. The initially successful Arras attack had come to a halt around the villages of Monchy and Oppy, and, as it was planned as part of the failed Nivelle offensive, was abandoned. General Allenby moved to Egypt, where he led a successful campaign against the Turks in Palestine, and activity on the British section of the Western Front turned to the north. Orders arrived from GHQ that the 8th Division was to be withdrawn from General Rawlinson's Fourth Army, and would join the Second Army in Belgium.

# XIV

# INTRODUCTION
# TO THE SALIENT

There were sound strategic reasons for Field Marshal Sir Douglas Haig to launch the next attack from the Belgian town of Ypres. Enemy submarines, based on the Belgian coast in Zeebrugge and Oostende, were taking a growing toll of British shipping, and the operation envisaged breaking out of the Ypres salient and heading towards the coast near the border with Holland, meeting up with an amphibious landing for which 1st Division were already in training. Submarines had a restricted range, and forcing them back to bases further east would limit the time they could spend on patrol.

The scheme, if successful, would also have the advantage of cutting off a large section of the German Army. A further factor, which was miraculously kept from public knowledge, was the morale of the French Army following the failure of the Nivelle plan. Several units had mutinied, stating that they would only act defensively, and refused to participate in any further offensives. General Pétain had assumed command, but until he could restore order, it was imperative to keep the enemy busy.

Ypres, a historic market town, was the only significant city in Belgium not under German occupation. The original British Expeditionary Force had fought an epic battle to defend it in October and November 1914, narrowly preventing a German breakthrough, but at the cost of many of the regular pre-war officers and men killed or maimed. Since then, it had remained in British hands, its fine buildings ruined, its moat a stinking lake of water polluted by gas attacks and explosives. It stood in the centre of a salient thrusting into the enemy lines, whose boundaries had fluctuated with the changing fortunes of the defenders and attackers. A salient can give an advantage to its garrison if it is on a promontory, but the Ypres salient was not. There are few hills in Belgian Flanders, but most of the higher ground was on the German side of the front line. Little could be hidden from enemy observers, and the defenders were vulnerable from three sides. To make things worse, the land drainage system, developed over centuries by the farm workers, had been destroyed by constant shellfire, and the land was waterlogged and swampy from flooded streams and ditches. Between Ypres and the coast, miles of low-lying land had been deliberately flooded by closing the sluice gates at Nieuwpoort, which at least gave the British some comfort that they were unlikely to be outflanked by an enemy attack on their left.

The 8th Division had managed to avoid being stationed at Ypres during the two and a half years since arriving at the front, but undoubtedly there were many among the ranks who had served there in other battalions, and as the trains rolled north, were making sure that their comrades knew exactly what was in store for them.

Most of June 1917, was spent in billets at Hazebrouck and Caëstre, where the battalion absorbed and trained new drafts. Seventeen new subalterns had joined since April, and much training was undertaken to familiarise them with their new commands. Medal awards were announced in the *London Gazette* – a bar to Lieutenant-Colonel Haig's DSO, a DSO for Captain Allfrey, and Military Crosses for Captains Hanbury-Sparrow, Allaway and Cahill, Regimental Sergeant-Major Weston and Lieutenant Hinde. Additionally, Sergeants Hole, Oakley, Leslie and Collins were awarded the DCM.

On 7 June, while the Berkshires were training, General Plumer's Second Army made a spectacular and successful attack on Messines Ridge, to the south of Ypres. Aided by the explosion of seventeen massive mines, the attackers gained and held the ridge which had been in enemy hands since November 1914. This action was an important prerequisite to the main attack on the salient, for it prevented the enemy dominating the right flank of the proposed assault.

One month later, on 5 July, the 2nd Royal Berkshires relieved the 1st Worcesters in Ypres. The massive medieval walls that surrounded the town were impervious to enemy shelling, and the battalion, less D Company, who had been detached to work with 171st Tunnelling Company, Royal Engineers, found themselves in dugouts beneath the ramparts at Lille Gate. On the following day, they moved up the Menen Road for a spell in the line, occupying trenches between Zouave Wood and Birr Crossroads. The enemy front line crossed the remains of the road about 1,000 yards away, near the ruins of Hooge Château.

The three days in the line were uneventful, according to the war diary, but the casualty returns show two men killed and seventeen wounded. On relief, the battalion returned to Dominion Camp, but B Company and one platoon from C Company remained behind, for they had been detailed to partake in a trench raid on the night of 10 July, which Lieutenant-Colonel Haig was going to lead in person.

The raiding party formed up in Kingsway Trench, with a strength of 168 of all ranks. The platoon from C Company had been included because of the presumed strength of the enemy, a decision which turned out to be fully justified. Zero hour was set for 1 a.m., and at 12.45 a.m., with 15 minutes to go, all was ready, but one unfortunate individual was killed by a stray shell while forming up.

The barrage opened punctually at 1 a.m., and the raiders immediately started to move forward, reaching the enemy line without any casualties except from over-eager men who pressed too closely behind their own barrage. The sections tended to bunch together at first in the darkness, but managed to regain their proper intervals by the time the German line was reached. Haig wrote in his report: '50 per cent of the company had never been in action before, and all things considered, the attack went very well, though there was some wavering when the enemy threw bombs, which they did from dugouts and shelters.'

It was difficult to identify the entrances to the enemy dugouts in the darkness, and after the raiders moved forward to the second objective, a machine gun team emerged and brought their weapon into action, but it and the crew were swiftly knocked out by Sergeant Sturgess.

Haig's report continues: 'The Germans put up a good fight in practically every instance, the consequence was only one prisoner was taken. With reference to this, one German fired at Pte Bowden, the bullet grazing the latter's arm. Bowden, knowing how essential identification was, showed great self restraint in not killing the man, who immediately put his hands up after firing. In one case two Germans offered to surrender, and then threw bombs. These were killed. Many dugouts were bombed and as these positions were strongly held, a good many Germans must have been killed. Those killed from hand to hand encounters estimated at 30.'

The left hand platoon reached Hooge Crater, which is now the site of the Commonwealth War Graves Cemetery. They found a number of dugouts which they bombed, and reported that the crater was 40 to 50ft deep, very muddy around the edges, and with a large pool of water in the bottom. There were a number of enemy dead in the trenches, killed by the barrage, which Haig described as 'excellent in every way. I am of opinion that the care taken by Major Duncan of the Royal Artillery to demonstrate the exact position of the

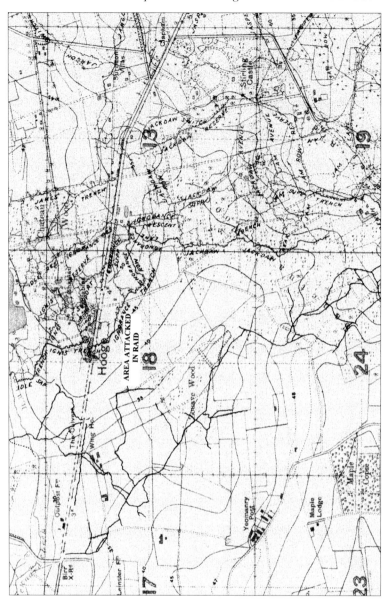

Map of the Hooge Château area.

barrage to all raiding officers on the morning of the 10th instant was largely responsible for the excellent direction kept by the troops in the raid.'

At 1.44 a.m., Haig ordered his bugler to sound the signal for withdrawal. All unused Stokes Mortar bombs and Mills bombs were rapidly thrown down the nearest dugouts, and the party retired in good order, covered by the troops in the front line, and sustaining no further casualties on the way back.

When the roll-call was taken, one officer, Lieutenant Hinde, was reported wounded and missing, with Corporal Giles and Privates Lawrence and Shield killed. Two officers and thirty-five men were wounded. Lieutenant Hinde's body was never recovered, and he is commemorated on the Menen Gate Memorial to the missing. Lieutenant-Colonel Haig estimated the enemy casualties at seventy to eighty as a minimum.

After the raid, the battalion moved to Tournehem, between Calais and St Omer, and spent a further two weeks in training before moving back to the forward area on 24 July. The main assault was planned to start on 31 July, and on the day before, the Berkshires moved to their forming up point at Halfway House, some 500 yards to the south-west of Birr Crossroads.

The 8th Division were to mount an attack on a north-easterly axis, crossing the Menen Road diagonally at Hooge Château, and, keeping the railway line on their left, advance towards Jaffa Trench which lay between Westhoek and the ruined station buildings on the railway line. Major-General Heneker planned an initial two-brigade assault, with 23rd Brigade on the left and 24th Brigade on the right. The 15th Division were to advance on the same axis, with the railway line forming the divisional boundary. On the right, the 18th Division would initially keep to the south of the Menen Road, crossing it at Clapham Junction and aiming for Glencorse Wood.

The 25th Brigade would remain in reserve until zero +6 hours, or when the two leading brigades had secured their objectives, and then leapfrog them to attack the Green Line about 1,000 yards further on. This attack would be made by the other three battalions in the 25th Brigade, with the 2nd Lincolns on the left, the 1st Royal Irish Rifles in the centre, and the 2nd Rifle Brigade on the right. The 2nd Royal Berkshires would be in reserve, but a platoon from A Company was loaned to the Royal Irish Rifles to assist them in mopping-up operations.

The Berkshires were to leave their dugouts at Halfway House, and advance in artillery formation, until they reached their forming up positions south of Oxford Street, and west of Halfway House at zero +4 hours. When the remainder of the 25th Brigade started their attack on the Green Line at zero +6 hours 28 minutes, the battalion was to move forward in support and send out patrols to establish contact with the 53rd Infantry Brigade on the right and the 45th Infantry Brigade on the left.

Once the 25th Infantry Brigade had secured their objectives, the Berkshires would move up with a cavalry squadron of the Yorkshire Hussars, pass through the newly acquired line, and send out fighting patrols in conjunction with the cavalry to locate the enemy, and, if possible, establish themselves on the Broodseinde Ridge.

Such was the plan, and, initially, it worked fairly well. The 23rd and 24th Brigades advanced at zero hour, 3.50 a.m., with the 2nd Northants taking Bellewaarde Lake. Beyond the lake, it was difficult to keep up with the artillery barrage, but the first objective, the Blue line, and the second, the Black line, were taken with little difficulty. However, they then encountered heavy rifle and machine gun fire from two blockhouses called 'Kit' and 'Kat', and from Glencorse Wood. The two brigades took shelter behind Westhoek Ridge and waited for 25th Brigade to pass through them.

At zero +4 hours, the waiting Berkshires set out from Halfway House, following the other three battalions of 25th Brigade. Lieutenant-Colonel Haig went off to confer with Brigadier Coffin, and the Adjutant, Lieutenant Forster, took charge of the advance. The enemy were shelling the old British front line with 5.9in shells, so Forster swerved them to the left across the Menen Road, where a short halt was made to reorganise. They pressed on through Château Wood with some difficulty owing to the terrain, and lost some casualties to enemy shelling and machine gun fire. They emerged into open ground just west of Jabber Trench at about 9.30 a.m., and again paused to reorganise, for the companies had become rather scattered in the wood. Lieutenant-Colonel Haig had still not returned, and Forster was growing anxious about him.

A message was received to the effect that the division on the right had been held up, so, in the absence of the commanding officer, Forster reported to Major-General Heneker, who confirmed the news about the right division, and told him not to make any further advance until ordered to.

Just after 11 a.m., orders were received to send one company to reinforce the 2nd Lincolns, and for one company to face right and establish a defensive flank. Accordingly,

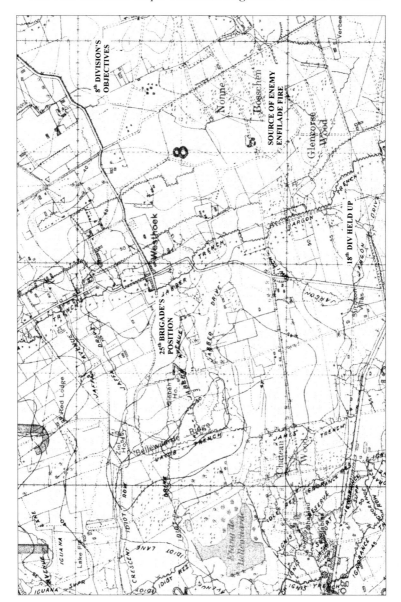

Map of the Jabber trench area.

C Company occupied Jabber Trench in support of the Lincolns, while D dug in along Jabber Drive, facing south. A and B remained with Battalion Headquarters at Ziel House.

The 18th Division, on the right, had been detailed to support 30th Division with their 53rd Brigade, who were to leapfrog 30th Division when they had secured Glencorse Wood. The 18th Division had established a proud reputation on the Somme. They were commanded by Major-General Ivor Maxse, who was particularly enthusiastic about training and more training. On 1 July, they had taken their objectives at Montauban, fought at Delville Wood, and in September 1916 had taken Thiepval Ridge.

This time, the division was not so successful. Troops of 30th Division had veered too far to the left, and entered Château Wood. Finding it clear of the enemy, and believing themselves to be in Glencorse Wood, they reported Glencorse to be in British hands.

Acting on this information, the unfortunate 53rd Brigade advanced confidently on Glencorse Wood, only to be cut down by a torrent of rifle and machine gun fire. The brigade included the 6th Battalion, Royal Berkshires, who suffered very heavy casualties before managing to establish themselves in Jargon Trench, just to the west of the wood, at about 10 a.m. The advance of the 30th and 18th Divisions ground to a halt.

On the 8th Division's left, the 15th Division had reached their objectives, taking Frezenburg and the Black line. The 23rd Brigade of 8th Division were in touch with them, so Major-General Heneker had to skew the right flank of his division back, and cancel any further advances, in order to compensate for the failure of the 18th and 30th Divisions.

The Berkshires were coming under fire from Glencorse Wood, and pigeon messages were sent back asking for artillery support. Casualties were mounting, including Lieutenant Ayres, RA, the Forward Observation Officer attached to the Berkshires, who was killed by a sniper. The enemy seemed to be forming up for a counter-attack, and a message to that effect was sent to the brigade, who replied that the 2nd Lincolns were being counter-attacked, and ordered Forster to withdraw D Company from Jabber Drive, and consolidate 300 yards east of Ziel House. Soon afterwards, a message arrived from the commanding officer of the East Lancs that they too were expecting a counter-attack.

At around 2 p.m. the enemy made a counter-attack with bombs. A platoon was sent forward to reinforce C Company, later followed by half of A Company. A message was received from Brigade Headquarters to consolidate and hold at all costs. Brigadier Coffin led by example, for he went forward and made an inspection of the front posts. Although under the heaviest fire from both machine guns and rifles and in full view of the enemy, he showed an utter disregard of personal danger, walking quietly from shell-hole to shell-hole, giving advice and cheering his men by his presence.

After the failure of the enemy counter-attack, things quietened down. The Berkshires remained in the area between Ziel House and Jabber Trench, apart from B Company, which was sent to reinforce the 2nd Rifle Brigade near the railway line. News arrived that Lieutenant-Colonel Haig had been wounded early in the day, and been evacuated, which explained his absence.

At 8.40 that evening, orders were received that the three attacking battalions from 25th Brigade would be relieved, but the Berkshires would remain, under orders from GOC, 24th Brigade. At 10.30 p.m. he ordered A, C and D Companies to take over the 2nd Lincolns' positions. It had started to rain earlier in the day, and by now the conditions were getting so bad that it took until 4 the next morning to complete the relief. A request was made for B Company to be returned to the battalion, and they rejoined at about the same time.

A very wet night was spent floundering in flooded shell-holes and scraping refuges in the mud, and the message from 25th Division that the Berkshires were to be relieved by the Loyal North Lancs must have been very welcome. However, the enemy commenced a heavy barrage with 5.9in and 9in shells which went on all afternoon, causing many casualties and making the relief very difficult. It was not until 6 p.m. that a very weary battalion trudged back to Pioneer Camp. Their mood was not improved by being told on arrival at Pioneer Camp that there was no room for them, and they were to move on to Winnipeg Camp. Stragglers were still turning up the following day.

The action had cost the lives of Second Lieutenant J. Lee and twenty-six other ranks. Three officers had been wounded, including Lieutenant-Colonel Haig, DSO, and 105 other ranks. Fifteen men were posted as missing. Medals were awarded for the raid on the enemy lines at Hooge on 10 July. Sergeant Sturgess, who had knocked out the machine gun post, was awarded the DCM, and Private Belcher received a Military Medal. Three officers, Captain Flint, Lieutenant Brown and Second Lieutenant Bayley received Military Crosses.

# XV

# THE HANEBEEK

August 1917 was reputedly the wettest in Belgium for seventy-five years. The rain continued for four days after 31 July, turning the battlefield into a swamp, and a quick resumption of the attack was out of the question until the terrain had dried out.

With the departure, wounded, of Lieutenant-Colonel Haig, the commanding officer, Hanbury-Sparrow returned from convalescent leave to take his place. In August 1914, he had been the junior subaltern in the 1st Battalion, Royal Berkshire Regiment, fretting that the war would be over before he reached the battlefield. Three years later, he was a lieutenant-colonel – albeit a temporary one – commanding the 2nd Battalion, having been twice wounded, awarded the DSO and the Military Cross, and been Mentioned in Dispatches. He was still only twenty-four years old. Such was the promotion of holders of pre-war regular commissions who had the fortune to survive. Most of Hanbury-Sparrow's seniors in the Regiment were now either dead, maimed, or had been promoted to even higher ranks.

After two days in Winnipeg Camp, cleaning up, the battalion moved to Steenwoorde Training Area, and spent a week training and absorbing a new draft of replacements. On 12 August orders were received that the division would resume the assault, in the sector where they had been in action two weeks earlier. On 15 August the battalion moved up to their assembly positions on Westhoek Ridge, just in front of the line of Jabber Trench where they had fought on 31 July. Today, the plan called for an advance of about 1,500 yards across the valley of the Hanebeek Stream, capturing an enemy strongpoint called 'Iron Cross Redoubt', and consolidating on the Green Line, which had been the division's objective on 31 July.

Hanbury-Sparrow detailed A, B and C Companies to make the assault, in two waves, each wave consisting of two platoons from each company. D Company was to follow, mopping up, and then to garrison Iron Cross Redoubt once it had been taken from the enemy.

When the Green Line had been reached, the first wave was to advance a further 70 yards and consolidate, with snipers and Lewis guns, and act as cover for the second wave whilst they dug in on the Green Line. Two companies of 2nd Rifle Brigade were to follow in close support, ready to reinforce if necessary. It was anticipated that there would be difficulties crossing the Hanebeek Stream, and twenty men from the 22nd Durham Light Infantry, who were the division's Pioneer Battalion, would accompany the Berkshires carrying portable bridging supplies.

Forster, the Adjutant, who had commanded the battalion on 31 July, had severe misgivings. If, he reasoned, the division on the right failed to take Polygone Wood, the Green Line position would be enfiladed by the enemy and would be untenable. Hanbury-Sparrow raised this concern with Major-General Heneker, who agreed, and suggested to Army Command that the attack by 56th (London) Division, on the right,

Major Forster, pictured before the war when he was a sergeant.

should commence one hour before that of the 8th Division, but this idea was rejected by General Gough.

Great difficulty was encountered in reaching the start line. The battalion moved off in single file, walking through the darkness on a path made of duck-boards. The guides were unsure of their way in the dark, parts of the column split off and lost their way, and it was 4 a.m. before everyone was assembled on the start line tapes. There had been considerable hostile shelling, but the casualties had been surprisingly light. An officer of the battalion holding the line told Hanbury-Sparrow that the hostile shelling during their four days in the line had reduced their numbers to less than 200. As they were meant to be the Berkshires' support, this caused him some consternation.

The assault on the Green Line started promptly at 4.45 a.m. The Hanebeek Stream was crossed without too much difficulty, and about fifty enemy prisoners were taken. It was then realised that the attack on the right had made little, if any, progress, and C Company had to be withdrawn from the assault to set up a defensive flank, while A and B continued with the attack when the barrage lifted, and the greater part of Iron Cross Redoubt was captured, together with a further fifty prisoners. The left company, under Captain Cahill, captured a further strongpoint known as 'Anzac', and reached the Green Line in certain places.

At this point, the attackers came under very heavy rifle and machine gun fire from Polygone Wood on the battalion's right, just as Captain Forster had predicted. The Royal Irish Rifles, on the Berkshires' left, had not reached the Green Line, but as they were exposed on their left, they set up a series of posts facing north.

Hanbury-Sparrow, who had set up his battalion headquarters in a German blockhouse near the Hanebeek Stream, could not ascertain what was happening, so went forward to find out. He found the remnants of the battalion sheltering in an old trench and series of shell-holes, under heavy fire, which made it impossible to reorganise. The casualties, together with the removal of C Company from the assault group had made the firing line perilously weak in numbers.

In fact, the Berkshires and Royal Irish Rifles were the spearhead of 8th Division, and were about 1,000 yards ahead of the divisions on either side. They were in an untenable position, and were now under fire from three sides, and even from the right rear. An enemy counter-attack on the Royal Irish Rifles forced them back, and then a second attack from the south-east obliged Hanbury-Sparrow to order a withdrawal. 'It is extremely hard to make out what happened on our front as no really reliable witnesses survived,' Hanbury-Sparrow reported. 'Our casualties on the crest of the ridge had been very heavy, and the Germans attacked in great force. According to the accounts of two men they appeared to come from a tunnel behind Anzac. The enemy suffered considerable casualties but our front was driven in, and the Division on our right appears to have given way.'

In fact, a reliable witness had survived, but his story did not come to light until he was released from a German prisoner of war camp after the Armistice. Second Lieutenant George Threllfell was a Royal Berkshire officer, but had been seconded to the 25th Trench Mortar Company. He moved up behind the infantry, but his section became separated from their ammunition-carrying party. He sent his sergeant to look for them, and moved up towards the front with the rest of his men, hoping that the missing carriers would join him there. The following narrative is taken from his statement after repatriation:

> The line I was following had borne over to the right in consequence of the right of the attack being held up, and after crossing the Hanebeek I arrived at the 'Iron Cross' Redoubt, which we had taken.
>
> A considerable number of casualties had occurred there, and the line there had become disorganised. I could get no information as to my ammunition party, and none of them joined us then or later. When the barrage moved on a position was taken up a little beyond and to the right of the redoubt. I took my section up slightly in rear of it, one gun being incomplete owing to casualties.
>
> The enemy were preparing for counter-attack on our right and front. As I could do nothing without ammunition I went up to the line to give what assistance I could. I was in a shell-hole with about six men on the left of our position facing the front, with our left in the air.
>
> The enemy in the front had the advantage of the higher ground, and were able to move up unobserved to within quite a short distance of us. We did all we could to prevent their movements, and inflicted a number of casualties on them, but they were able to bring a superior fire to bear, and we were also exposed to fire from the right.
>
> Half of my party had been killed when the enemy commenced moving down to our left along what must have been a trench leading to the redoubt. They got practically level with our left and were only about fifty yards away. I fully expected their attack would come first from that direction, and my attention was chiefly focussed on it. Thus I had not observed them coming up from the right front, and did not know of their attack until it was too late, the first intimation being some shouting to our right, and some of our men coming out to surrender, the others having retired. It was then too late for me to get back, as they were almost on top of us.

There was a complete mix-up of units, with men from the Royal Irish Rifles and 1st Londons mixing with the Berkshires. Once again, Brigadier Coffin rallied them to the west of the Hanebeek Stream, and a series of outposts was established in an old trench. By now the Berkshires were down to four officers, one of whom was wounded, and about 100 men. Hanbury-Sparrow was concerned that they were the only obstacle between the advancing Germans and the British artillery batteries, but, to his intense relief, the enemy counter-attack stopped when they had recovered the Iron Cross Redoubt.

At about 3 p.m. enemy troops were spotted massing for another counter-attack in Polygone Wood, and a pigeon message was sent asking for artillery support. The attack developed at 3.30 p.m., but ammunition was so short that Hanbury-Sparrow ordered the

Lewis guns to cease fire, and only marksmen were to use their rifles. The bodies of the dead were searched for more ammunition, which was sent up to the marksmen, who were doing very well in slowing down the enemy assault, which was making slow progress as the attackers were forced to keep under cover.

At 4.30 p.m. the requested artillery barrage opened up on the ridge, causing the enemy considerable casualties, but by 5.30 p.m. the enemy were only 600 yards from the Berkshires' firing line. Hanbury-Sparrow's report continues:

> This attack, in the opinion of those present, would have been comfortably repulsed, but at this time the Division on our Right were seen retiring in disorder, exposing our Right Post to enfilade fire, and ultimate destruction. The left flank was already in the air and retirement became necessary. This was effected with very few casualties, in spite of heavy machine gun fire. As the Division on our right had last been seen retiring on Westhoek it was anticipated that the right would be held by them. This, however, was shortly found not to be the case.

The Berkshires were now down to about sixty men, and, together with about twenty men from the Lincolns, moved to the right and formed a defensive flank. A report was received that they were in touch with the Londons, but this proved to be erroneous, and there was a considerable gap in the line, which Brigadier Coffin partially filled by mobilising all the personnel in his Brigade Headquarters, and signallers, clerks, messengers and staff officers enthusiastically joined the battle. Brigadier Coffin noted that Lieutenant Cohen, RE, the Brigade Signalling Officer, was seen happily shooting away, and carefully putting the cartridge case away in his pocket when he had scored a hit. Coffin also ordered up two companies from the 2nd Northants, his reserve battalion, and they made their way up from Jaffa Trench through a heavy enemy barrage which wounded both company commanders. Second Lieutenant Bailey took command, although himself wounded in four places, and brought the two companies into the line where they reinforced the Berkshires and filled the gap on the right.

Meanwhile, the enemy had brought troops up by bus to a position behind the Anzac strong-point, and they were advancing in lines, threatening to overwhelm the defenders by their very numbers. However, they were spotted by the divisions' massed machine gun companies. 'As the dense waves of German infantry surged down the open slopes towards the Hanebeek,' recorded the 8th Divisional History, 'the machine guns opened a furious barrage over the heads of our own infantry. The Artillery Forward Observation Officers also saw their chance, and a few minutes later the artillery joined in. It was a perfect bit of work. The counter-attack hesitated, halted, and then melted away.'

After dusk, the 2nd Royal Berkshires were relieved by the 2nd Northants and went into reserve. There were sufficient survivors to reorganise the battalion into four platoons and a headquarters, with the strongest platoon numbering thirty men. The fighting strength was three officers and 115 men. When the first retirement had been made, a considerable number of wounded men and at least one officer had fallen into enemy hands and become prisoners, which was somewhat balanced by the 100 enemy prisoners that had been captured at the Hanebeek Stream and Iron Cross Redoubt.

Two company commanders, Captains Cahill and Howse, had been killed, together with sixteen other ranks. Seven officers, including the other two company commanders, Captains Young and Hales, had been wounded, together with 231 other ranks, eight of whom died from their injuries. Five officers and 120 other ranks were missing. In fact, the final death toll was 101 who were killed or died of wounds on 16 and 17 August 1917. The majority have no known grave, and are recorded on the Memorial to the Missing at Tyne Cot Cemetery.

It was little comfort that the Berkshires' Adjutant, Captain Forster, had predicted exactly what the outcome would be if the attack by the division on the right failed to take

Lieutenant Harold Howse, killed in action, 1917.

Polygone Wood, or that Major General Heneker's suggestion to Sir Hubert Gough, the Fifth Army commander, had been rejected. Gough had virtually wiped out 1st Battalion Royal Berkshires in the battle of Loos on 28 September 1915, by insisting on an ill-judged attack, and he had now repeated it with the 2nd Battalion.

The 8th Division were now placed under the orders of II Anzac Corps, and left Fifth Army. In a farewell message, which was presumably not intended to be ironic, General Gough pointed out 'that it was no fault of theirs that they had failed to retain all the ground won on the 16th August, and that their fine success in going forward over all difficulties of ground was due to their great spirit and their good discipline and training.'

The 25th Brigade's commander, Brigadier-General Clifford Coffin, was deservedly awarded the Victoria Cross. He had seemed to be everywhere during the critical hours of the enemy counter-attack, coolly encouraging the men and leading them by his own example, although under heavy shell and sniper fire. The citation covered both this action, and his similar exploits on 31 July.

The depleted battalion was taken by bus to Caëstre, in the back area, to re-form and refit. Three officers and 159 other ranks arrived on 20 August, and there were now sufficient men to organise the battalion into two companies, called 'A/B' and 'C/D'.

# XVI

# PLOEGSTEERT TO PASSCHENDAELE

On 21 August, the 8th Division was inspected by Field Marshal Sir Douglas Haig. After the casualties suffered in the two actions, the infantry could only muster a total of 3,950 men of all ranks, the equivalent of one complete brigade. Haig gave the division many words of encouragement and thanks, and, in the words of the Divisional History 'inspired all ranks by his generous appreciation of what they had done.'

Hanbury-Sparrow recorded the occasion somewhat differently:

> When, two days later the Division paraded its shattered ranks before Sir Douglas Haig, there was a dull fury in your head against Gough and the gilded staff of the Fifth Army. Between the lot of them the British Army had just escaped the most humiliating and catastrophic defeat of its history. But what of the Field-Marshal who was inspecting the ranks with his air of grave serenity? What of him? All to whom he was introduced he looked straight in the face. Always it appeared as if he were about to speak, but all he did was to regard the person with his clear eyes as if he sought to imprint his face for ever on his memory, and then, shaking hands, would pass on in silence, with his inscrutable gravity. Surely this man must see Gough as you saw him, outclassed by his task and utterly school-boyish? Yet such was the power of Sir Douglas's demeanour that as your eyes followed him round the three-sided square of the Division you began to have doubts of the rightness of your judgement about his General. But when you looked at the depleted battalions and thought how all these lives had been fruitlessly lost, your mood changed again. You didn't know what to think. You wobbled, mistrustful of Gough and mistrustful of your own judgement.

The period at Caëstre was all too short, for with the campaign on the salient still in progress, a division could not be rested for very long. On 27 August General Heneker took over command of the Ploegsteert Sector in II Anzac Corps, which 8th Division was to hold. The territory was newly conquered, for the successful assault on Messines Ridge in June 1917 had driven the enemy back to beyond the River Lys. The respective front lines followed the line of the river, the British on the west bank and the Germans on the east. There was, however, plenty of work to do, for there had been little time since the ground had been won from the enemy to develop the defences. Communication trenches, drains and dugouts needed to be constructed, together with tasks such as burying telegraph wires and building company headquarters and strong-points. Much work had to be done on the captured German trenches so that fire-steps and sentry posts looked east instead of west.

After the pounding they had taken on 16 August, however, the Berkshires remained in reserve until 11 September, when they moved forward to hold a line near Warneton, with the village of Deûlemont opposite them on the enemy bank of the river. The front line was lightly held, and there was no intention of mounting a serious attack, but sufficient aggressive activity was kept up to prevent the enemy withdrawing troops from their sector to assist at the Passchendaele battle. On four nights between 8 and 18 September, when the wind was favourable, 'L' Special Company, Royal Engineers, delivered massive gas attacks by the use of Livens Projectors, which had been introduced earlier in 1917 for the Arras attack. However, the main activity was a 'demonstration' on 20 September.

Meanwhile, the incessant rain had prevented any progress in the salient since the setback on 16 August, but a comparative dry spell had allowed the ground to become passable, and the third phase of the advance was scheduled for 20 September. To aid this attack, VIII Corps, which the 8th Division were now part of, were ordered to induce the enemy to believe that the main attack was being delivered along the Corps Sector north of the River Lys. The 25th Brigade were in the line at the time, and, at 5.40 a.m., which coincided with the real attack on the salient, 1,200 smoke candles were set off, together with a heavy artillery and machine gun barrage. The Royal Engineers had manufactured hundreds of dummy soldiers, and these were pulled upright at the appropriate time by means of ropes. The enemy were confronted by lines of attacking infantry men advancing through the smoke, and unleashed a terrific fusillade on the dummies, knocking most of them down. Papers captured after the war revealed that a heavy British attack had been repulsed!

The ruse must have helped, for the attack on the salient went well. Second Army had been entrusted with the Menen Road sector, and drove the enemy from Polygone Wood, where their defenders had been so effective in frustrating 8th Division's attacks on 31 July and 16 August.

New drafts arrived, were fitted into the depleted battalion, and taught their duties. Hanbury-Sparrow wrote: 'Sometimes it frightened you, this terrific power that discipline held over modern man. We'd get our drafts of reluctant but sensible conscripts, and of returned wounded undergoing God alone knew what agonies of fear, and in a few weeks we'd turn them into troops as brave, if not as skilful, as any the battalion had ever had.'

One of the newly joined officers was Second Lieutenant Charles Morris, who, after a few weeks training in Portsmouth was appointed Platoon Commander of No.4 Platoon in A Company. He was eighteen years old, and typical of the young subalterns at the time. He has left an unpublished diary, written up in a school exercise book, and held in the archives of the regimental museum. He arrived on 2 October, and his first impressions were very favourable:

> Walked to 8th Division reinforcement camp and from there went to the Berkshire camp about 3 miles walk. Arrived about 11.10. Did not do anything today. Have a fine semicircular hut very warm and comfortable. Nice comfortable bed made of wood and canvas. Good mess. Colonel a fine chap. Col A A H Sparrow DSO MC bar to the DSO. Captain Ayres is my company Captain. Very fine chap. A Coy is my coy and No 4 Platoon is my platoon.

Morris's first visit to the front line came three days later, when his platoon was sent to assist the Royal Engineers.

> Went up the line tonight. Left camp at 6.15 by motor lorries and went to Nieppe and Le Bizet (very ruined, and fine ruined church) to motor car corner. Then R.E. guide took us for a 3 ½ hour walk to no mans land and we widened a drain running in the River Lys from one of the strong posts. The ruins of La Basse Ville were just on our left about 300 yards away. Mr Hope Lumley was in charge and we got back to motor car corner at 2.30 there were no lorries and we had to walk all the way back to camp the men were quite done some of them and I carried one of their rifles. Lieutenant. Lumley gave away all his cigarettes. We eventually arrived back at 5.10 in the morning. I had a good cold supper and went to bed at 6.40 and got up at 12. We covered about 8 miles.

Working parties could be dangerous as well as fatiguing. On the night of 11 October, Morris's mentor, Lieutenant Hope-Lumley, was out with a working party.

I was awakened at 1.40 in the morning by Yeats and he told me that Hope-Lumley had been killed and 4 men wounded and 1 missing of A Coy working party. He was hit in the head by a piece of shell which took off the back of his head so he died instantly. He was found just by the side of a shell-hole. Everybody is very upset about as he was such a nice fellow − a real gentleman in every way. He was buried this afternoon at a British Cemetery near Steenwerck − I watched his body carried out of the camp on a stretcher. As I write this on my bed I can see all his belongings and equipment on his bed ready to be packed up − it's very sad indeed, and everybody's awfully sorry. He lived at Pangbourne on the Thames in his own cottage and I believe his wife and child live at St John's Wood at present. I liked him immensely from the very moment I met him.

It was the eighteen-year-old Morris's first exposure to the loss of a comrade.

Shelling and sniping continued to take their toll. On 15 October, the Regimental Sergeant Major, John Campbell, from Hillingdon, was killed by shell-fire, together with Sergeants Gibbard and Connor. Two days later, Sergeant Lewis and three privates were killed while on a working party. All seven are buried in Prowse Point Cemetery, on the edge of Ploegsteert Wood.

The routine of spells in the front and working parties lasted until 29 October, when the Berkshires were relieved by the 1st Sherwood Foresters and moved to Ypres, where they spent two days attached to the Canadian Corps to provide working parties for the Canadian Light Railway Company. The Canadians specialised in building and running the 60cm-gauge railways, which carried ammunition and supplies from the main railheads up to the front.

Meanwhile, on the salient, the BEF had been gradually pushing forward in the most appalling conditions of mud, rain and desolation. On 10 November, the 1st Canadian Division took the remains of Passchendaele Village, and the campaign officially ended. It had not achieved the grand design of securing the Belgian coast, but it had achieved its secondary function of taking the pressure from the French armies, and giving General Pétain the opportunity to resolve his morale problems.

The divisions who had fought their way up to Passchendaele were overdue for relief, and on 17 November the Berkshires made their way through the wasteland to relieve Princess Patricia's Canadian Light Infantry to the north-east of the site of the village. The slurry was so treacherous that the only practical means of movement was by walkways made of duck-boards laid on the mud. Falling off could be fatal, especially for men laden with equipment.

Hanbury-Sparrow describes the end of his journey to the front:

The duckboard track across the swamps came to an end and the way took the line of the squelching, shell-devoured lane that ran straight up the bank to Passchendaele. The going was fairly good, for your feet, inches deep in running mud, could feel traces of the once metalled surface. Ahead, the jags and stumps of the village proclaimed the prize [the Canadians] had wrested from the Germans. On either side was written the cost. For far to north and far to south, dotted haphazard where they had fallen, lay the unburied dead of the Dominion. There seemed to be hundreds and hundreds of them.

Any illusions that the 8th Division had arrived too late for the party were soon dispelled. The positions were under heavy shell-fire, including gas. Battalion and brigade headquarters were in captured concrete blockhouses, each with three rooms, which measured about 12 by 14ft. The thick roofs were capable of withstanding direct hits from

An artist's impression showing an infantry attack on a German pillbox.

6in shells, which was as well, for the barrage, recorded the Divisional History, was more severe than any the division had yet experienced. As the enemy had built the blockhouses, and knew exactly where they were, hits were frequent, the terrific jar of the impact compelling their inmates to keep standing as the best way to lessen the concussion.

The conditions for the men in trenches were equally unpleasant. 'The trench was only breast high and very wide and most of it was shell-holes. It was terrifically cold and we could not sleep that night. We had absolutely no cover at all and all we did was to sit in the trench,' Second Lieutenant Morris noted in his diary.

The shelling continued the next day, the only respite was a raid by German aircraft, witnessed by Morris.

> Early in the morning the Boche came over in large aeroplanes about 5 of them and they hung about for two hours until one of them was crashed by one of our men. Captain Flint and I were in the trench when he was about 100 feet up and he must have seen us looking at him because we saw him swing his gun over and fire straight at us. We threw ourselves flat against the side of the trench and we could see the bullets striking the other side of the trench only about 2 feet away.

Battalion headquarters was still being heavily shelled, and in the afternoon the high explosive changed to gas shells. Hanbury-Sparrow was badly affected, as was Major Allaway, the second in command, and the adjutant, Lieutenant Brown, who had recently taken over from Captain Forster when he had gone to England on a senior officer's course.

Major-General Heneker had decided that two days in the front line was enough for each brigade, and at 9 p.m. that day, the Berkshires were relieved by the Sherwood Foresters from 24th Brigade. Morris's diary probably reflects the view of the whole battalion as they made their way back:

> We were awfully pleased to get away from Passchendaele. I led the company out and it was an awful walk falling in shell-holes and tripping over dead men in the road. We left Wieltje

at midnight and got into camp at 3 in the morning. Had dinner and went to bed at 4. You could stand on the ridge at Passchendaele and look 5 miles without seeing a single blade of grass. All there are is a few tree stumps and pill boxes and one or two duck board tracks, there are shell-holes everywhere and bits of men lying about – old German and English rifles and equipment.

Lieutenant-Colonel Hanbury-Sparrow, DSO★, MC, had been so badly affected by the gas that he was forced to relinquish his command. His place was taken by Lieutenant-Colonel Colin Stirling, DSO. Like Hanbury-Sparrow, he was only twenty-four, and had been commanding the 2nd Scottish Rifles in 23rd Brigade until he was wounded on 31 July. Now recovered, he was attached to the Berkshires. He made a favourable first impression on Second Lieutenant Morris: 'A jolly decent chap in every way,' he confided to his diary. The Berkshires' former commander, Lieutenant-Colonel Roland Haig, who had been wounded on the same day as Stirling, had returned from hospital as a brigadier-general, and was appointed to the command of 23rd Infantry Brigade.

The Berkshires had ten days out of the line near Poperinge, and moved back to the hated Passchendaele sector on 29 November. They had been practising the attack, for there were two enemy strongholds to the east of the ruined village, which, if captured, would give good observation over the enemy rear areas. The 25th Brigade were ordered to capture them, in conjunction with an attack on their left by 32nd Division, and a 'demonstration' on the right flank by 33rd Division.

The journey up to the start line was a nightmare. The battalion had been waiting for dusk at Meetcheele, a hamlet some 1,000 yards west of Passchendaele, which was now merely a map reference, for nothing of it remained. At dusk, A Company, which was to be the reserve, set off along the duckboard walkway to reach their assigned waiting point to the west of Passchendaele. In the darkness, they lost their way, and did not reach their position until 9 p.m., after losing a lot of men to shell-fire.

B and D Companies, who were to make the main assault, set off along the walkway at 7.15 p.m. There was intermittent shelling, and the leading men found that a portion of the walkway had been shattered by shell-fire, and there was a large gap of glutinous mud to cross. The first platoon, under Second Lieutenant Giddings, the commander of B Company, managed to get over, but as more men tried to get across, the mud became worse, and the other platoons were floundering in the morass. Giddings decided to go forward with his platoon, leaving Second Lieutenants Upton and Tremellen to try to get the rest of the men across the gap and sort them into their respective sections again.

By now, men from the 2nd Lincolns and 2nd Rifle Brigade were waiting to use the track, so Lieutenant-Colonel Stirling went forward, found that the Berkshires had managed to reorganise themselves, took charge and led them up to the tapes which marked the start line. He had difficulties finding the tapes, for they had become so saturated with mud that it was difficult to make them out in the dark, but at last, satisfied that the two companies were in the right place, he reported the battalion ready at 11.30 p.m. After their fight with the mud, the condition of the men's uniform and equipment must have been dreadful, but they had a two-hour respite before zero hour at 1.55 a.m. to clean their rifles and scrape the worst of the mud from their trousers and boots.

C Company were not expected to take part in the attack, but had moved forward by a different route to form a defensive flank on the right of the Berkshires' sector, facing the area where 33rd Division were to mount the 'demonstration' or dummy assault to distract the enemy.

At zero hour, 1.55 a.m., the two companies moved forward, B on the left and D on the right. Lieutenant Upton noticed that the 2nd Lincolns, on his left, seemed to be bearing too far to the left, so he veered his left-hand platoon towards them to try to stay in touch. For three minutes, the advance went undetected by the Germans, but suddenly, at

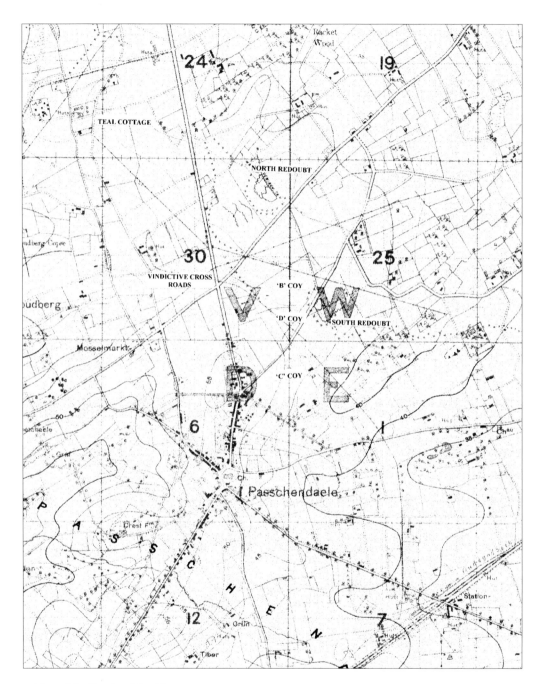

Map of the Passchendale village area.

1.58 a.m., a display of red, green and golden flares went up, and the enemy opened a heavy but hurried and badly aimed fusillade of rifle and machine gun fire, which, Stirling noted, did not cause many casualties. However, six minutes later, at 2.04 a.m., the German artillery responded to the flares with a heavy bombardment on Vindictive Crossroads, to the north of Passchendaele village. Unfortunately, the reserve and support platoons of B Company were caught by this barrage, sustaining heavy casualties. Company headquarters were knocked out, and Lieutenant Giddings was knocked over and dazed.

Meanwhile, Sergeant Sturgess had led No.5 Platoon into the Southern Redoubt, and heavy fighting was in progress. They were joined by the leading platoon of D Company, and accounted for many of the enemy with rifle and bayonet, but also took heavy casualties themselves. The problems caused by B Company's left flank veering to the left to try and keep touch with the Lincolns now became apparent, for there were insufficient men to maintain the hold on the redoubt. Eventually the attackers were forced out, and dug in to the south-west of the complex.

While this was going on, the rest of B Company, under Lieutenants Upton and Tremellen, had succeeded in capturing a portion of the trench which connected the north and south redoubts, killing the occupants and capturing three machine guns. This section of trench should have been an objective for the 2nd Lincolns, but after veering too far left, they had lost heavily from shellfire, and all their officers had become casualties.

On the right flank, where C Company were supposed to have a purely defensive role, a platoon under Lieutenant Smith fought their way towards the group dug in near the South Redoubt, and managed to link up with them, after first taking thirty prisoners, including an officer, and capturing another machine gun.

The left flank of 25th Brigade's attack had failed. The 2nd Rifle Brigade had lost their commanding officer, Lieutenant-Colonel Brand, who had been wounded by a rifle bullet when trying to find the forming-up tapes. As well as suffering from the intense barrage, they made the unpleasant discovery that Teal Cottage, a German strongpoint on their left flank, was still in enemy hands. The plan had called for this to be taken by 32nd Division

A Lewis gun team in action.

before the attack started, but they had failed to do so. The Rifle Brigade now found themselves under fire from this strongpoint, and were forced to form a defensive flank on their left. By now they were so depleted by casualties that it was out of the question to attack the North Redoubt, their objective, for they would have been enfiladed by the Teal Cottage machine gunners.

Daybreak found B and D Companies occupying shell-holes to the south-west of South Redoubt, with C Company forming a flank on their right. The remnants of the 2nd Lincolns were dug in on the Berkshires' left, while the 2nd Rifle Corps formed a defensive flank on the left. The attack by the 32nd Division appeared to have failed. Stirling decided to go back to Mosselmarkt, where the Lincolns' Battalion Headquarters was situated, and try and find out what was happening. On the way, he came across a wounded orderly with a message from C Company timed at 3.45 a.m. to the effect that they were in place and all was well. This was the first that he had heard from them since they left for their start line the previous evening. When he reached the Lincolns' HQ, Stirling learned that the Lincolns and the Rifle Brigade had not gained their objectives.

During the day, the enemy made several attempts to dislodge the Berkshires from their posts, but they were repelled without too much difficulty. However, at about 4.10 p.m. an SOS was sent up by the Rifle Brigade on the left, which Stirling, who had by now returned to his own headquarters, repeated. The British artillery responded with a heavy barrage which scattered a large enemy force who were forming up for a counter-attack. By 5 p.m. the Germans appeared to have given up, and all went quiet. Stirling decided to extract his exposed forward units as soon as darkness fell, and Lieutenant Upton succeeded in bringing them back safely at about 9 p.m., and established a more tenable line.

The 25th Brigade were now due for relief, but the guides who had been detailed to lead the incoming battalion had become casualties. Stirling detailed Lieutenant Burne, the signalling officer, to take men from his headquarters staff and look for the reliefs. The 8th Battalion, King's Royal Rifle Corps, from 14th Division, were found, and guides from the Berkshires' companies led them on from battalion headquarters to the new positions. The weary troops of 25th Brigade returned to Junction Camp near Ypres.

Stirling attributed the limited success of his battalion to the Lincolns veering too far left, which was understandable, for their officers had become casualties. The overall failure of the brigade's attack was due to the unaccountable failure of 32nd Division to capture Teal Cottage, which prevented the 2nd Rifle Brigade from assaulting the North Redoubt.

The Berkshires had lost Lieutenant Troup killed, and Second Lieutenants Giddings and Wait missing. In fact, both Giddings and Wait had been killed, and all three are commemorated on the Memorial to the Missing at Tyne Cot Cemetery. Second Lieutenants Grove and Osbourne had been wounded, together with Second Lieutenant Morris, whose diary, and short military career, had come to an end. Thirty-five other ranks had been killed, thirty-three were missing and eighty-three wounded. When the missing were accounted for, a total of fifty-one had lost their lives, most of whom have no known grave, and are commemorated at Tyne Cot.

The Berkshires celebrated an early Christmas in 1917, on 23 December, for they returned to Passchendaele on 24 December for another week in the line. However, all was quiet, with no attacks planned or any significant enemy activity taking place.

# XVII

# THE SPRING OFFENSIVE

The battalion spent the first two months of 1918 holding the line near Passchendaele, with the other units of the 25th Brigade. Every few days the division's brigades would rotate, and a welcome few days would be spent out of danger near Poperinge. Both sides had been exhausted by the autumn campaigns, and as the winter weather precluded any serious chance of attacks, the periods in the line were relatively quiet.

The campaign had far-reaching effects, for the Prime Minister, Lloyd-George, was sensitive to the political risks of another battle of attrition with heavy casualties, and would not sanction reinforcements to the Western Front. Very few units were at anything like full strength, and the Army Council took the decision to reduce the number of battalions in an infantry brigade from four to three. This would mean the disbanding of 142 battalions, whose troops could be used to reinforce the remainder. The theoretical front-line strength of an infantry division would reduce from 12,000 men to 9,000, although in practice none of the divisions would have been able to muster anything like this number since the Somme campaign in 1916. To further add to the strain on the BEF, four divisions had been sent to assist on the Italian front, and a further 25 miles of front line south of the River Somme had been taken over from the French.

As all the infantry units in the 8th Division were regular army battalions, none were required to disband, but an order was received on 27 January to transfer the 1st Scottish Rifles to the 20th Division, 1st Royal Irish Rifles to the 36th Division and the 2nd Lincolnshire Regiment to the 21st Division. As both the Royal Irish Rifles and the Lincolns were leaving 25th Brigade, the 2nd East Lancs were transferred from 24th Brigade to make the third battalion. For the remainder of the conflict, the 25th Brigade would consist of the 2nd Royal Berkshires, 2nd Rifle Brigade and 2nd East Lancashires. The decision to disband so many battalions caused much resentment, for the displaced men had naturally formed loyalties to their old units, and now found themselves parcelled out to new ones. The 6th Battalion, Royal Berkshires, who had been in the 18th Division, and, it may be recalled, had lost heavily on 31 July 1917 on the right of the 8th Division, were among those disbanded. Their 650 men found themselves distributed to the 1st, 2nd and 5th Royal Berkshire battalions, so at least they remained in the same regiment. Others were not so fortunate.

On the enemy side, the surrender of Russia had enabled Germany to reduce its strength on the Eastern Front, and the railway network was busy transferring divisions and artillery to the west. It was becoming obvious that the enemy was planning an attack as soon as the weather permitted, for the American Expeditionary Force under General Pershing was beginning to arrive in France, and General Ludendorff, the German chief of staff, was well aware that he would be outnumbered once the Americans had completed their build-up.

In anticipation, the BEF was reorganised for defence rather than attack. General Gough's Fifth Army, with twelve infantry and three cavalry divisions, was sent to take over the

Lieutenant Mant leads his men from the trenches, believed to have been taken in 1918.

French sector south of the Somme, and a new concept was put in place, in which the front line was lightly held, and the defenders would make a fighting withdrawal when attacked. This would lead the attackers into a 'battle zone' some two or three miles deep, where the artillery and machine guns could deal with them. As part of the plans, the 8th Division was placed under the direct command of Haig's GHQ, to be used as a rapid reinforcement to any section of the line which was attacked. To this end, the division was to be based at St Omer, which had good rail network connections to all sectors of the British front. On 11 March 1918 the 2nd Royal Berkshires boarded trains to St Omer, and marched to billets in nearby St-Martin-au-Laert, where an intensive training programme commenced.

The 8th Division's staff and transport officers had been warned that the whole division might be ordered to move anywhere on the Western Front at short notice, and contingency plans were drawn up. Moving a division by rail was not an easy task, as explained in the Divisional History:

> The allotment of trains and entraining stations and the determination of the precise manner and order in which each train would have to be filled were in themselves a highly complicated piece of work, and involved a whole host of subsidiary problems. Where horses should be watered; how many days' rations would be required to issue to units in advance, and what proportion should be carried on the man; the allocation of cookers and teams to the different trains in such a way that all should be in order on arrival; the precise number of wagons which could be allotted to the ordnance; the ultimate disposition, even, of the divisional laundry – such were the kind of problems which had to be thought out in advance, the proper solution discovered, and the necessary orders and instructions issued accordingly.

The expected attack came on the equinox, 21 March 1918. Three German Armies, the Second, Seventeenth and Eighteenth, with sixty-seven divisions between them, attacked the southern part of the front held by the British Third Army and the whole of the Fifth Army's sector, which stretched 31 miles from the Flesquières Salient in the north to the junction with the French Sixth Army on the River Oise. Preluded by an intense artillery and gas shell bombardment, and aided by thick fog, the Germans soon overwhelmed the front line defenders, and by midday were across the planned 'battle zone' in many places. The Fifth Army started to fall back, and the troops on the Third Army's right wing were obliged to fall back to prevent a gap opening up, which would enable the Germans to outflank them.

The afternoon of 21 March was the 2nd Royal Berkshires' Regimental Sports Day, held to celebrate the anniversary the next day of the Battle of Tofrek, one of the Regiment's proudest battle honours. However, at 4 p.m. the events were abruptly cancelled when orders arrived to embark on the allotted trains the next day. Everything was hastily packed, and the battalion marched to nearby Arques, and boarded the trains the next morning. Major-General Heneker was advised that his division would be allocated to XIX Corps, and he would come under the command of Lieutenant-General Sir H.E. Watts.

The CWGC headstone for Captain (acting Lt-Col.) Colin Robert Hoste Stirling DSO and Bar MC, Commanding Officer of 2nd Battalion at St Sever Cemetery, Rouen.

While the 8th Division had been in transit, the Fifth Army had been forced back. There had been insufficient time and manpower to construct the various lines of defence to the rear of the battle ground, and in many places the planned trenches were just surveyors' stakes laid out by the Royal Engineers. Lacking a proper line, General Gough decided to hold the enemy on the Somme to the south of Péronne. The 8th Division, as they arrived, were to establish defences on the west bank between Villers-Carbonnel and Béthencourt. The troops on the east bank, fighting a desperate rear-guard action, would cross the river and reorganise while the 8th Division held the line. It was now 23 March, and the 2nd

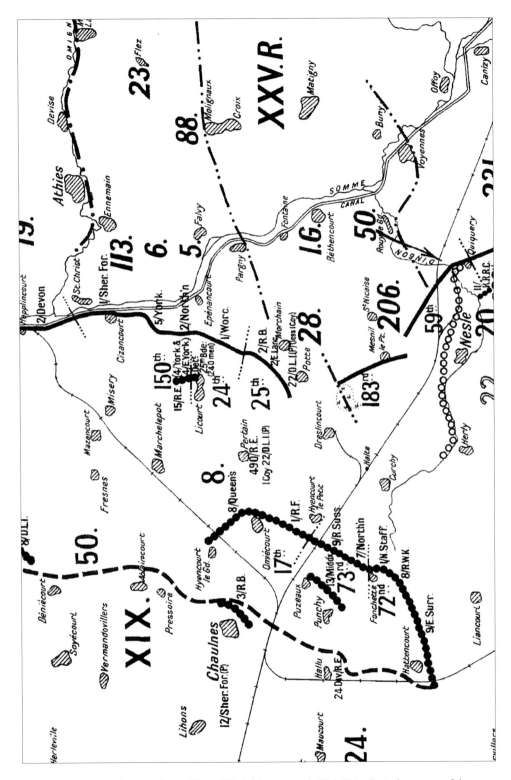

Situation on 25 March 1918. The 2nd Royal Berkshires are with 25th Brigade in the centre of the map.

Royal Berkshires, 2nd East Lancs and 2nd Rifle Brigade had reached Chaulnes, after leaving their trains at Rosières and marching eastwards towards the sounds of the battle.

The 25th Brigade's sector was between Rouy-le-Grand and Pargny, which included the bridge over the river at Pargny. The Berkshires were in the centre, and the three battalions advanced in open order through the 50th Division, who withdrew through them. They came under heavy shell-fire, and when they arrived at the river bank found the enemy were almost at the east bank, driving the retreating troops before them. The brigade's machine gun company placed their guns to cover the bridge at Béthencourt, which had been partially demolished, but it was still possible for infantry to cross it in single file. Initially, General Heneker had ordered all three battalions into the line, but subsequently decided to keep the Berkshires in reserve, so they withdrew from the river bank, with two companies in Monks Quarry and two in Morchain Wood.

As soon as it was light on the following day, 24 March, the enemy began their attack, crossing the Somme Canal north of Béthencourt at Pargny by felling trees across the water and by constructing rafts. The brigade immediately counter-attacked, and the Berkshires were once again ordered forward. A fierce battle ensued, especially around Monks Quarry, in which Lieutenant-Colonel Stirling was mortally wounded. However, the enemy had crossed the Somme further south, and were advancing in strength around the 8th Division's right flank. Brigadier Coffin ordered a fighting retreat, and by about 2.30 p.m. the brigade were occupying an old trench system near Potte and Morchain.

The situation was becoming so serious that Major-General Heneker sent in his last reserves – the 490th Field Company, Royal Engineers, and the 22nd Durham Light Infantry – as reinforcements. The Durham Light Infantry were the 8th Division's Pioneer Battalion, who would normally have been digging fortifications or repairing roads. Together with the sappers, they exchanged their tools for rifles and became infantrymen. Orders arrived at 10 p.m. to the effect that 25th Brigade would launch a counter-attack in the morning, in conjunction with an attack to be launched on their right flank by the French and the British 24th Division. This was intended to retake the river line to the south.

By the close of the day's fighting on the Fifth Army's front, the 8th Division History noted:

> The retreat was continuing on both flanks; while in the centre, where was the 8th Division, some 6 miles of the river line was holding firm. To the north, the westward bend of the Somme still offered some security to the flank of the troops holding the river defences; but their southern flank lay open, and it was clear that unless the river line could be regained it would only be a matter of time before they too were compelled to fall back.

The enemy renewed his assault at 6.15 a.m. on 25 March. The Berkshires had moved away from the brigade's right flank to leave the way clear for the expected attack by 24th Division, and the defenders were very thin on the ground. The attack by the French and 24th Division failed to materialise, because the French divisions had been unable to get in position, and had asked for a postponement of three hours. After three hours, when still nothing had happened, it transpired that no definite orders to attack had been issued to them. The delay was fatal, for the enemy found the gap that had been deliberately left open for the counter-attack, and started to pour through it.

The brigade was in danger of being outflanked, so Brigadier Coffin withdrew his headquarters to Omiécourt at about 10 a.m. and ordered the rest of the brigade to fall back on the village, which was completed by noon. However, the withdrawal continued, and by 3 p.m. the 25th Brigade was concentrating around Chaulnes. The 'front line', if it could be called that, for the situation was very fluid, was being held by the 23rd Brigade on the left, 24th in the centre, and 17th Brigade, which was part of 24th Division, on

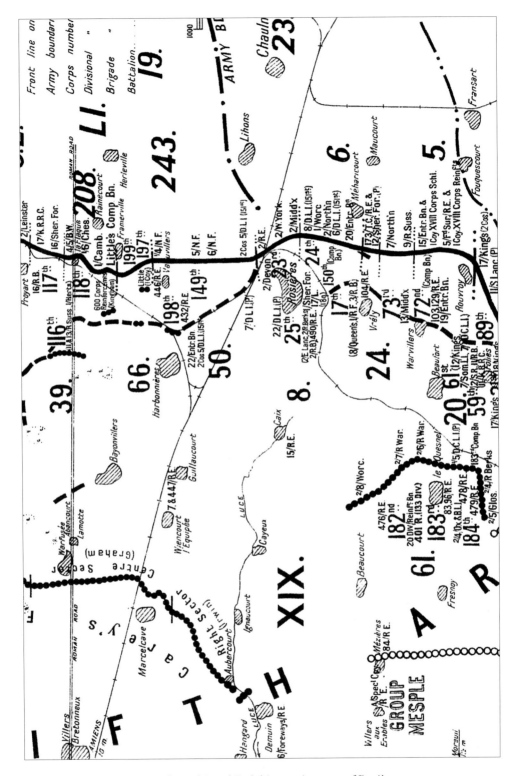

Situation on 27 March 1918. The 2nd Royal Berkshires are just west of Rosières.

the right. The 25th Brigade were temporarily out of the battle to reorganise, while the stragglers, numbering about 300 to 400, were placed under the command of Major Mitchell of the 22nd Durham Light Infantry to protect the right flank of 17th Brigade.

During the afternoon of 25 March, orders arrived from XIX Corps that a new line of defence was to be established, and the 8th Division would be responsible for the sector between Chaulnes and Estrées. The 50th Division was on the left, and the 24th Division on the right. The withdrawal to the new line commenced at dusk, and was carried out successfully and in good order. Two brigades, 23rd and 24th, were in the line and the 25th (including the Berkshires) were in reserve at Lihons. The enemy attacked in considerable force on the morning of 26 March, but were driven off with heavy losses.

Nevertheless, the right of the British line was still being driven back, and there was a risk of a gap being driven between the BEF and the French Army. The 25th Brigade were ordered to remain at Lihons and act as rearguard until the other two brigades had withdrawn past them to a new line at Rosières. Lieutenant-Colonel Armitage, on 8th Division's General Staff, drove up to Lihons and met Brigadier Coffin. Everything was quiet, but there was occasional shelling on the position, and the enemy was reported to have reached Chaulnes. Armitage then went north, and found Brigadier Haig (the Berkshires' former commanding officer) with both 23rd and 24th Brigades retiring in good order. The 25th Brigade remained at Lihons until 5.30 p.m. and then withdrew safely to Rosières.

Changes had been made in the higher command. At a conference at Doullens, it had been agreed that General Foch would be appointed Generalissimo on the Western Front, to co-ordinate the Allied Armies, and prevent misunderstandings such as the counter-attack on 25 March which did not materialise. General Gough was removed as commander of the Fifth Army, after being made the scapegoat for the current situation. Gough had made questionable decisions in the past, but considering the weakness of his forces, and the strength of the German attack, he had actually done a good job in handling the retreat and preventing it from becoming a rout. General Fayolle, commander of the French Northern Army Group, was placed in charge of all forces south of the River Somme, including the British units which had been part of Fifth Army.

The 26 March ended with a message from the Corps Commander:

> Under instructions from the French C-in-C, to 5th Army, the XIX Corps will maintain at all costs the line we are now on until the arrival of French troops who are on their way to relieve us. For this purpose every available man will be put into the fight, and the Corps Commander looks to all ranks to make one more supreme effort and maintain to the last the magnificent fighting qualities and endurance already displayed throughout the battle.

The enemy mounted a furious attack on the 8th Division's sector at 8 a.m. on 27 March. The division fought back, and the first two waves were driven back by artillery fire, but the third wave managed to penetrate the defences on the right, until a counter-attack by the 1st Sherwood Foresters drove them out again. The line was maintained, and the enemy held off, making no further serious attacks. However, on the left, the 50th Division were giving ground, and the headquarters staff of all three brigades, together with the 15th Royal Engineers Field Company and the 24th Trench Mortar Battery, were banded into an *ad hoc* unit to defend the northern flank. They made a heroic bayonet charge, and captured thirty prisoners and three machine guns before handing the newly regained ground back to 50th Division.

The situation was not looking good on either flank. Due to a misunderstanding, the Third Army, on the north bank of the Somme, had retired too far. It had been intended to mount a stand at Bray-sur-Somme, which was approximately opposite the left flank of the 50th Division, but instead they had fallen back to the confluence of the Somme and Ancre, some 6 miles to the west. The only force preventing the enemy from crossing the river behind 50th and 8th Divisions was an improvised one of some 350 men with armoured cars who were holding the river crossings. On the southern flank of the 8th Division, the withdrawal had continued, and by the evening of 27 March had reached Montdidier. The highly strategic city of Amiens was within the enemy's reach, and the loss of its railway facilities would severely hamper Allied movement along the Western Front.

At about 8 p.m. on 27 March, news reached General Heneker that the enemy had succeeded in crossing the Somme at Cérisy, and was advancing southward. He called his fellow commanders of the 50th and 66th Divisions to a conference, and they agreed that unless a retirement was ordered at once, the remains of their divisions would be surrounded and cut off. Their concerns were passed back to Fifth Army headquarters, who forwarded them to General Foch. At 3.30 a.m. on 28 March he authorised a further withdrawal, and the 8th Division fell back to a line between Vrély and Caix, with the 50th Division on their left. To the south, the remnants of three British divisions, 20th, 30th and 36th, without artillery support, were struggling to hold the enemy on the Roye to Amiens road.

The new line did not hold for long. The enemy was crossing the Somme in force, and linking with their forces south of the river to press the 50th Division, who fell back on the afternoon of 28 March, when the Germans reached Caix, which was being held by 23rd Brigade. The 8th Division were once again compelled to withdraw; the 24th and 25th Brigades managed to get clear without difficulty and fell back to Moreuil, but the 23rd Brigade suffered heavy losses, for many of their scattered units did not receive the order to retire until it was too late.

The division remained at Moreuil, with the survivors from the 23rd and 24th Brigades going into billets for a night's rest. They had been fighting continuously for a week, and the Divisional History records that the two brigades were now so utterly exhausted that they were quite unfit to move. The 25th Brigade, including the Berkshires, were somewhat fresher, for they had been in reserve at Caix and had taken the opportunity to rest. They were ordered to hold a portion of the wood north of Moreuil, but on arrival Brigadier Coffin found it occupied by French troops, so decided to keep his men in reserve.

At about 5.30 p.m., the French were observed to be retreating from the wood. Coffin ordered the 2nd Royal Berkshires to mount a counter-attack. The Berkshires found the wood already occupied, but fought a rearguard action protecting the right flank of XIX Corps before falling back to the high ground north-east of Moreuil. Meanwhile, the division's other two brigades, 23rd and 24th, had been ordered north to assist the 24th Division at Berteaucourt.

Brigadier Coffin attached his brigade to a French regiment, whose commander was intending to hold the river crossing at Castel. Coffin found the French holding the position in force, so moved the brigade to the neighbourhood of Rouvrel, where cookers and rations were found. When the units had been fed, reorganised and rested, welcome news arrived to the effect that the Canadian Cavalry Brigade had delivered a successful counter-attack on the enemy in Moreuil Wood, where the Berkshires had been the day before. However, they asked for infantry assistance, and Brigadier Coffin sent the 2nd West Yorkshires up to help them.

Meanwhile, XIX Corps ordered General Heneker to relieve the cavalry in the wood with the 8th Division. He placed Brigadier Grogan in overall command of the 23rd and 24th Brigades, who were sent to take over the wood, with 20th Division on their left and the French on their right. The situation in Moreuil village was obscure. The 25th Brigade remained in reserve, and Brigadier Coffin was ordered to take some rest, for he was in a condition of collapse from lack of sleep.

Grogan's troops discovered that the enemy was holding the village, and the British line to the north ran along the western edge of the wood rather than the eastern edge. The night of 30 March was quiet, but at first light patrols sent into the wood started to encounter enemy scouts. The Germans started to form up to attack the wood and, despite being bombarded by the 8th Division's field artillery, mounted a heavy attack at 1 p.m., breaking through on the left and forcing the 2nd Devonshires out of the wood.

At 2.30 p.m. the 2nd Royal Berkshires and part of the 2nd East Lancashires, with Major Griffin of the Berkshires in overall command, were hurried forward from their reserve position and mounted a successful counter-attack, driving the enemy back and restoring the line. The Berkshires continued into the wood, but General Heneker ordered them to withdraw, because he was planning a heavy artillery barrage on the wood during the night, in preparation for a further counter-attack the next day. Griffin's force, who were now very wet and exhausted, were relieved by the 23rd Infantry Brigade.

The planned counter-attack was delivered at 9 a.m. on 1 April by the 2nd Cavalry Division. They swept round the north of the wood, and proceeded across the 8th Division's front. According to the Divisional History, the assault 'provided another example of the success with which mounted troops can be used in the concluding stages of a protracted battle. A large number of the enemy were killed, many prisoners captured and valuable territory regained.'

By now, the enemy attackers were just as exhausted as the defenders, and had the additional handicap that their supply routes were growing longer with each advance. Despite some tense moments, the British line had not broken, General Ludendorff had not achieved his breakthrough, and Amiens was still in Allied hands. However, the British Army had suffered enormous casualties, and it would take some time to reorganise and re-equip the shattered divisions. In the Somme valley, the British line was now several miles behind the positions from which the 'big push' of 1 July 1916 had been launched.

In the early hours of 2 April, the 8th Division were relieved by the 133rd French Division, and marched back to the Cavillon area west of Amiens to rest and regroup. General Heneker sent a message to the troops: 'On being withdrawn from the front line to rest and reorganise after the strenuous nine days of fighting in which the division has taken such a distinguished part, I desire to convey to all ranks my admiration of their behaviour and fighting spirit. While every hour was full of heroic deeds, and it is perhaps invidious to refer to any particular unit by name when all have done so well, I feel I should record certain outstanding operations.' The message goes on to list six events, one of which was the counter-attack by the 2nd Royal Berkshire Regiment and 2nd East Lancashire Regiment at Moreuil Wood.

*Author's note: This chapter has essentially told the story of the 8th Division or 25th Brigade. The war diary of the 2nd Royal Berkshires from 23 to 31 March is somewhat unhelpful, for it simply repeats 'Battalion took part in rear-guard actions', and was probably written up early in April. The narrative is mostly gleaned from the 25th Brigade's report of the action, and the 8th Division's history. No individual diaries or letters from the period have come to light.*

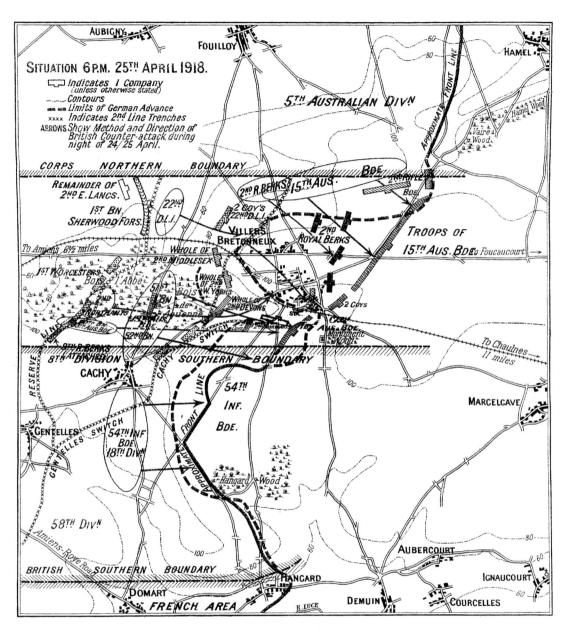

Map of Villers–Bretonneux.

# XVIII

# VILLERS-BRETONNEUX

The 8th Division remained in the Cavillon area for a week, while drafts arrived to replace the casualties. The actions since 23 March had cost 250 officers and 4,693 other ranks. The Berkshires had lost their commanding officer, Lieutenant-Colonel Stirling. Severely wounded, he died two months later in hospital at Amiens on 29 May. In addition to Stirling, three officers had been killed, three taken prisoner, and twenty-one wounded. Thirty-five other ranks had lost their lives, eighty-eight were missing and 182 wounded. The final death toll, when the missing had been accounted for, was eighty-two officers and men. Few of them have graves; they are commemorated on the Pozières Memorial to the Missing.

The action had also cost the lives of two earlier commanders of the 2nd Royal Berkshires. Lieutenant-Colonel Feetham, who had brought the battalion from India and commanded it for the first few months of the war, had risen to the rank of Major-General. He was killed on 29 March while commanding the 39th Division. Additionally, Lieutenant-Colonel Hill, who had led the battalion in 1915, was killed on 23 March while commanding the 1st Royal Berkshires in action at Léchelle Wood.

The German offensive had been halted just short of the village of Villers-Bretonneux. It occupied a summit position on the straight Roman road between St Quentin and Amiens, and, had it been captured, would have given the enemy excellent observation over Amiens and its surroundings, which could then have been bombarded with impunity. Preventing the enemy from gaining this prize became a major concern in this sector of the front.

However, the second phase of Ludendorff's plan opened further north, on the River Lys. The 8th Division were placed under immediate notice to move to that sector, and there was a confusing period of orders being issued, countermanded, and then cancelled. For a few days the division was assigned to the Anzac Corps under General Birdwood, but then, on 17 April was transferred to III Corps. On the same day, thirteen officers were drafted into the 2nd Royal Berkshires, mostly from the Manchester Regiment. They had little time to settle in, for on 20 April the Berkshires found themselves designated as 'centre attack battalion' in the line just north of Villers-Bretonneux. Major Griffin, who had joined the battalion in January, was promoted to lieutenant-colonel and assumed command.

Everyone was on full alert, for interrogations of German prisoners and deserters all indicated that an assault was imminent. A sergeant-major from the 4th Guards Division, captured by the 1st Sherwood Foresters on 22 April, informed his questioners that the attack was planned for 3 a.m. the next day. A heavy bombardment was delivered on the probable enemy forming-up locations, but the assault did not take place.

The next day, 23 April, was punctuated by enemy bombardments of gas shells. Aircraft reconnaissance confirmed that large bodies of troops were moving up towards the front line, and more prisoners asserted that an attack was imminent.

The following morning, 24 April, five German divisions launched an attack on an 8,000-yard front, which included the whole of the 8th Division's sector, and extended southward to Hangard Wood, which was being held by the 58th Division. It opened with a very heavy artillery bombardment, starting at 3.30 a.m., with both high explosive and gas shells supplemented with mortars. It lasted over two hours, and was, the Divisional History comments, 'the heaviest bombardment that the Division had yet experienced.'

At 6 a.m., the enemy started to lay down thick smoke all along the line, which mingled with the early morning mist to produce a dense fog. The defenders could hardly see further than 20 yards, but were soon set upon by enemy tanks. Already depleted by the bombardment, the units in the front line had little chance, for the tanks positioned themselves across the trenches, and enfiladed the defenders with their machine guns. The tanks were followed up by an attack from the 4th Guards Division.

Fortunately for the Berkshires, they had been stationed in the second line of defence, occupying the valley to the north of the village, but the 2nd Middlesex and 2nd West Yorks suffered heavily as they were driven back into the gas-filled ruins of Villers-Bretonneux. By 9.30 a.m. they were through the village, and manning positions on the western slope, attempting to prevent the enemy from debouching from the ruins. Further to the south, the 58th Division had been driven back towards the village of Cachy.

The 25th Brigade, holding the 8th Division's left, or northern, flank, were now vulnerable, because they had been outflanked on the right. The foremost battalion, the 2nd Rifle Brigade, found that their two forward companies had been surrounded. Despite putting up a fierce resistance, they soon ceased to exist, with their men either killed or taken prisoner. The Berkshires, to the rear of the Rifle Brigade, had swung round to the right to face the enemy in the village, and the two surviving Rifle Brigade companies, B and D, fell back and joined forces with them.

By midday, when the fog cleared, the enemy had gained possession of the whole village, and was busy installing machine gun posts along the northern, western and southern perimeters. However, these boundaries were still under intense British artillery fire, which effectively kept the Germans bottled up in the village and prevented a breakout.

Major-General Heneker was determined to dislodge the enemy from the village, but was unwilling to order a direct counter-attack, for the newly installed machine guns would soon cut the assault troops down, causing heavy casualties with nothing gained. He was confident that he could maintain the current position during the day, and proposed to Corps headquarters that a night attack would be the best option. Corps agreed, and placed the 13th and 15th Australian Brigades under Heneker's command to assist.

The plan called for the 54th Brigade, which was part of the 58th Division, to launch an attack in conjunction with the 13th Australian Brigade, which would strike eastward between Villers-Bretonneux and Hangard Wood, regaining the lost positions. Meanwhile, the 15th Australian Brigade, who were in position on the high ground to the north of the village, and had so far not been involved in the action, would strike diagonally south-eastwards, across the back of Villers-Bretonneux. While these attacks were taking place, the 8th Division were to hold their current positions and keep the enemy confined in the village.

The conditions, according to the Divisional History, were ideal for a night attack, for there was sufficient light for the troops to maintain their positions, but it was too dark for the enemy to aim a machine gun. The Australians advanced across the Berkshire's front, aided by flares put up by uneasy German defenders. As soon as a flare went up, the position was rushed by a platoon, and the occupants bayoneted or taken prisoner. At 4.30 a.m. the Australians reported that the old front line had been recaptured, and sixty prisoners taken.

The village, however, was still full of the enemy, who had now realised that they were practically surrounded. Heneker ordered Brigadier Coffin to send the 2nd Royal Berkshires to clear the village from the north.

Lieutenant-Colonel Griffin led the Berkshires forward at 6.30 a.m., and they soon made their presence felt, clearing a large area of the village and capturing 300 prisoners and thirty-five machine guns. The Divisional History recorded: 'The brilliant work by the 2nd Royal Berkshires in this engagement was acknowledged by a message from 5th Australian Division: "Well Done, Royal Berks." '

By this stage of the war, the ANZAC and Canadian Corps justifiably considered themselves as elite units, with a somewhat scathing opinion of British formations, so to receive a 'well done' from an Australian divisional commander was a rare honour.

By nightfall on 25 April, the original lines were reoccupied and the enemy had been cleared from their gains, and showed no inclination to continue the fight. The 8th Division spent a quiet day until they were relieved on 27 April by the 4th Australian Division.

The action, although successful, had been costly. Three officers, Second Lieutenants Mossman, Cooper and Moore, had been killed, together with sixty-six other ranks. Seven officers and 183 men had been wounded, and a further eight were missing.

# XIX

# DOWN ON THE AISNE

One of the positive results to come out of the German spring offensive – so far as the Allies were concerned – was the appointment of Marshal Foch as supreme commander for the Western Front theatre. While Haig and Pershing would retain command of the British and American forces respectively, overall strategic direction would come from Foch. This move would hopefully avoid situations such as the misunderstandings between Gough and Pétain, which had almost led to the loss of Amiens.

The new spirit of co-operation led to a decision which profoundly affected the 2nd Royal Berkshires. The four British infantry divisions which had received the worst battering in the German onslaught were to be sent to a quiet part of the French sector in order to absorb the influx of replacements, retrain, reorganise, and be brought back to full fighting efficiency once more. In return, a French army was sent to reinforce the BEF.

The March offensive, followed by the action at Villers-Bretonneux, had cost the 8th Division 390 officers and 8,210 other rank casualties. By the end of April, 329 officers and 7,567 other ranks had been drafted in as replacements, making the division a prime candidate for the respite, together with 21st, 25th and 50th Divisions, which had also suffered heavy losses. They were banded together in IX Corps under Lieutenant-General Sir A. Hamilton Gordon, and started to move down to the new area on 3 May. Divisional Headquarters was established near Fismes, on the River Vesle. The 25th Brigade left on 5 May, the 2nd Royal Berkshires travelling by train to billets at Loupeigne. The Corps became part of the French Sixth Army, which was commanded by General Duchêne.

The countryside was a complete contrast to the flat, muddy misery of Flanders. Captain Sidney Rogerson, of the West Yorkshire Regiment, was serving as a staff officer in the 23rd Brigade, and this eloquent description of the new surroundings comes from his book, *The Last of the Ebb* (London, 1937):

> To the battered, battle-weary troops, whose only knowledge of France was based on their experience of the northern front, the Champagne country in the full glory of spring was a revelation. Gone was the depressing monotony of Flanders, drab and weeping, with its mud and mists, its pollards and its pavé: gone the battle-wrecked landscapes of Picardy and the Somme, with their shattered villages and blasted woods. Here all was peace. The countryside basked contentedly in the blazing sunshine. Trim villages nestled in quiet hollows beside lazy streams, and tired eyes were refreshed by the sight of rolling hills, clad with woods golden with laburnum blossom; by the soft greenery of lush meadowland, shrubby vineyards and fields of growing corn. Right up to within 2 miles of the line civilians were living, going about their husbandry as if ignorant of the close proximity of war.

There was little time to admire the scenery, however, for there was much to be done. The majority of the new drafts were only eighteen years old, and their training in Great Britain had been rudimentary. The NCOs started to lick them into shape, while parties of the more experienced men were sent to training schools for snipers, handling of Lewis guns, hand grenades, signalling, and the other skills which were needed to form an effective front line battalion again.

Alas, the respite was to be short. The Corps commander was informed by General Duchêne that the British divisions should take their place in the front line. There was a storm of protest from all levels, for the whole reason for sending IX Corps to Champagne was that they were no longer battle-ready, and needed time to regroup and retrain. Hamilton Gordon's objections were over-ruled by the French high command, and the 8th Division was ordered to occupy a portion of the front line running along the River Aisne between La Ville aux Bois and Berry-au-Bac. The 50th Division were to their left, and the 21st Division on the right. The 25th Division was kept as Corps reserve. Hamilton Gordon was informed that this was a very quiet sector of the line, there was no possibility of an attack, and his men would be free to carry out their training programmes while holding the line.

On 12 May, the 2nd Royal Berkshires took over a sector from the 4th Battalion of the French 358th Infantry Regiment. It was very quiet, for their predecessors had, by mutual consent, arrived at a 'live and let live' understanding with the enemy, and the peace was only disturbed by desultory rifle shots and an occasional artillery round. Despite the calm, the more experienced officers and other ranks were very uneasy. There had been so little action that the defences had not moved for three years, and the position of every trench and gun pit would have been precisely plotted by the enemy artillery, and, if they chose, could be bombarded with impunity. Another problem was that the River Aisne was some thousand yards behind the front line. Although it had many temporary bridges across it, it would pose a formidable obstacle if a rapid withdrawal became necessary. These concerns were passed up through the levels of command, but once again rejected by the French, who reassured the British that no attack was possible, and told them politely to stop panicking.

Soon, the observers noticed ominous signs of enemy preparation. The frequency of artillery shelling had gradually increased, but instead of barrages, it seemed to consist of single ranging shots, as if newly arrived batteries were checking their calibration. There were sounds of hammering in the enemy lines at night, particularly noticeable in the Berkshires' sector, where no-man's land was at its narrowest. What appeared to be black notice boards had been erected, and it was feared that these were direction signs for tanks.

The three divisional commanders were very concerned about the vulnerability of their men in the event of an attack. The lesson learned from the spring offensives had shown that the front line should just consist of lightly held outposts, and provision made to retreat to a 'battle zone', forcing the enemy to extend their supply and communication lines, and losing their immediate artillery support. The position of the River Aisne, and its associated canal system, limited the battle zone to some 2,000 yards in depth. Major-General Heneker, commanding the 8th Division, protested strongly, and was backed up by General Campbell of the 21st Division and General Jackson of the 50th Division. They proposed a battle zone south of the river, with only lightly held outposts in the front line. The river bridges would be destroyed as soon as the outpost line could withdraw, and then the artillery and machine guns would be used to devastating effect when the enemy attempted to cross the river.

This plan was rejected by the French Army Command. The front line was to be held in strength, and the area north of the river was to be held at all costs. No destruction of the bridges was to take place, unless by the express permission of General Duchêne. The Corps Command were also informed that there were no intelligence reports that the Germans were planning an attack.

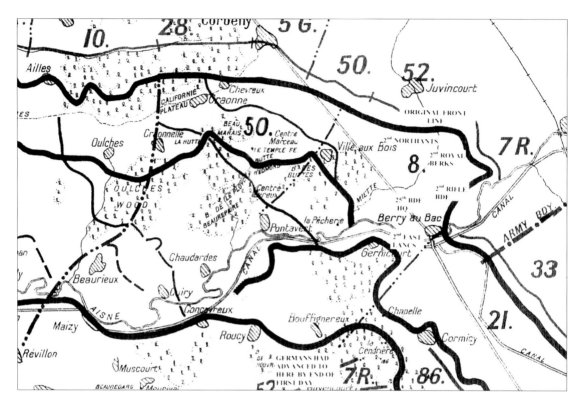

Map of the Aisne Battle.

They would not have been so complacent had they known of the plans of General Ludendorff. The next phase of the operations to end the war in Germany's favour would comprise a massive attack on exactly that sector of the front line which the British were holding. The operation had been in the planning phase for some weeks, and it was an unexpected bonus for the Germans that it was now occupied by divisions which had already been virtually destroyed in the earlier offensives. Seven German divisions who had distinguished themselves in the March offensive had been withdrawn from the line, brought up to strength, and rested. A concentration of artillery had been assembled, allowing eighty guns per kilometre of front, and Colonel Bruchmüller, acknowledged as the Germans' expert in planning artillery attacks, was called in to direct them. In order to avoid alarming the British, the new batteries had been brought in at night, carefully concealed, and only allowed a single calibration shot before the assault.

The 2nd Royal Berkshires were in a dangerous position, right in the nose of a salient, and close to the enemy lines. On their right were the 2nd Rifle Brigade, in an equally exposed position, with their right flank on the north bank of the River Aisne. The Berkshires' left bordered a swampy stream called La Miette, which separated them from the 2nd Northants of 24th Brigade. Lieutenant-Colonel Griffin reported to Brigade HQ how impossible the position was 'should the Germans make an attack, as they had direct observation of our whole line from Hill 108 on our right, and from rising ground on our left between our left and the Miette stream'. Behind the two battalions were two companies of the 2nd East Lancs, in support, together with 25th Brigade Headquarters on the north bank of the river. The other two companies of the East Lancs were positioned on the south side of the Aisne, in reserve.

The German attack commenced punctually at 1 a.m. on 27 May, when 1,000 artillery pieces opened fire in unison. Captain Rogerson, quoted earlier, recalled that 'the night was rent by sheets of flame. The earth shuddered under the avalanche of missiles. Ever above the din screamed the fierce crescendo of approaching shells, ear splitting crashes as they burst, and all the time the dull thud of detonations.'

As well as high explosives, Bruchmüller had specified a large proportion of gas shells: 80 per cent of the long-range bombardment, 70 per cent to the rear of the front line, and 40 per cent of the creeping barrage were to be gas, and soon it started to drift into the dugouts, forcing the men to wear their masks. Additionally, certain batteries had been detailed to take out the Allied guns, precisely located because they had been in the same gun pits for over two years. It was not long before all the guns north of the river had been destroyed, and their crews had become casualties.

The barrage lasted three hours before the German infantry, supported by captured British tanks, attacked the British positions in force. As on 21 March attack and at Villers-Bretonneux on 24 April, there was a thick early morning mist to aid them: many British officers were convinced that the enemy had a secret method of producing mist to order.

Captain Rogerson reported scenes of men stumbling out of their dugouts, shaking from the bombardment, unable to see properly because of the fog and the need to wear their gas masks, only to find themselves surrounded by the enemy. The 2nd Royal Berkshires were completely overwhelmed; the only clue to their fate was a pigeon message which arrived at Divisional Headquarters at 6.05 a.m.:

*Message timed 5.15 am. HQ 2nd R Berks. Regt. Consisting of Lieutenant-Colonel Griffin, Captain Clare, RSM Vokins, Sergt Trinder, Corpl Dobson, Ptes Stone, Gregory, Slee and Quartermaster, surrounded. Germans threw bombs down dugouts and passed on. Appeared to approach from right rear in considerable strength. No idea what has happened elsewhere. Holding out in hopes of relief.*

There was no chance of relief. The two divisions north of the river, 50th and 8th, were fighting desperately for survival, with the majority of their infantry battalions in the same predicament as the Berkshires. Bewildered survivors who had managed to avoid

Captured British positions on the Aisne canal, seen from Hill 180. The village of Berry-au-Bac is in the background.

being captured made their way back to the Aisne, and scrambled across the bridges only yards ahead of the victorious Germans. It can have been of little consolation to Generals Heneker and Jackson that the situation they had predicted had come to pass.

The Royal Engineer Field Squadrons who had survived the gas attacks were unable to contact Duchêne's headquarters for permission to destroy the bridges but, on their own initiative, managed to blow up or burn all twenty-two in the 8th Division's sector, and fifteen out of nineteen in the 50th's sector, despite suffering heavy casualties. The enemy were still able to cross the river virtually unopposed, for the infantry battalions and artillery batteries who might have stopped them if they had been positioned on the south bank had been lost with nothing gained.

General von Unruh was chief of staff in the attacking German Corps, and contributed a chapter to Rogerson's book describing the battle from the other side. He was sympathetic to the British in his narrative:

> The English, who could usually be relied upon to hold out in shell-holes, firing to their last cartridge, were given no opportunity by the violence and activity of our combined artillery and trench-mortar fire to display their customary coolness. They were up against 'force majeure', and, first blown out of their trenches and then surrounded, sentry posts, Lewis gun teams, and whole platoons saw that resistance was hopeless and were reluctantly obliged to surrender. Everywhere one could see groups stumbling down from the high grounds to be taken prisoner by our waiting troops.

The officers and men named in the pigeon message were all captured. After the war, repatriated officers were required to appear before a Board of Inquiry to explain the circumstances of their capture. Captain Clare's evidence, preserved in the National Archives, confirms General von Unruh's statement:

A German trench mortar team passing the old 8th Division front line near Berry-au-Bac. The 2nd Battalion were at this location.

The bridge at Pontavert, with German Infantry being ferried across the Aisne. The vital crossings were seized within three hours of the opening assault.

The Germans launched their attack at 1 am on 27/5/18 by dropping a tremendous barrage, covering the ground from Btn HQ and including our two rear companies; (one in close support and one in reserve) and then back to and including the Divisional Artillery and the Aisne bridges. Our two forward Companies were almost untouched. We were defending in depth as well as breadth. About 3.30 am reports came from our rear Companies that Germans were all round them in very large numbers, and had attacked from Hill 108 and from our left. This we soon confirmed as Germans were visible from Btn Observation Post everywhere in large numbers, and had overcome our forward Companies by excess of trench mortars and machine guns. Under such circumstances with no artillery support, chances of a scrap were absolutely useless. Orders were given by our CO for 'every man for himself' and he, I and others of Btn HQ waited at Btn HQ on the chance of a counter-attack by the Btn in support at Guyencourt. A pigeon message was sent to Division about 4 am stating the position. This message appeared in the Times account of the 8th Division about 28/9/18. I was captured with Colonel Griffin at 7 am 27/5/18.

Lieutenant MacDonnell's statement is also held in the National Archives. He was commanding C Company, who were in the front line. 'On 27 May I held up the enemy during his attack until, having lost three officers and more than half of the other ranks, all communication with flanks and rear being cut off, I managed to fight my way back with the remainder of my company to the Miette River, where I was captured in an attempt to cross the said river.'

The German regiment which had attacked in the Berkshires' sector was the 72nd Reserve Regiment. Their version of the action, from the Reichsarchiv Band 32, corroborates the two officers' statements.

The 1st Battalion [a German regiment contained three battalions, and was roughly equivalent to a British brigade] with aircraft cover, mortars and mostly captured tanks were sent to clean up the area between the Miette and the site of Ferme de Mauchamps. There was a lot of hand to hand fighting and use of grenades but by 0515 they had finished, they then went into reserve. By 0700 the 2nd Battalion had taken 600 prisoners and 4 artillery pieces. The 2nd

Two 2nd Battalion prisoners of war, believed to have been taken in 1918. Both are still wearing their 'China Dragon' cap badges to maintain regimental identity.

and 3rd Battalions then tried to cross the Aisne. Two footbridges were blown up in front of them but one bridge remained intact though under heavy machine gun fire. At 0940 storm troops from the 2nd Battalion took the bridge. By 1000 all of the battalion were across.

For all practical purposes, the 8th and 50th Divisions had ceased to exist. The 21st Division, being south of the Aisne, had fared better, for they had not faced the main thrust of the enemy attack, and their lines of withdrawal had been easier. The 25th Division, having been in corps reserve, was still intact, but could do little to withstand the assault of seven German divisions. The roads were choked with fleeing French refugees, interspersed with groups of stragglers from the 8th and 50th Divisions who had made their escape across the river, and latched themselves on to any officer or NCO they could find, in the forlorn hope that they knew what was happening.

The German assault had not only fallen on the British. The French XI Corps, defending the ridge of the Chemin des Dames between Vauxaillon and Ailles, had also been overwhelmed, and were retreating southward towards Fismes. By nightfall on 27 May, the enemy were occupying a salient thrust deep into the Allied lines, some 10 to 12 miles in places, and threatening the town of Soissons. In the British sector, the 21st Division, backed up by the 25th Division, was still holding out at Guyencourt, but was outflanked on its left.

Not all of the battalion, however, had been in the line. Lieutenant Rooke collected about sixty-five Berkshires who had been attending the Corps' Lewis gun training school, and attached himself to the 23rd Brigade, as he could find no-one from 25th Brigade to report to. It was later established that both Brigadier Husey and his Brigade Major, Captain Pascoe, had been killed, and the brigade headquarters overrun by the enemy. Husey had only recently taken over from Brigadier Coffin, VC, who had been promoted to command a division. The Berkshires' assistant adjutant, Lieutenant Barrett, gathered another sixty men from the transport lines and helped to establish a defence line near Ventelay, protecting the 21st Division's left flank. No details of what they achieved have been recorded, but Lieutenant Rooke is listed as being wounded on 27 May.

General Ludendorff had planned this operation to advance only as far as Fismes. It had been intended as a feint, to convince the French that Paris was threatened, so that all available reserves would be withdrawn from Flanders to defend the capital. Then, Prince Rupprecht's army group would launch an attack on Flanders. However, the Aisne attack was proving so successful that on 28 May Ludendorff issued orders to continue the advance as far as the River Marne at Château-Thierry. Progress was swift, and by 1 June the enemy were occupying about 10 miles of the north bank of the Marne from Château-Thierry to Dormans, and then a line running north-east to the city of Reims. During this time, the remnants of the 8th Division, under the leadership of Brigadier Grogan, had established a number of strongpoints which were, in their turn, overrun. Undoubtedly some of these were manned by stragglers from 2nd Royal Berkshires, but no individual stories have survived the fog of war.

The British despatched 19th Infantry Division to join IX Corps, and there were enough survivors from the 8th Division to form a composite battalion, which was given the title '1/8th Composite Battalion', and attached to the 19th Division. The 2nd Royal Berkshires' war diary states that three officers and 120 other ranks from the Berkshires went to make up this battalion. Two days later, a second composite battalion, the '2/8th', was formed from 'drummers, cooks, drivers and reinforcements'. Both battalions remained with the 19th Division until 12 June, when they rejoined the other remnants of the 8th Division and moved north to Mérélessart, near Abbeville.

The battalion digest of service gives the following casualty statistics:

|  | Officers | Other Ranks | Total |
| --- | --- | --- | --- |
| Killed | 2 | 1 | 3 |
| Died of wounds | 0 | 1 | 1 |
| Wounded | 3 | 51 | 54 |
| Missing | 19 | 655 | 674 |
| Total | 24 | 708 | 732 |

The total fatalities confirmed at the end of the war shows ninety-one killed or died of wounds in the period 27 May to 12 June, so some 580 officers and men must have been taken prisoner. Thirty-nine of the fatal casualties occurred on 27 May, and another forty on 11 June, when both the composite battalions were in action. Very few of the casualties were identifiable after the war, and the majority are commemorated on the Soissons Memorial to the Missing, having no known grave. The 8th Division had lost 366 officers and 7,496 other ranks killed, wounded or taken prisoner. The 'rest and recuperation' holiday was over.

In all, the BEF had suffered 29,000 casualties, and the French army 98,000. The Germans had advanced far further than they had planned, and caused a degree of panic in the French Chamber of Deputies, who feared that Paris was about to fall. The attack did not, however, achieve its aim, for very few reserves were moved south from the Flanders area, and the Rupprecht offensive was called off.

There was some compensation for the British when General Duchêne, who had rejected their advice and warnings, was removed from the command of the Sixth Army by Marshal Foch.

# XX

# REBUILDING AGAIN

On 14 June, the remnants of the 8th Division, less the two composite battalions, who were still attached to the 19th Division, boarded trains for a 200-mile journey via Paris to Abbeville, where Divisional Headquarters were established at nearby Huppy. The composite battalions followed a few days later, and on 19 June the 2/8th Battalion arrived at the divisional area.

'For the third time in little more than two months, the division had suffered terrible casualties,' the Divisional History commented. 'During this period there was kept at British GHQ a daily return showing for each division of the British Army the number of its losses since 21 March. On this list the 8th Division now held the proud yet unenviable position of 2nd place, with the 50th Division less than 300 in front, and the next division more than 1,000 behind.' All nine of the division's battalion commanders had become casualties.

One of the fatalities of the Marne débâcle was Major Harold Forster, who had been commanding the 2nd Northamptonshire Regiment. He had come up through the ranks in the Royal Berkshire Regiment, and was commissioned into the 2nd Royal Berkshires as a Second Lieutenant in September 1915. He had held various positions – sniping officer, company commander and adjutant – and had won the DSO, Military Cross and bar. It was he who warned Hanbury-Sparrow of the fatal flaw in General Gough's strategy at Third Ypres. The 2nd Northamptons had been on the Berkshires' left flank, beyond the Mette stream, and Forster was one of their many casualties. He is buried in Terlincthun British Cemetery at Wimille.

The manpower situation, exacerbated by the losses from the German offensives, was even more serious. In June, seven divisions were shown as 'reduced to cadre', meaning that they existed as an administrative unit only, with no fighting units. Their men were drafted to other divisions to bring them up to strength. The 8th Division, being a regular army unit, was to be built up, absorbing the displaced men.

On 18 June, twelve second lieutenants joined the Berkshires, and on 21 June Major Auberon Isaac MC joined and took command of the battalion. Isaac had served with the 2nd Battalion in India, returning home in 1912 to join the 3rd Royal Berkshires, the training unit at Portsmouth. Soon after the outbreak of war, he joined the 1st Battalion in France, travelling out with a party of ninety-four reinforcements. He was rapidly promoted to captain and company commander, winning a Military Cross. He joined the staff in the middle of 1915, becoming staff captain in the 6th Infantry Brigade, and later brigade major in the 2nd Brigade. He was thirty-one years old, and assumed the rank of lieutenant-colonel with his new position.

The three infantry brigades were sent to training areas near the coast at Le Tréport. Brigadier-General Pollock McCall set up his 25th Infantry Brigade Headquarters at Hautebut, and intensive training commenced. McCall had been appointed to the

Captain Isaac seen here on horseback whilst 'riding to hounds' prior to the war.

command of the 25th Brigade following the death of Brigadier Husey on 27 May. The weather was glorious, and the men's training was punctuated by swimming in the sea whenever possible, together with inter-battalion football matches, boxing tournaments, and a divisional horse show.

Fortunately, the British sector of the Western Front remained fairly quiet. Prince Rupprecht's army group was still poised opposite the Ypres sector, but the enemy's attention was focused on the unexpected success of the Marne assault. This, it will be recalled, had only been planned as a feint to draw the Allied reserves south to protect Paris, and enable Rupprecht's force to break through in Flanders. In terms of ground gained, the German offensives had achieved spectacular results, but they had not achieved a breakthrough. Both the British and French armies had retreated, but the defence lines had never disintegrated, and all the enemy had achieved was to lengthen his supply lines at the cost of heavy casualties and expenditure of material. When German soldiers had captured British supply stores on the Somme, they were demoralised to discover the abundance of food rations. They had been receiving letters from their families at home telling them of desperate shortages, and that their loved ones were existing on a diet of turnips, but the German propaganda machine had been informing them that the British supply situation was just as perilous as their own. The contrary evidence before their eyes told a different story.

To add to the enemy's problems, the strength of the American Expeditionary Force was now building up. Their first few divisions were completing their familiarisation and training with British and French units, so the manpower advantage that the Germans had achieved by the Russian capitulation, which enabled them to transfer divisions from the Eastern Front, was being eroded. On 18 July, four American divisions launched an attack from Villers-Cotterêts and started to drive the enemy eastwards from the Soissons– Château-Thierry line. At the same time, the French Army struck northwards across the Marne. The turning point of the 1918 campaigns had arrived.

The next day, 19 July, the 8th Division received orders to join VIII Corps in General Horne's First Army. They had actually been placed on 24 hours' notice to move as early as 9 July, but in fact were left in peace to continue training for a further ten days.

The 2nd Royal Berkshires boarded trains at Feuquières during the evening of 19 July, and arrived at Pernes at midnight before marching to a camp in Bois d'Ohlain, where they spent two days before relieving units of 52nd Division in Corps Reserve at Mont-St-Eloi. The 8th Division was housed in Durham and Lancaster camps, and the intense training continued.

The Berkshires' training was interrupted on 27 July, when the battalion was granted a holiday to commemorate the anniversary of the battle of Maiwand, in 1879, when men of the 66th Regiment had fought a desperate last stand in the Second Afghan War. A battalion sports day was held, enlivened by the attendance of the 8th Divisional band. Similar celebrations for Tofrek Day on 22 March had been cut short by the order to proceed at once to the Somme to counter the German spring offensive, but no crisis occurred to disturb Maiwand day, which made a welcome break from routine for all ranks.

On 5 August, it was back to the war, and the 25th Infantry Brigade took over a sector at Acheville. The 2nd Royal Berkshires were moved by truck from the camp at Mont-St-Eloi to Neuville-Saint-Vaast, which was in ruins. From there, they had to cross Vimy Ridge on foot. Although the ridge had been in Allied hands for a year, it was still hazardous, and the men went across in pairs spaced 35 yards apart, for groups would be spotted and shelled. On reaching the trenches, they relieved the 2nd West Yorks, who were feeling very pleased with themselves. When they had been disembarking from their trains at Pernes on 19 July, they had been strafed by a low-flying enemy fighter plane, and officers and men had been forced to execute a most undignified dive for cover. Fortunately, there had been no casualties. However, during their spell in the trenches, they had managed to bring down an enemy aircraft with rifle and Lewis gun fire. It was most unlikely to have been the same one, but revenge was sweet! The Berkshires took the sector over, and settled down for a quiet week, with very little enemy activity to report.

It was a different story further south. Whilst the Berkshires were manning the trenches, the British, French and American armies had launched the first of what was to become a series of rolling attacks on the enemy. It was becoming increasingly apparent to the German High Command that they were going to lose the war on the Western Front, and General Ludendorff described the Amiens assault on 8 August as 'a black day for the German Army'. Haig and his army commanders planned a series of attacks with limited objectives, called 'bite and hold'. A corps or division would make an advance, and then consolidate their gains, regroup and rest while a neighbouring unit did the same. In this way, the enemy was kept on the defensive, and not given time to recover. Haig was optimistic that he could finish the war during 1918.

# XXI

# THE OPPY SECTOR

The Berkshires came out of the trenches on 12 August, and on the following day orders arrived from Corps that the Division was to increase the size of its sector by relieving 52nd Division on the right. This brought the frontage up to 9,000 yards, so it was necessary to keep all three brigades in the line instead of having one in reserve. The 25th Brigade were responsible for the Méricourt sector in the north, the 23rd Brigade in the centre, and the 24th were holding the Oppy sector in the south, which had been in 52nd Division's area. However, things were so quiet that Major-General Heneker allowed the brigades to keep one battalion at a time out of the line for training and rest.

The 2nd Royal Berkshires were the first battalion in the 25th Brigade to be out of the line, but it was hardly a rest. D Company were loaned to the 185th Tunnelling Company, Royal Engineers, for a week of labouring, and the rest of the battalion prepared new dugouts to be the headquarters of the brigade and battalion staff and signal detachments. This came to an end on 21 August, when they went back into the line, exchanging with the 2nd Rifle Brigade.

The 21 August was a significant day down on the Somme front, as the Third Army had launched a successful attack north of the River Ancre. In fact, it was proceeding so satisfactorily that the left flank was extended northwards, and on 26 August the Canadian Corps attacked in the River Scarpe sector, rapidly regaining the high point of Monchy-le-Preux. The 51st Division also attacked to the north of the Scarpe, reaching the village of Roeux, which had resisted so many gallant attacks in the 1917 Arras battle.

This was bringing the reopened battle to the edge of the 8th Division's sector, and the German troops ranged against them must have been feeling very uneasy, for their left flank was giving way. On 29 August, the division was ordered to send fighting patrols forward to engage the enemy and test their resistance. The 2nd Royal Berkshires sent forward B Company to advance along a communication trench known as Belvoir Alley, while at the same time D Company probed Brough Alley, which ran about 300 yards to the north of Belvoir Alley. Each company was reinforced by a team from the brigade's trench mortar company.

The two groups cautiously advanced eastwards, encountering some resistance, which was overcome. After about 1,000 yards, they established a new line of defence based on Cup and Chop trenches, where they remained until 31 August. The action had cost the lives of Lieutenant Carlisle, attached from the Royal Army Service Corps, and seven men, together with two officers and twenty-six men wounded.

There was a respite on 1 September, when the battalion was relieved by 2nd Rifle Brigade, and travelled back to Ecurie Camp by truck for a week out of the line. On 4 September, a parade was held, the battalion was inspected by the corps commander, Lieutenant-General Sir Aylmer Hunter-Weston. The general presented two NCOs, Sergeant Albury and Sergeant-Major Turvey, with the DCM for gallantry and devotion to duty. Four days later, on 8 September, the brigade commander presented medals to Number 8 Platoon, B Company, who had won the rifle competition.

The battalion went back into the line on 9 September, relieving 2nd East Lancashires in the right brigade sector. It was quiet until 15 September, but on that night, after a heavy bombardment, the enemy raided a post on the right of the Berkshires' line, which cost one man killed and five missing. As the post-war records show two men killed on that day, Privates Cook and Bye, one can speculate that the remaining four became prisoners of war.

On 19 September, Lieutenant-Colonel Isaac was called to a meeting of battalion commanders at Brigade Headquarters, and learned that orders had been received to advance the line a distance of 600 yards, which meant capturing and occupying the trenches known as Whine, Gavrelle Support, Cheapside, Chutney, Curry, Chestnut and Cheddar. The 2nd Royal Berkshires would attack on the right, the 2nd East Lancs on the left, and the 2nd Rifle Brigade would hold the current line and act as reserve. The attack would be made under a barrage, and the division on the Berkshires' right would also take part, advancing in parallel, and a joint post would be established on the east of Whine Trench.

A and C Companies were to lead the attack, with C targeting Whine Trench on the right. They were to occupy the trench, and establish contact with the left hand unit of 49th Division at the junction of Whack Trench. A Company's objective was Cheapside Trench and part of Gavrelle Support, and the junction of the two companies would be the intersection of Whine and Cheapside Trenches.

2nd East Lancs would be attacking on the north side of the Gavrelle to Fresnes road, and one of A Company's platoons was detailed to join up with them. B Company was to provide support, occupying South Gavrelle Trench, while two platoons of D Company would hold the existing battalion line in Crab, Cod and Crawl Trenches. The other two platoons would act as ammunition carriers. Battalion headquarters moved up, and was re-established among the ruins of Gavrelle village.

The creeping barrage started on time at 11 p.m., and the two assault companies moved forward. The enemy sent up SOS flares, and about four minutes later their barrage came down. It turned out to be not so heavy as expected, and there was very little opposition, but a heavy barrage fell on South Gavrelle trench as soon as B Company entered it. The barrage also caused communication problems, for the telephone wires to the forward companies were cut several times.

The first reports to Lieutenant-Colonel Isaac indicated that all was going well, except that opposition was being met at the junction of Cheapside and Whine, but it was hoped that it would soon be cleared. However, at 5 a.m., the situation became more critical. C Company reported that 49th Division on their right had been driven back behind Square Wood, and 15 minutes later a second message warned that the enemy was getting around the Berkshires' right flank and had also launched a counter-attack on the junction of Whine and Cheapside. C Company then withdrew to Gavrelle Support, and A Company was driven back down Cheapside, where they established a bombing block. By daybreak, the two companies had established themselves in Gavrelle Support trench, and across to Chutney Trench, with an outpost about 50 yards down Cheapside.

Although the failure of the attack had been due to 49th Division allowing the enemy an opportunity to outflank C Company, the battalion was ordered to make a second attack the next evening.

The orders for the next attack were similar to the night before, except that D Company would attack on the right, with the same objective – Whine Trench – that C Company had had. A Company would push up Cheapside, and make good their original objective. B Company, which had suffered a lot of casualties from the bombardment on South Gavrelle Trench, was to loan a platoon to support the left of D Company, while the remainder of the company would join C Company in holding the old line. The only significant change of tactics was that one platoon of C Company would act as escort to

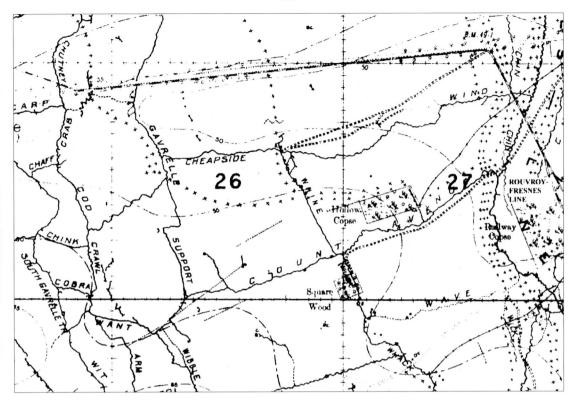

Map of Hollow Copse area.

a detachment from the 25th Machine Gun Company, who were to establish a post about 500 yards short of Whine Trench.

The second attempt was far more successful. The barrage was timed for midnight, and fell on Whine Trench. D Company crept forward, and, when the barrage ceased after 15 minutes, were in position to jump into the trench. The Germans were still down in their dugouts, showed no inclination to fight, and were marched back to Battalion Headquarters. By 2 a.m., the company commanders reported all objectives had been achieved, and they were consolidating. Patrols were sent out, and one, under the command of Sergeant Mead, encountered a group of about twelve enemy troops. Mead ordered his men to open fire, killing three, and capturing three. The others bolted into the night.

Two German officers and forty-seven other ranks had been taken prisoner, and five machine guns had been captured. However, the two actions had cost the lives of Second Lieutenant Frank Finch, and eight other ranks. Finch was the son of the late Lieutenant-Colonel Finch, who had been killed in 1915 whilst commanding the battalion during the attack on Fromelles.

On the night of 24 September, the 2nd Rifle Brigade took over the captured trenches, and the Berkshires returned to Ecurie Camp for rest and training. There was a parade and inspection by Major-General Heneker on 30 September, and he presented medals and parchment certificates to men who had been decorated for the recent actions.

After the rest period, the Berkshires went back into the line, relieving the 2nd East Lancs in the left-hand brigade sector, north of the remains of the Gavrelle to Fismes road. Intelligence reports indicated that the enemy was evacuating the trenches opposite the divisional front, so a reconnaissance patrol was sent out on the night of 3 October, which found that the German positions were still held.

Lieutenant Frank Marshall Finch, the
son of Lieutenant-Colonel Finch. Both
were killed in action while serving with
the 2nd Battalion.

Hollow Copse, some 300 yards in front of Whine Trench, sat between the British lines
and the strong enemy position called the Rouvroy–Fresnes Line. The copse was a maze of
old German dugouts and strong-points, but the division was uncertain as to how strongly
it was held, or indeed if it was occupied at all. C Company was given the objective of
clearing the copse and establishing a new line on the eastern edge. They moved forward
on the night of 5 October.

Three platoons of C Company left their positions in Whine Trench at 9.30 p.m.
Captain Barrett, the adjutant, went forward and took up a position at the junction of
Whine Trench and Count Avenue to relay progress reports back to Lieutenant-Colonel
Isaac. As the men left the trenches, the British artillery barrage opened up, but was
reported to be 'rather weak'.

At 9.40 p.m., Barrett reported that three hostile machine guns had opened up in the
copse, and were firing at the attackers. This was followed 10 minutes later by a report that
the machine guns' fire had ceased. Battalion Headquarters then sent a message forward
via the adjutant to the effect that if little opposition was being met, the company should
push forward to the Rouvroy–Fresnes line, and if it was found to be unoccupied to take
possession of it.

The next message from C Company was a request for more bombs and rifle grenades,
and reported that they were still west of the copse. An hour later, at 11 p.m., the company
commander reported that the copse was strongly held by machine guns, and two platoons
were busy digging in about 80 yards to the west of the copse, but the third platoon,
commanded by Second Lieutenant Gosling, was working its way along the south side of
the copse, but nothing had been heard from them for an hour.

At midnight, the fourth platoon of C Company, who had not been engaged so far,
moved up to the junction of Count Avenue and Whack Trench with fresh supplies of
grenades. They were ordered to move along Count Avenue and try to establish what had
happened to Gosling's platoon. They reached Gosling's men, who had worked their way up
to the south-east corner of the copse, but were being held down by machine gun fire from
inside the copse, and from a short length of trench which ran from Count Avenue into the
eastern edge of the copse. At this point, the company commander decided there was little
chance of gaining the objective, and ordered Gosling to withdraw, which he did.

Two nights later, on 7 October, it was D Company's turn at the copse. The attack was made in the early morning, and Captain Richardson, the company commander, reported that his men had left Whine Trench at 5 a.m. No.16 Platoon moved quickly along the northern edge of the copse, and established themselves on the eastern edge by 5.15 a.m. Richardson reported that the objective was secured at 5.25 a.m., and that four prisoners from the German 83rd Regiment had been captured. The dugouts were searched, and a further prisoner was taken, together with a machine gun. Shortly afterwards, a group of about forty men ran from the north-east corner of the copse back towards the German lines, but they were engaged by Lewis gun fire. The copse had been taken in less than an hour, with one man killed and three wounded.

Lieutenant-Colonel Isaac was keen to exploit the success, and ordered C and D Companies to continue down Count Avenue and Wind Trenches. C Company reported a group of enemy working towards them down Wind Trench, and a quick artillery barrage was ordered to cut them off, which it did. Orders then arrived from the 25th Brigade to attempt to occupy the Rouvroy–Fresnes line.

D Company chased the enemy along Count Avenue, but not without loss, for Sergeant Bradford was killed, but at 8.40 a.m. Captain Richardson reported that he had reached the junction of Count Avenue and the Rouvroy–Fresnes line, and a patrol was working their way northwards along it. The patrol made contact with a party from the 2nd Rifle Brigade, who had been working their way southwards, but a German bombing party then made a counter-attack which pushed the Berkshire patrol back to the junction with Count Avenue, where Second Lieutenant John Maurice was killed by a sniper.

While this was happening, C Company were engaged with a German strong point in Wind Trench, but at 9.40 a.m. they reported that they had destroyed it and were moving up the trench. An hour later they entered the Rouvroy–Fresnes line and started bombing their way southward towards D Company's position. At this stage large numbers of enemy troops were seen running away eastwards towards Fresnes, and Lieutenant-Colonel Isaac ordered his reserve B Company to send two platoons up Wind Trench, and another up Count Avenue to reinforce the two forward companies. The fourth platoon was to remain in reserve in Crab Trench.

The Berkshires' D Company continued to occupy the newly captured section of the Rouvroy–Fresnes line between Wind Trench and Count Avenue until the late afternoon, when they were relieved by 2nd Rifle Brigade, who also took over the positions in Hollow Copse. D Company retired to the ruins of Gavrelle to rest.

Meanwhile, C Company were frustrated in their efforts to move north along the Rouvroy–Fresnes line by an enemy strongpoint at the junction with Chalk Trench. It was getting dark, and the men were attacking uphill. Finally, a determined effort was made by a bombing party, who rushed the position, with Lewis gun teams supporting them on either flank. The enemy fled, but many were cut down as they ran. One wounded man was taken prisoner.

So ended the 2nd Royal Berkshires most successful day of the war. Hollow Copse had been captured, together with over 3,500 yards of enemy trench. Two German officers and forty-four other ranks had been captured, with many more killed. The Berkshires' losses amounted to one officer killed (Second Lieutenant Maurice) and three other ranks killed, with fourteen wounded.

Other units in the 8th Division had also done well, and the Rouvroy–Fresnes Line had been secured all along the division's front. General Horne, the First Army commander, sent a message to the corps commander:

Please tell Major General Heneker and the 8th Division that the way in which the successful operations of yesterday were conducted reflects great credit on all ranks. Since the 8th Division has occupied its present extended front I have been much impressed by the fine offensive spirit displayed.

# XXII

# IN HOT PURSUIT

The next obstacle for the 8th Division lay about 3,000 yards ahead: the Quéant–Drocourt line. The Divisional History described it as a formidable system – 'an elaborate arrangement of trenches well protected by several thick rows of barbed wire' – but the German Army was disintegrating, and it was imperative to keep the pressure up. After a brief overnight rest from their exertions in gaining their section of the Rouvroy–Fresnes line, the Berkshires moved forward.

Fighting patrols went out from A and C Companies, and by 7 a.m. on 10 October a scouting patrol under Second Lieutenant Strange was reported to have reached a position about 500 yards short of the first big barbed wire entanglement. Lieutenant-Colonel Isaac ordered A Company to move forward from the Rouvroy–Fresnes line, and to form the battalion's advance guard. The remaining companies then moved up, with D taking over the positions vacated by A.

By 9 a.m., A Company had established two platoons on the rise overlooking the ruined village of Izel, and the scouts had moved forward to the edge of the barbed wire on the western edge of the village. During the day the rest of A Company moved forward, and by 4 p.m. all four platoons plus Company Headquarters were dug in overlooking the obstacle. Two Lewis gun teams had moved forward to join the scouts, and had been positioned close to a gap in the wire which had been left for a lane running south-west from the village to run through the entanglement. Vigorous patrolling took place during the night, and six enemy machine guns were located and captured.

Major-General Heneker was short of artillery. He had been obliged to lend one of his artillery brigades to an adjoining division, and the rest of his guns were having difficulty moving across flooded ground in the valley of the River Scarpe. Accordingly, he decided to support a two-battalion attack by the 2nd Devonshires and 2nd Middlesex to the north of Vitry-en-Artois. If a breakthough could be achieved there, he was hopeful of rolling up the enemy line and enabling the rest of his division to take the remainder of the sector.

The attack went in at 5 a.m. on 11 October, and was entirely successful. Enemy prisoners revealed that they were in the process of abandoning the Quéant–Drocourt line, and had planned to just leave isolated machine gun crews behind as a rearguard. The attack had caught them unawares, and they were now retiring in disorder. Major-General Heneker ordered his artillery to shift their barrage northwards along the enemy line, and by 7.20 a.m., the first platoon of the Berkshires' A Company had made their way unopposed through the wire, occupying the empty German trenches.

By midday, the rest of the battalion had joined them, including Lieutenant-Colonel Isaac's headquarters. After a short rest, C Company formed up in fours and marched north eastwards, following the enemy along the road to Esquerchin. By mid-afternoon they had reached the village of Cuincy, and by that evening all four companies and battalion headquarters had established themselves in ruined houses and German huts. To the south east, the city of Douai was in flames, and massive explosions could be heard.

Everywhere bore evidence of a hasty retreat by the enemy, with meals left uneaten in the billets, and personal possessions lying about. The Germans had time, however, to lay countless booby traps, typically an innocuous plank of wood left on a road surface would have a wire connected to a nearby mine, so the advancing men had to proceed very warily. The Divisional History notes that the 185th Tunnelling Company, Royal Engineers, whose normal employment had been curtailed by the welcome change to open warfare, made safe 1,395 mines and booby traps in the 8th Division's sector. Apart from the booby traps, however, the battalion history records that the main roads were generally in good condition, and, although bridges had been blown, the work had been inefficient and they were generally passable. Bridges on side roads had been left intact.

The 2nd Royal Berkshires spent two days in Cuincy, protecting the 25th Brigade's front, while the 8th Division consolidated and brought supplies forward for the next advance. There was intermittent shelling from the enemy artillery, but this, it was noted, came mostly from long-range guns, indicating that the Germans' field artillery had retreated out of range. A battery of 18-pounders came forward to support the Berkshires, together with the 2nd East Lancs. Patrols were sent out during the night of 13 October, but four men from C Company, under 2nd Lieutenant Eastman, went too far, were surrounded by the enemy and were captured.

The following day, the Berkshires pushed forward to the canal which bisected Douai, and established outposts on the west bank, before being relieved by the 2nd Rifle Brigade and moving back to brigade reserve. Meanwhile, the 2nd Middlesex Regiment advanced through the city centre. The 8th Divisional History records what they found:

> The place was empty, except for a deserter from the German rear guard. All the civilians had been evacuated. Every building concealed a scene of utter and wanton destruction. Everything of value had been removed and such things as had been left – furniture, crockery, pictures and the like – had been smashed to atoms. The inside of the beautiful organ in the cathedral had been torn out and its reeds lay scattered in a heap on the floor.

The 2nd Middlesex raised their flag next to the French tricolour over the town hall, and four years of enemy occupation came to an end.

Although nobody knew at the time, the war for the 2nd Royal Berkshires had ended. As brigade reserve they took the rear position as the 2nd Rifle Brigade and 2nd East Lancs moved forward to Roost-Warendin on 18 October, and then Marchiennes the next day, where they exchanged with the East Lancs to become brigade support. The corps commander then granted 8th Division a well-earned rest, while the Canadian Corps tackled nearby Valenciennes. The Berkshires moved forward to Tilloy, some five miles from the Belgian border, on 21 October, and went into billets in the village until 3 November.

The twelve days were spent resting, training and regrouping, but, to thank the villagers for their hospitality, the battalion arranged a fête and sports day on 3 November. The list of events included 100m races for boys and girls, skipping races, blindfold races, an egg and spoon race, and a horse and driver race for teams of one boy and one girl. The programme concluded with a threadneedle race for soldiers and village girls over eighteen, which must have been fun!

Afterwards, the Mayor, Monsieur Berteaux, gave a speech of thanks which was translated and recorded in the battalion Digest of Service:

> To the Colonel and Officers of the 2nd Royal Berkshire Regiment.
> Gentlemen,

Before terminating the Fête which you have been good enough to organise today for the children of Tilloy, I beg your leave to address them a few words.

My dear little Children,

You are French, and without quite realising why, you are already proud to bear this glorious name. You used to enjoy yourself with the natural carelessness of your age, when a Vampire formed the hateful project in order to tear away from you the name of French. Envious of your wealth, which was the fruits of your fathers' labour, he conceived the design to make Germans of you and his dispositions were all ready to attain his criminal purpose in a very short time.

He trampled over Belgium, crushing the innocent persons and children like you, and putting everywhere terror into the hearts of the population. Most of the grown-ups that are here can remember the day of 24th August 1914, when the whole population fled before the Barbarians. After that day we became their slaves. But a powerful friend looked after us, and would not allow the realisation of such a crime. He came, and notwithstanding fear of danger, devoted himself wholly, and shouted in the face of the Pirate 'Stop there – you will go no further.' He joined his efforts with those of your fathers and brothers, and we were saved.

This powerful friend you see now amongst you. Not being satisfied to have saved you, he wishes, on the other hand, to make you forget the miserable life which the wicked Germans made you endure, and to give you proof of his good heart and generosity, he is offering you this fete, thus giving you another page of his whole friendship.

My dear little Children, you will remember religiously his passage in Tilloy, and you will join your wishes to those I express myself that any further troubles should be spared to him, that he might triumph over all the obstacles, and that he should be victorious in the cause of humanity against the Barbarians in order to enable us to resume our friendly connections such as have been established by the Cordial Entente.

Now, my dear Children, shout with me as loud as you can, and with all your heart: Vive l'Angleterre; Vive the 2nd Royal Berkshire Regiment.

Tilloy, 3rd November 1918

J. Berteaux, le Maire

The mayor's sentiments would hardly earn him any plaudits in today's European Union, but it must have been an emotional moment for the battalion to receive such heartfelt thanks for all the pain and sacrifice of the past four years, for the next day would be the fourth anniversary of the 8th Division's march to Southampton and embarkation for France.

After leaving Tilloy, the Berkshires marched north-eastwards towards Mons. Just to the south, the Canadian Corps had successfully attacked the city of Valenciennes, and the enemy was in full-scale retreat. Mutiny had broken out in the German Navy, and the German High Command was urging the Kaiser to go into exile. Diplomatic efforts to achieve an armistice were taking place, and, on 11 November, when the battalion had reached Pommeroeul, news arrived that the war was over. The Berkshires were on the left flank of the 8th Division, but the 2nd Middlesex found themselves in Mons, where, for the British Expeditionary Force, the war had started. Some of the men in the 2nd Middlesex had been serving with their 4th Battalion in Mons on that same day. They had come full circle.

# XXIII

# THE FINAL MONTHS

Rumours were circulating that the battalion would take part in the occupation of the Rhineland, under the terms of the armistice, but they came to nothing. Instead, the 8th Division was to be stationed at Tournai, and the 2nd Royal Berkshires found themselves billeted at Esplechin, a town on the Belgian border between Lille and Tournai.

There was little to do, except for parades and sport, which must have seemed rather an anti-climax after the momentous events of 1918, with a near defeat in March turned into a decisive victory by the end of October.

On 20 November, a letter arrived from the Mayor of Reading addressed to Lieutenant-Colonel Isaac:

Town Hall, Reading
14th November 1918
Dear Sir,

On behalf of the Council and Citizens of the County Borough of Reading, I tender you and the officers, non-commissioned officers and men of the 2nd Royal Berkshire Regt hearty congratulations on the successful issue of the fight for Right, in which you have been engaged, and sincere thanks for the great gallantry and wonderful patience, with which, during the long period of the war, you have sustained the honour of England and of the Royal County, whose name you bear.

Yours faithfully
Stanley Hayward, Mayor.

Lieutenant-Colonel Isaac thanked the mayor for his letter and informed him that all ranks had been inspired by the support from Reading and the County of Berkshire. He also wrote a letter of thanks to Lady Constance Pasley, who had organised gifts and comforts for the men of the battalion during the conflict:

Dear Lady Constance,

Now that the terms of the Armistice are being complied with, and peace is in sight, I cannot allow the moment to pass without a letter of thanks and appreciation for all that has been done for this battalion by you during the long period of hostilities.

I write, therefore, on behalf of all ranks of the battalion under my command, to thank you, Miss Allfrey, and other Ladies who have so generously helped us during the last four memorable years.

Throughout the campaign a continual stream of gifts have been received, and the thoughtfulness, labour and expense entailed have been very greatly appreciated by us all. No one could have done more for the comfort of the troops, and many games would never have been played but for the very material assistance you have given us.

Many incidents of the Campaign may fade from our memories, but the part you have played can never be forgotten.

Would you please convey to all who have so generously helped, our keen appreciation and sincere thanks.

I have caused a copy of this letter to be placed in the records of the Regiment.


Yours sincerely,
[signed] A.G.F. Isaac, Lt-Col.
Comdg 2nd Royal Berkshire Regt.


The four years of war had played havoc with the army's personnel system, for the battalion was now populated with pre-war regulars who had served their time, Kitchener volunteers who had signed up 'for the duration', former men from the territorial battalions, and conscripts under the Derby scheme. It was the same for the officers, few of whom could call the Royal Berkshires their 'parent' regiment, and many Berkshire officers had been seconded to other units. Additionally, many of them were holding ranks far above their substantive level, for example, Lieutenant-Colonel Isaac's rank was only an acting one, for he was actually a captain and brevet-major.

On 7 December, the battalion marched to Tournai, and took part in a parade the next day to mark the royal visit by His Majesty King George V. There was a review in the main square, and the king then inspected a guard of honour formed by the men in the 8th Division who had been serving since 1914.

A week later, the battalion went to the polls to cast their votes in the general election. It was, noted the war diary, the first time the battalion had voted since the enfranchisement of the army.

Classes were set up to prepare the men for civilian life, and a steady stream of individuals who had served the longest went home in batches for demobilisation. Priority was given to former coal miners, for the nation was still desperately short of fuel.

The world wide influenza epidemic was taking its toll of both civilians and soldiers alike. One of the saddest casualties was Captain Charles Nugent, who had come from India to France with the 2nd Battalion in 1914. He was wounded at Neuve Chapelle in March 1915, but then recovered to serve in both the 1st and 5th Battalions through 1916 and 1917, rising to the rank of acting major, and was often acting battalion commander when the regular CO was away. He was gassed in March 1918, but again recovered to rejoin the 2nd Battalion in September of that year. After surviving so much, he succumbed to influenza in the 4th Canadian Casualty Clearing Station on 19 November, and is buried in Valenciennes Communal Cemetery.

The 1914 survivors of the 8th Division, under the command of Sergeant-Major Huggins DCM, parade at Tournai in December 1918 before His Majesty King George V.

The Cadre of the 2nd Battalion march from Reading Railway station on Saturday 17 May 1919 en route to Brock barracks. They have their rifles at the slope with the battalion colours in the centre. It is of interest to note that all the rifles still have the working parts covered in canvas to protect them from dirty conditions.

The survivors of the 2nd Battalion who fought throughout the war. From left to right, front row: Acting RSM F. Vockins, Lt W. Weston MC, Capt. H. Quick MC, Acting RQMS W Booker. Middle row: Cpl Evans, Pte Bursan, L/Cpl Allen, Pte Allwood, Pte Cripps, L/Cpl Hunt. Back row: Pte Dines, Pte Chandler, Sgt Smith, Pte Chapman.

The British government had decided to intervene in the internal conflicts in Russia, and volunteers were called for to join an expeditionary force to be despatched to Archangel. Five officers and over 100 men, who had presumably not had enough of war on the Western Front, came forward, and a company of Royal Berkshires was formed which became D Company of the 1st Battalion, Oxford and Buckinghamshire Light Infantry. The force landed at Archangel in May 1919, and became part of General Grogan's Brigade. They were engaged in a number of skirmishes and inconclusive actions along the Dvina River. The battalion was evacuated from Russia in October 1919 and arrived back in Liverpool on 4 November.

The men left behind in Belgium were part of a constantly shrinking unit, as drafts of men either went home to England for demobilisation, or moved to other regiments or battalions according to their circumstances. There were some reasons to celebrate, for the *London Gazette* in February announced a DSO for Lieutenant-Colonel Isaac, a Military Cross for Second Lieutenant Strange, and the DCM for Private Taylor and Lance-Corporal Long.

By 3 May, the battalion, now stationed at Ath, had been reduced to cadre, and entrained for Dunkirk with the band playing and the colours proudly displayed. By 9 May, they had

Private Gillespie was killed in action on 1 July 1916. His mother and sister visited his grave in the CWG cemetery at Ovillers shortly after the war.

arrived at Southampton, and marched to Sandown Camp, where the wartime mobilisation equipment and transport was handed in to stores.

On 17 May, the cadre arrived in Reading by train at 2.15 p.m., where the mayor entertained them at a civic reception, attended by the lord lieutenant of Berkshire, after which the 2nd Battalion, Royal Berkshire Regiment, marched along the Oxford Road to Brock Barracks. It was all over.

The cost had been high. The 2nd Battalion suffered 1,474 fatalities, about one and a half times its original strength. The statistics for the wounded are notoriously hard to compile for Great War units, but it is generally accepted that a ratio of one killed to two injured provides a reasonable approximation. If so, about 3,000 officers and men would have been wounded, some of whom would have made a complete recovery, while others were maimed or disfigured for life.

# SELECTED BIOGRAPHIES

Almost every man in the battalion would have had a tale to tell and would have been worthy of inclusion here. However, we have had to be very selective and the existence of a photograph or the winning of a medal have had to be key criteria for selection. The exceptions are Private Angier and Private King, whose families have provided us with extensive biographical details, which has justified their inclusion here.

### 17410 Private Horace G. Angier

Horace Angier was born on 23 October 1894 at 12 Vansittart Street, Deptford, south-east London. He was the third child of Frederick William Angier and Keziah Jane Angier. 'Holly', as he was known, had various jobs on leaving school and at one time worked as a kitchen porter.

His family, originally from London's East End, lived at 4 Walker Street, Limehouse. They then moved via Bermondsey to 23 Wellfield Road, Streatham, where Holly attended Wellfield Infants' School. He went on to attend Sunnyville School and was a regular at the Band of Hope Sunday School.

Sometime after the turn of the century the Angier family moved once more, to 58 Corsehill Street, Streatham, and it remained an Angier household until 1998. It was from this home that Holly left for the Great War in 1914, enlisting at the age of twenty at Lambeth into the 2nd Battalion Royal Berkshires. On joining the battalion he was placed into A Company, where he became the company runner, and it was while carrying out this duty he lost his life.

On 1 July 1916 in Mash valley, he was sent with a message to the Machine Gun Team at the Glory Hole at La Boisselle. On reaching his destination a shell exploded amongst them killing him and the entire machine gun team. Almost a year later, the Red Cross found an eye-witness who gave a true account of what happened to Private Angier and the Machine Gun Team. 19937 Private Hubert Hemmings, 2nd Royal Berkshires, gave a statement to the British Red Cross from his bed in the Red Cross Hospital at Torquay:

> On July 1st 1916, at Albert, in the Glory Hole, Private Angier was killed by a shell which came over and killed all the machine team. Private Angier had only been there a few minutes, having been a runner with a message to the team. I was doing sentry duty and saw it all happen and afterwards heard enquiries made for the runner. It was in the middle of a summer morning. The 2nd Royal Berks had a terrible time from the Germans and when they were relieved that night, only 36 left the trenches.

Private H.G. Angier is buried in the Ovillers Military Cemetery, Plot 17, Row G, Grave 6.

*Far left:* Private Angier.

*Left:* Sergeant Burrows.

### 7882 Sergeant Ernest Frederick Burrows, DCM

Ernest Burrows was born in Burnham, and lived in Farnham Common. He enlisted in the Royal Berkshire Regiment at Maidenhead, and served with the 2nd Battalion in India, where he was a recipient of the Delhi Durbar Medal.

By the time the battalion had returned from India, he had been promoted to sergeant, and he went to France with the battalion on 5 November 1914. He distinguished himself at the battalion's first big action at Neuve Chapelle, where his company led the attack. He was awarded the DCM for 'conspicuous gallantry and coolness while engaging the enemy'.

He remained with the 2nd Battalion, and was promoted to company sergeant-major. He was killed at Iron Cross Redoubt on 16 August 1917. His body was never identified, and he is commemorated on the Tyne Cot Memorial to the Missing near Passchendaele.

His DCM and Delhi Durbar Medal are displayed with his campaign medals in the Regimental Museum at Salisbury.

### 7620 John Christopher, DCM

John Christopher's family lived at 37 Cranbury Road, Reading, just five minutes' walk from the regimental depot in Brock Barracks. In 1894, he joined the regiment as a boy bandsman, and qualified as a bandsman a year later. He served in the South African War and was posted to the 2nd Battalion in 1906, where he received his Good Conduct Badge and Delhi Durbar Medal.

As a bandsman, Christopher automatically became a stretcher bearer when the battalion was in action, and at Fromelles on 9 May 1915, he 'went out many times during the day under very heavy fire to bring in wounded men. He was conspicuous among the stretcher bearers for his coolness and courage in the performance of these hazardous duties.'

His actions were rewarded by the DCM, and the *Berkshire Chronicle* reported:

> People passing along Oxford Road could not fail to notice the string of flags across the bottom of Cranbury Road with the central banner and inscription 'Cranbury Road welcomes its hero.' The event has created much excitement, and small boys march up and down the road singing patriotic songs and giving three cheers for Mr Christopher and saluting the flags.

John Christopher survived the war and transferred to the Labour Corps in January 1918.

*Right:* Private Christopher.

*Far right:* Lieutenant-Colonel H.M. Finch, pictured here as a Major with the 1st Battalion in Ireland before the war.

## Lieutenant-Colonel Herbert Marshall Finch

Lieutenant-Colonel Finch was born in Sonning in 1866, the eldest son of Revd Thomas Finch. He was educated at Winchester, and after serving with the militia, was gazetted as a lieutenant in the Royal Berkshire Regiment in 1886, aged twenty. During his time in Bermuda, he married Florence Pierremont in 1895. They had four children, three boys and a girl.

He saw active service in South Africa, and was awarded the Queen's Medal with three clasps, and the King's Medal with two. By 1906 he had been promoted to major, and commanded the depot at Brock Barracks from 1907 to 1911, before being posted to Aldershot as second in command of the 1st Battalion.

He went to France with the 1st Battalion in August 1914, and during the retreat from Mons distinguished himself at the battalion's first clash with the enemy at Maroilles Bridge. He participated in the actions on the Marne and Aisne rivers before the BEF was shipped north to take part in the defence of Ypres. He briefly found himself in command of the battalion when Colonel Graham was seriously wounded, but the following day Finch was himself wounded, and forced to hand over command to Captain Lucas. His conduct during this battle earned him the DSO.

After recovering, he was appointed to the command of the 2nd Battalion, joining them on 4 May 1915. Five days later he was killed leading the battalion at the battle of Fromelles. His eldest son, Frank, also lost his life while serving with the 2nd Battalion in 1918.

## Major Harold Thomas Forster

Forster was born at Christchurch, Hampshire on 6 November 1878, and enlisted in the Royal Marines in 1897, serving until 4 October 1899. Ten days later he joined the Royal Berkshire Regiment.

Harold Forster was a cricketer of some note, playing first-class cricket for Hampshire in 1911. He was a left-hand bat, with a bowling style that was described as 'left arm slow medium'. In his opening game for Hampshire he took 9 wickets for 92 runs. He was a sportsman within the battalion as well, taking part in most sporting activities, as was reported in the regimental journal, The China Dragon.

His pre-war service was all with the 1st Battalion, either at home, which included Ireland, or Gibraltar. He was married in Dublin in 1905 and subsequently had two children. At the start of the war he was serving with the 1st Battalion at Aldershot and he was with them when they went to France on 12 August 1914.

He remained with the battalion until 26 May 1915, when he received a commission as a second lieutenant and was posted to the 2nd Battalion. He was further promoted to lieutenant on 18 December 1915. He remained with the 2nd Battalion for three years, serving as sniping officer, company commander, and as adjutant from 22 October 1916 until 7 April 1918. He was awarded the Military Cross in July 1916, followed by a Bar in September 1917. On the same date he was gazetted for a DSO, when he took command of the battalion when Lieutenant-Colonel Haig was wounded. In early 1918 he was posted to the 2nd Battalion Northamptonshire Regiment and in April 1918 was promoted to acting major. On 29 May he was reported missing and his death later presumed from that date. He was killed on the Bouleuse Ridge, near Ventelay in France. On 16 September 1918 he was awarded a Bar to his DSO. In addition to these awards he was mentioned in dispatches five times. He is buried at the Terlincthun British Cemetery, Wimille.

After his death his will showed a gross value of £707 2s 0d. He bequeathed his watch and chain to his son Willie 'when he is of age', and his medals to 'Dear little Vic'. He went on to say 'claim my war medals, kiddie, and then my sons will have something to remind them of their father's glorious death in fighting so that they may live in dear old England as free men.'

### Second Lieutenant John Arthur Gray, DCM (formerly No.7901)
John Gray joined the regiment at Maidenhead in 1905, aged eighteen. He was 5ft 3in tall, and gave his trade as a woodcarver. After basic training, he joined the 1st Battalion in Ireland, where he proved to be an above-average soldier, passing courses in signalling, gaining his education certificates, and trained as mounted infantry on a course in Aldershot. In 1909, he was posted to India to join the 2nd Battalion, where he rose steadily through the ranks, becoming a sergeant in 1912.

At the battle of Fromelles in May 1915, when all his company officers had become casualties, Gray took command of the company, rallied the men under heavy fire, moving from place to place regardless of his own safety, and gave a splendid example of coolness and courage, for which he was awarded the DCM.

After a spell as company sergeant-major in Brock Barracks, Gray returned to the 2nd Battalion. He was recommended for a commission, and the examining officer reported that he was 'well educated, and a good leader of men'. After a spell at an officers' training unit in England, Second Lieutenant Gray returned to the battalion in November 1916.

Gray was among those killed in the assault on Pallas Trench on 4 March 1917, and is buried in Sailly-Saillisel British Cemetery. The chaplain wrote to his parents: 'He was an awfully good fellow and was always ready to do one a good turn. The Regiment loses in him a good officer, and many of us who knew him have lost a friend.'

*Opposite left:* Major Harold Thomas Forster in the hockey team, middle row, second from right.

*Opposite right:* 2nd Lieutenant John Arthur Gray DCM (formerly No.7901).

*Right:* Private James Haunts.

*Far right:* Arthur John Howells.

## 6963 Private James Haunts

James Haunts was born in Reading, but spent most of his childhood in Woolwich. As his father was a retired soldier he followed in his footsteps, joining the Royal Berkshires in January 1903. From 1903 to 1904 he served in Dublin. In 1904 he joined the 2nd Battalion Royal Berkshire Regiment and served in Egypt and India before becoming a reservist in 1911.

After leaving the regiment he emigrated to Canada, working on a farm and marrying the farmer's daughter Ellen soon afterwards. On the outbreak of war in 1914 he was still a reservist and was called back to active duty. He reported to Levis, Quebec and in his words was declared 'Fit, Fit, Fit' and was soon on board the ship *Teutonic* bound for England. On arrival he rejoined his regiment and was one of the first reinforcements to the 1st Battalion, who were already in France. He was wounded while with the 1st Battalion and shipped back to England. After recovering from his wounds he was posted to his old pre-war battalion, the 2nd Royal Berkshires.

By now he had become a corporal, but Haunts was again wounded in 1917, this time more seriously, in his leg and shoulder. He managed to crawl back to the trenches and was evacuated back to England. This was the end of the war for him and in 1918 he returned to Canada, where he spent six months in the old military hospital in Kingston, Ontario. After discharge from hospital he spent a short while working for Canadian Locomotive, after which he took up employment as an officers' mess orderly in the Royal Military College, Kingston.

## 220288 Company Sergeant-Major Arthur John Howells, DCM★

Company Sergeant-Major Howells was a Welshman who had already distinguished himself in the Boer War. He was born on 28 October 1875 in the parish of Llantrisant, Porth, Glamorgan. He was the son of Howell Rees Howells, a stonemason and Joan Howells (*née* Williams), who died in 1881. His father remarried. He enlisted in 1898 as a private, no. 5771, in the South Wales Borderers, and was posted to the 2nd Battalion at Pembroke Dock where he remained until September 1899. This was followed by postings to Dublin, South Africa (Boer War), Bulford, Aldershot and finally Chatham in 1910, where he transferred to the reserve.

Whilst in South Africa he was wounded at Modderfontein on 29 January 1901. He then went on to win the DCM (*London Gazette* 23 April 1901, AO 163/01). The citation reads:

> During the Boer attack on Modderfontein Private Howells stayed with a wounded comrade
> outside our lines, and four times during the day crossed 800 yards of fire swept ground to

fetch him water, and other things, and the last time brought away his rifle and ammunition to prevent it falling into enemy hands.

After leaving the Army he became a carpenter in Ebbw Vale and also enlisted in the Territorial Force as a sergeant instructor in the 3rd Battalion, Monmouthshire Regiment. On 20 September 1913 he married Miss Ada Florence Shergold at St Peter's Church, Stournton, Wiltshire. In March 1917 his son William was born.

On the outbreak of war he was mobilised as 1122 Sergeant Howells, 3rd Battalion Monmouthshire Regiment, and went to France with them in February 1915. The 3rd Monmouths were disbanded in August 1916, and Howells was transferred to the 2nd Battalion Royal Berkshire Regiment as a company sergeant-major, and allocated the number 220288.

He was awarded a bar to his DCM for his bravery in the assault near Passchendaele on 2 December 1917. His citation reads: 'For conspicuous gallantry and devotion to duty in taking command of his company when all the officers had become casualties, reorganised them after an attack, and beating off a counterattack with heavy loss to the enemy.'

Howells was one of the many casualties of the enemy assault on the Aisne position in May 1918, when he was killed in action 'somewhere between Reims and Soissons'. He has no known grave and is commemorated on the Soissons Memorial to the Missing. (Panel 23, Column 1) His medals are on display at the South Wales Borderers Museum at Brecon.

### Lieutenant-Colonel Gerald Ponsonby Sneyd Hunt

Gerald Hunt was born in 1877 the son of Robert Ponsonby Carew Hunt and Ada Mary Hunt, and educated at Harrow and the Royal Military Academy, Sandhurst. He joined the 1st Battalion Royal Berkshire Regiment in the West Indies in 1897. Promoted to lieutenant in May 1900, and transferred the same year to the 2nd Battalion in South Africa, he served with this battalion until the end of the Boer War. He was awarded the Queen's Medal with three clasps and the King's Medal with two.

He was promoted to captain in February 1905, and went to France as a company commander with the 2nd Battalion in November 1914, but was wounded in February 1915 at Fauquissart. Promoted major in September 1915, he commanded the battalion after the death of Lieutenant-Colonel Finch. He was in command of the battalion during the engagement at Bois Grenier, for which action he was mentioned in dispatches.

From December 1915 to April 1917 he commanded the 173rd Territorial Brigade, and then returned to France in command of the 1st Battalion Royal Berkshire Regiment. He was again mentioned in dispatches, this time in connection with the fighting around Cambrai, and was awarded the DSO.

He was killed in the German Spring Offensive of March 1918, and was recommended for a posthumous Victoria Cross, for most conspicuous courage and devotion to duty near Manancourt. During intense hostile rifle and machine gun fire, he personally supervised the task of placing his own men and those of other units to the best advantage. He showed at all times a clear appreciation of very difficult circumstances, and when other troops had fallen back, realising that it was of the utmost importance to hold on, in order to gain valuable time, and by his own magnificent example in the front line, he inspired all ranks to further heights. He refused to spare himself, although frequently begged to do so by his fellow officers, and continued to organise his line, up to the moment of his death on 23 March 1918. He is buried in Varennes Military Cemetery.

### 9612 Private Charles Richard King

Charles was born on 28 December 1892 in West Street, Henley-on-Thames. He was the fifth of eight children of Samuel and Eliza King. At the age of seven his father died of heart disease whilst the family were living at 23 Albert Road, Henley.

2nd Lieutenant Arthur Maybury,
DCM (formerly No.7330).

Initially, Charles was employed as a general labourer for a Mr Atkins, who owned the Remenham Dairies in the Market Place, Henley, but on 6 November 1911, at nearly nineteen years of age, Charles, like his older brother Alfred before him, enlisted in the Royal Berkshire Regiment at Brock Barracks, Oxford Road, Reading. This was the start of what was to be an extraordinary period of military service for Charles over the next eight years, in which he served in the 2nd, 3rd and 5th Battalions of the Royal Berkshire Regiment.

Charles joined the 2nd Battalion at Meerut in 1911, and was still serving in India when the battalion was recalled to form part of the 8th Division. By now the war was six weeks old and Charles' older brother Alfred William King Private 7707 in the 1st Battalion of the Royal Berkshire Regiment had already been killed in action during the battle of the Aisne on 16 September 1914.

While the battalion was manning the trenches at Bois Grenier, Charles was shot and wounded on 7 September 1915, and taken to No.2 Casualty Clearing Station and admitted to hospital, where his injury was diagnosed as a gunshot wound to his left shoulder. He was evacuated to a hospital in Birmingham, returning to the 2nd Battalion on the Somme in April 1916.

He survived the action at Ovillers on 1 July 1916, but after several periods in hospital with a neck injury and trench foot, returned to England in May 1917 for treatment. He then spent a period with the 3rd Battalion at Portsmouth, training new recruits, before returning to France and joining the 5th Battalion, where he was promoted to Lance Corporal. He was injured once again during the battle of Cambrai in November 1917, and hospitalised in Bristol, rejoining the 5th Battalion in March 1918. He was posted as missing following a trench raid in May 1918, but had in fact been taken prisoner. He was repatriated in January 1919, and found employment with the Great Western Railway as a signalman. He died in 1962.

## Second Lieutenant Arthur Maybury, DCM (formerly No.7330)

Sergeant Maybury went to France with the 2nd Battalion in November 1914. He had distinguished himself as a marksman, winning at total of 53 rupees' prize money at the Meerut Rifle Club meeting in 1907. He surpassed this in 1911 and 1912, when, at the Bengal-Punjab Rifle Association meeting, he was the champion shot for two years running, winning the Viceroy's Cup and 500 rupees in prize money.

He was awarded the DCM in 1916, not for any particular action, but for 'consistent good work since his battalion arrived at the front. He is cool and reliable under all circumstances.'

Maybury was recommended for a commission and, after officer training, was posted to the 5th Battalion Royal Berkshire Regiment in January 1917. He soon distinguished himself leading a bombing raid, and bringing in a wounded man, Private Taplin, who had lain in a shell-hole for 20 hours.

Second Lieutenant Maybury was posted missing after the 5th Battalion took part in an attack on Monchy during the battle of Arras on 19 July 1917. His body was never recovered, and he is commemorated on the Arras Memorial to the Missing.

### 6365 Sergeant Frank Edward Parker, DCM

Frank Parker joined the regiment in London in 1901, having been born in Lambeth. He took part in the Delhi Durbar, and by the time the 2nd Battalion went to France he had become a sergeant in the Signals Section.

He was awarded the DCM at Neuve Chapelle on 14 March 1915, for displaying conspicuous courage and coolness while laying telephone cables and maintaining communication while under fire.

Sadly, Parker did not live long to enjoy his medal, for he had contracted tetanus, although the records do not specify whether this was the result of a wound or if he had cut himself while laying the cables in the muddy ground. He was evacuated to England, but died in hospital in Leicester on 24 March 1915, aged thirty-two. He is buried in Welford Road Cemetery, Leicester.

### Lieutenant Arthur Pritchard

Arthur Pritchard was a cocoa planter by trade, with previous service in the British South African Police, from which he was discharged in 1903. He then joined the Cape Mounted Rifles and served until 1905. On the outbreak of war he was in Costa Rica and it was from there that he made his way back to Great Britain. He enlisted on 13 October 1914 and became a trooper in the 1st Life Guards (Household Cavalry). He went to France with that regiment on 11 November 1914, but on 26 May 1915 was commissioned into the Royal Berkshire Regiment. After officer training he was posted to the 2nd Battalion where he received his first wound, at Neuve Chapelle on 23 June 1915, after which he appeared before a number of medical boards.

Proceedings of Medical Board (London District) 15 July 1915:

> The Board found that during heavy shellfire Lieutenant Pritchard had sudden headaches which have continued since, he had an attack of diarrhoea for 6 days and after that sleep failed him and his nerve gave way. He had an attack of Malarial fever on July 12th 1915 [He has lived in the tropics for 15 years.] His sleeplessness continues, he easily gets tired and complains of nervousness. His headaches are lessening. They concluded that he was suffering from Traumatic Neurasthenia.

He appeared before a further medical board on 15 February 1916. The report stated: 'This Officer's condition is improving but the course of Musketry practice, which he had whilst on leave, upset him very much. He suffered from severe headaches, insomnia, with exhausting and terrifying dreams and feelings of extreme restlessness.' A further medical board 1 May 1916 reported: 'he now sleeps satisfactorily and his physical condition is normal. Now fit for General Service.'

On 7 November 1916 he joined the 3rd Battalion Royal Berkshire Regiment, and from there he was later posted to the 2/20 London Regiment. During his sick leave, Pritchard applied his mind to an idea he had come up with, the pistol bayonet. In late

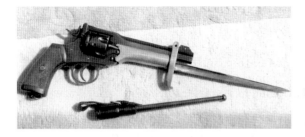

*Above:* The Pritchard Greener 'Pistol bayonet' invented by Lieutenant Pritchard.

*Right:* Sergeant Bernard Charles Shea DCM.

1916 he approached John Wilkinson-Latham of Wilkinson's Sword with the idea of utilising the Wilkinson factory for the manufacture of his bayonet. From Pritchard's sketches, a prototype was made by Waterers, the cutlery division of Wilkinson's. It was constructed of a brass or gunmetal grip, with the tip of an 1897 infantry officer's sword providing the blade. He later developed the idea in conjunction with W.W. Greener of Pall Mall to produce the Pritchard-Greener Pistol Bayonet. A very limited number were manufactured and it is not known if any were ever used in action.

In 1917 he applied to relinquish his commission due to wounds received, stating to the board that 'in 1914 I was in perfect health'. After the war he moved to Kuela Perak Estate, Teluk Anson, Lower Perak, Federated Malay States, where he resumed his former occupation.

### 7862 Sergeant Bernard Charles Shea, DCM

Bernard Shea joined the regiment as a boy soldier in 1906. He studied hard, and achieved a first-class Certificate of Education in 1907. He was a member of the 2nd Battalion Gymnastic Team, and was a good singer, often performing at concerts. By the time the battalion had reached France, he had become a sergeant.

At the battle of Fromelles, Lieutenant Druitt, his platoon commander, gave the order to attack, and both he and Shea climbed out of the trench. Druitt was immediately hit in the chest, and died instantly. Another bullet knocked Shea's rifle from his grasp. Without pausing, Shea led the platoon in a charge across no-man's land, but half way across, he collapsed when a bullet passed through his abdomen and broke his right hip joint. The rest of the men lay down to avoid the hail of bullets, but Shea angrily ordered them to continue the attack.

He lay out in the open with the other wounded until nightfall enabled them to be rescued. Shea was awarded the DCM. His soldiering days might have been over, but he recovered from his wound, and remained with the regiment after the war. He was later attached to the Egyptian Army, where he obtained a commission, and also served in the Second World War. His DCM is displayed in the Regimental Museum at Salisbury, together with his campaign medals from both wars, the King George VI coronation medal, and the Egyptian Order of the Nile.

### Lieutenant-Colonel A.A. Hanbury-Sparrow, DSO★, MC

Hanbury-Sparrow was born in 1892 and, after attending Sandhurst, embarked on his career as a regular army officer by joining the 1st Battalion Royal Berkshire Regiment in

*Far left:* Colonel Hanbury-Sparrow marching at the head of he ANZAC parade in Sydney, 1972.

*Left:* Sergeant Sturgess DCM, the champion boxer.

Aldershot. Promotion in peacetime was slow, and when the battalion was mobilised on 4 August 1914, he was still the junior subaltern. The battalion was short of a transport officer, and to his dismay, Colonel Graham appointed him to the vacancy. Transport officers, along with quartermasters, were usually long-serving senior NCOs with a wide experience of horses and army organisation, who received commissions to take up the post.

However, Hanbury-Sparrow successfully managed the transport during the exhausting retreat from Mons to the River Aisne, until a 'proper' transport officer was posted to the battalion, and he resumed command of his platoon.

He was awarded his first DSO at the first battle of Ypres, in which he was severely wounded. After recovering, he was posted to the 2nd Royal Berkshires, and the rest of his fighting career is told in the main text. After being gassed near Passchendaele, he did not return to active service until after the war, when he joined the 1st Battalion in Persia. He resigned his commission in 1926. He published his memoirs, *The Land-locked Lake*, in 1932, and served in the Home Guard during the Second World War. He later emigrated to Australia, where he continued to march in ANZAC memorial day parades until his death in 1982.

### 8536 Sergeant Albert Sturgess, DCM★

As well as winning the DCM twice, Sturgess was a first-class shot and a keen boxer. After his initial training, he was posted to the 1st Battalion, who at that time were serving in Ireland. In October 1907 he came second in the musketry course at Kilbride Camp, winning a prize of 20s. The following year, he completed the annual course on the Curragh Ranges, when he qualified as a first-class shot. In addition to being a marksman, he was very fit and came to prominence as a boxer.

At the battalion sports day to celebrate Tofrek Day in 1908 he fought and beat Private Roberts in the lightweight competition, winning a 10s prize. He passed his second-class Certificate of Education in 1912, and soon after was posted to the 2nd Battalion in India, returning with them on the outbreak of war. During the 3rd Ypres campaign, he was twice awarded the DCM, the first during the trench raid at Hooge on 31 July 1917. The citation reads:

> For conspicuous gallantry and devotion to duty during a raid on enemy trenches. He attacked a machine gun single handed, putting it out of action and killing and dispersing

*Above:* Sergeant
Henry Venn DCM.

*Right:* Lieutenant
L. Tremellen.

the team with bombs. He afterwards carried a wounded comrade back to our lines, having shown throughout the operation great dash and a fine disregard of danger. (*London Gazette*, 17 September 1917)

During the attack by 25th Brigade at Passchendaele he led his platoon in the attack on the Southern Redoubt, winning a bar to his DCM 'for conspicuous gallantry and devotion to duty in leading his platoon forward although wounded, capturing a redoubt by a bayonet charge and himself killing many of the enemy. The success of this part of the attack in which the enemy suffered heavy casualties was due to him.' (*London Gazette* 4 March 1918).

A report of the award of the Bar to the DCM appeared in the local newspaper:

The bar to the DCM has been awarded to Sergeant Albert 'Dick' Sturgess, brother of Mrs Gibbs of 8 Bright Street, Reading. Sgt Sturgess who belongs to the Royal Berks has been with that Regiment for about eleven years. He came from India with his battalion soon after the outbreak of war, and proceeded straight to the front. He has seen a great deal of fighting, and has twice been wounded. He was injured on the first occasion in the back and afterwards in the arm and left side. The Berks NCO is a very fine boxer. In India he won the championship which was open to all the forces stationed out there, thus securing a handsome silver cup and several other honours fell to his lot. Whilst at Reading he secured quite a number of prizes. He has four other brothers with the colours. Two are prisoners of war, and are both wounded. Both belong to the Royal Berks'

He remained in the battalion after the war, but transferred to the 4th (Territorial Army) battalion in 1922, remaining there until 1928. His comrades were sorry to see him go, and the regimental journal, *The China Dragon*, reported:

On his leaving the Regiment a special social evening was held in the Sergeants' Mess. A presentation was made from all the ranks by Major Sharpe, who spoke highly of the services rendered by Sgt Sturgess. He responded in a very modest way, being obviously moved by the reception and sentiments of his comrades. He presented the mess with a framed photo.

He died in London in June 1929. His post-war number was 5328145.

### Lieutenant L Tremellen

Second Lieutenant Tremellen was initially posted to the 3rd Battalion after graduating from Sandhurst in 1916, but then joined the 1st Battalion on the Western Front in January

1917. He was wounded in the action at Oppy Wood in May 1917, but after recovering was sent to join the 2nd Battalion.

He was badly wounded during the German spring offensive on 25 March 1918, losing an arm, which ended his active service for the time being. By the spring of 1919 he had recovered sufficiently to join the 3rd Battalion in Ireland.

His next posting was to Tanganyika, where he was appointed aide-de-camp to the governor, Sir N. Byatt, until 1922, when he rejoined the 2nd Battalion in Dublin. He spent the next fifteen years serving in both the 1st and 2nd Battalions in India, Sudan and Palestine, but at the outbreak of war in 1939 he was serving in the depot at Reading. He became chief instructor at the 61st Division School, but when the 10th Battalion Royal Berkshires was formed, he became second in command to Lieutenant-Colonel Sawyer. He later commanded the 9th Battalion, after which he was promoted to brigadier and commanded 158th Brigade in 45th Division. This was followed by command of the 206th Independent Infantry Brigade.

### 7951 Sergeant Henry Venn, DCM

Henry Venn was born in Sunninghill, Berkshire, and enlisted in the regiment at Reading. He was a noted marksman, winning a prize of 5s at the All Ireland Rifle Meeting in 1906. He was a member of the winning team for the Lord Roberts Cup at the Curragh in the same year.

He was posted to the 2nd Battalion at the end of 1906, and Captain MacDonald, his company commander, reported:

> Venn has more intelligence than the average young soldier, but does not always use it. Sometimes inclined to be too positive that he has got every shot off exactly right. The human error must always be considered even with the best shots. Inclined to despondency if shooting badly, and sometimes mistrusts the coach. Has all the makings of a brilliant shot.

By 1913, Venn had become a sergeant, and was detached to serve as an instructor at the Pachmiri School of Musketry, but he had returned from this posting by the time the battalion was sent to France. At Neuve Chapelle, he took charge of a machine gun section and organised blocking parties after the officer in charge had been wounded, for which he was awarded the DCM. He had himself been wounded, however, and died from his injuries two days later, aged twenty-eight. He is buried at Wimereux Cemetery, near Boulogne.

# APPENDIX II

# THE 2ND BATTALION ROYAL BERKSHIRE REGIMENT
## (THE OLD 66TH)

The 66th Regiment of Foot was formed from the 2nd/19th Regiment (now the Green Howards) in Northumberland in 1758, under the command of Colonel Sandford. In 1782 the 66th received the County Title of the 66th (Berkshire) Regiment. Its early days were spent in England, Ireland and Jamaica, where it was called upon for active service against bands of rebellious slaves. They remained in Jamaica from 1763 to 1773 returning to England that year. After service in Scotland they spent some time in Ireland, before returning to the West Indies in 1785, when they received new colours. In 1793 they crossed the Atlantic for a posting in Gibraltar. Further postings followed in Halifax, Nova Scotia, and Jersey. They were in Jersey when war broke out between England and France in May 1803.

The hostilities made it necessary to raise more units, and in 1803 the 2nd/66th was formed and went on to fight in the Peninsular War in Spain, earning immediate laurels for the regiment by their splendid fighting in the battles of Douro, Talavera, Albuera, Vitoria, Nivelle, Nive, Orthez and the Pyrenees. In the meantime, the 1st/66th had gone to Ceylon and India, where they fought in the Nepalese war before finally ending up on the island of St Helena guarding Napoleon. It was on this island that the 2nd/66th joined them and the two battalions were merged to reform as the 66th Regiment of Foot. They were present on the island in 1821 when Napoleon died and the 66th had the joint honour with the 20th of Foot of providing the pall bearers at his funeral.

The battalion then went to Canada via Ireland where they were actively engaged in putting down several rebellions. They returned to England in 1840 after thirteen and a half years in Canada. Between this time and 1870 the regiment repeated its travels and in January 1870 orders were received to move to India where they received new colours in 1872. They had various postings around India for the next eight years, until in February 1880 they were ordered on active service to Southern Afghanistan.

On 27 July 1880 the regiment took part in the disastrous Battle of Maiwand, followed by a gruelling retreat to Kandahar by the survivors. The Regiment lost 275 men killed at Maiwand and the colours were lost, but the battle today is remembered for the heroic stand of the last eleven, who stood back to back and fought to the last, their heroism being recognised by their enemy. The Maiwand lion today stands in Forbury Gardens, Reading, as a permanent reminder of the actions of the 66th on that day.

What remained of the regiment returned to England, where they were stationed on the Isle of Wight. In August 1881 Queen Victoria presented them with new colours. They then returned to Ireland carrying out garrison duties, returning to England in 1892. The only excitement they experienced during this time was when a couple of companies went to Penzance to aid the civil power in the Newlyn Fish Riots.

In 1898 they went to South Africa and they were there when the Boer War broke out. They remained in South Africa throughout this campaign, mainly being deployed manning blockhouses. The detachments rarely came together to fight as a complete unit, but on one of those occasions Private William House won the Victoria Cross during an attack on Mosilikatse Nek, on 2 August 1900.

When the hostilities in South Africa ended in 1902, the regiment went to Egypt, but a detached company was stationed in Cyprus. They remained there until 1906, when they transferred to India, where they remained until the outbreak of the First World War.

After the First World War the battalion found itself in Dublin, but a detached company of volunteers went to Archangel with the expeditionary force sent to aid the White Russian army. Postings followed to Plymouth, Wiesbaden, Aldershot, Shorncliffe, Palestine, Alexandria, Moascar and a detachment in Cyprus.

In 1937 they went to Lucknow in India, and were still there when the Second World War started. For the next three years they were garrisoned in India, where they were deployed for internal security duties in aid of the civil power. They were not committed to action until they joined General Slim's Fourteenth Army in 1944. They fought at Shwebo, Kabwet, The Singu Bridgehead and Mandalay, including the attack on Fort Dufferin, and many other actions.

After the cessation of hostilities, the battalion remained in Burma and on 3 January 1948 they were the last British battalion to leave the country when Burma gained independence from Great Britain, embarking on HMS *Scythia*. From Burma they went to Egypt, where after a short period they were sent to Eritrea where they took part in a campaign against the Shifta rebels.

The reduction in size of the British Empire enabled the government to introduce defence cuts, and in common with the rest of the Army the regiment had to reduce to one battalion. The amalgamation parade took place in Asmara, Eritrea, on 5 March 1949, with the new battalion being redesignated the 1st Battalion. And the proud history of the 'Old 66th', the 2nd Battalion Royal Berkshire Regiment, came to an end.

# APPENDIX III

# VISITING THE
# BATTLEFIELDS TODAY

We have selected five actions in which the 2nd Battalion of the Royal Berkshire Regiment took part. The criteria for selection have been accessibility of the terrain today and a reasonable certainty that we can identify the location of the battalion's position from trench maps and/or information in the unit diaries. The sites can easily be approached by car.

**Gouzeaucourt Wood** (Action 4 April 1917, Chapter 13)
*Nearest large town: Cambrai or Bapaume*
*Approx 4 miles south of the N30, Cambrai–Bapaume Road, midway between the two towns*
From Bapaume take the D7 via Bertincourt to Metz-en-Couture, continue on the D7 towards Gouzeaucourt Village. Stop at the Metz-en-Couture Communal Cemetery British Extension (on the right of the road just before reaching Gouzeaucourt Wood). Find the grave of Second Lieutenant J.A. Grimes, MC, Plot 2, Row H, Grave 23.

Standing with your back to the gravestone, look half right, past the lone tree, for the battalion forming-up area, some 800 yards south of the tip of Gouzeaucourt Wood. The battalion, on the immediate right of the 20th Division, with the 2nd Battalion Rifle Brigade on their right, advanced to the southern end of the wood, then through the wood, across the road, to their objective near the northern end of the wood.

To get to the battalion objective, continue along the D7, towards Gouzeaucourt Village, passing through the wood, to a crossroads. Take a left turn and drive for around 500 yards (the main body of Gouzeaucourt Wood runs some 500 yards to the left of this road), to where a spur of the wood reaches the road. The battalion occupied a line running along the edge of the spur. The 2nd Rifle Brigade occupied a defensive flank line, some 300 yards to the right of the road from the crossroads, to join up with the Royal Berkshires.

**Attack on Pallas and Fritz Trenches** (Action 4 and 5 March 1917, Chapter 12)
*Nearest large town: Bapaume*
From Bapaume take the N17, south through Sailly-Saillisel and Rancourt. About 1,000 yards south of Rancourt, pull in 100 yards or so past the D20 on the right. Looking across the road you will see St Pierre Vaast Wood stretching towards Rancourt on the left, with Moislains Wood, a relatively small copse, to the right. The German front line ran along the edge of St Pierre Vaast Wood, across the face of the gap between the two woods and continued south some 200 yards in front of Moislains Wood. The British front line ran parallel to it, some 200 yards to the west. The Royal Berkshire Regiment attack was on Pallas and Fritz trenches across the gap between the woods.

Continue south down the N17 and just before Bouchavesnes take a right-hand turn onto the D149 towards Moislains. After around 1 mile a track on the left of the road leads off to the gap between Moislains Wood and St Pierre Vaast wood, which leads to the point on Fritz Trench occupied by the battalion.

**Attack on Villers-Brettoneux** (Action 25 April 1918, Chapter 18)
*Nearest large town: Amiens*
From Amiens take the N29 (Amiens–St Quentin road). At Villers-Bretonneux take a left turn onto the D23 to the Australian Memorial. The memorial is situated to the west of Villers-Bretonneux. Walk up to the memorial through the cemetery, then turn to your right until you reach the chain-link boundary fence. You are now overlooking the ground which the battalion crossed to enter the northern end of Villers-Bretonneux.

**Attack on Ovillers** (Action 1 July 1916, Chapter 9)
*Nearest large town: Albert*
Take the D929 (Albert–Bapaume road) from Albert. Turn left onto the D104 (Bouzincourt road). Towards the top of the rise, on the right, a road leads off past the cemetery to Ovillers-la-Boiselle. The battalion assembled for the attack in trenches some 300 to 400 yards to the north of this road, facing due east towards the village of Ovillers. The assault crossed the land now occupied by the cemetery, where several of the casualties are buried.

On 3 July the 5th Battalion Royal Berkshire Regiment made a similarly unsuccessful attack on Ovillers, advancing over the ground to the right and left of the road leading to the village. Much of the ground covered was that attacked by the 2nd Battalion some three days earlier, where many of the unburied casualties were noticed.

**Operations North of Passchendaele** (Action 1 and 2 December 1917, Chapter 16)
*Nearest large town: Ypres*
From Ypres take the N8 (Menin road) and at Geluveld turn left to Beselare. At a T-junction take a left turn to Passchendaele. Continue to the north of the village, where on the outskirts, the road forks and take the right fork. The battalion were on the right of the brigade front line, which stretched from 100 yards to the east of the fork in the road to a point some 250 yards up the road.

# APPENDIX IV

# COMMANDING OFFICERS

| Rank on appointment | Rank on Leaving | Name | Age on appointment | Date from | Date to | Reason for Leaving |
|---|---|---|---|---|---|---|
| Lt-Col. | Brig(T) | E. Feetham | 48 | 30/4/1911 | 2/4/1915 | To command a brigade. (KIA 29/3/18Cmdg 39th Div) |
| Major | Major | R.P. Harvey | 42 | 2/4/1915 | 4/5/1915 | Reverted to 2/I/C. KIA 9/5/1915 at Fromelles |
| Major | Lt-Col. | H.M. Finch | 49 | 4/5/1915 | 9/5/1915 | KIA at Fromelles |
| Captain | Lt-Col. | G.P.S. Hunt | 37 | 9/5/1915 | 20/12/1915 | To command a brigade. (KIA 23/3/18Cmdg 1st Royal Berks) |
| Major | Lt-Col. | A.M. Holdsworth | 40 | 20/12/1915 | 1/7/1916 | Died of wounds, Somme |
| Major (6th Rifle Brigade) | Lt-Col. | R. Haig | 43 | 4/7/1916 | 31/7/1917 | Wounded at 3rd Ypres |
| Major | Lt-Col. | A.A. Hanbury-Sparrow | 25 | 31/7/1917 | 22/11/1917 | Wounded at 3rd Ypres |
| Major (1st Scottish Rifles) | Lt-Col. | C.R.H Stirling | 24 | 22/11/1917 | 24/3/1918 | Wounded. Died of wounds 29/5/1918 |
| Major (2nd Lincolnshire Regt) | Lt-Col. | J.A. Griffin | 26 | 25/3/1918 | 27/5/1918 | Prisoner of War |
| Major | Lt-Col. | A.G.F. Isaac | 31 | 21/6/1918 | 11/11/1918 | In command until cadre returned to Reading |

# APPENDIX V

# FATAL CASUALTIES

## Chart of Fatal Casualties by Month

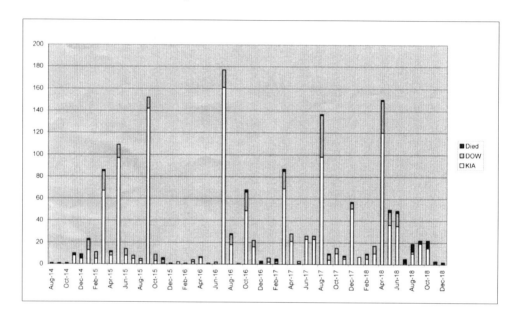

## Princess Charlotte of Wales (Royal Berkshire Regiment)
## 2nd Battalion Casualties by Month and Year

| Year | Jan | Feb | Mar | Apr | May | Jun | Jul | Aug | Sep | Oct | Nov | Dec | Year Total |
|---|---|---|---|---|---|---|---|---|---|---|---|---|---|
| 0 | | | | | | | | | | | | | 0 |
| 1914 | | | | | | | | 1 | 2 | 1 | 10 | 9 | 23 |
| 1915 | 23 | 11 | 87 | 12 | 98 | 14 | 7 | 4 | 150 | 9 | 6 | 1 | 422 |
| 1916 | 2 | 1 | 4 | 5 | 1 | 2 | 166 | 25 | 10 | 66 | 21 | 4 | 307 |
| 1917 | 6 | 5 | 85 | 28 | 2 | | 26 | 134 | 10 | 14 | 8 | 55 | 373 |
| 1918 | 7 | 10 | 16 | 148 | 51 | 49 | 5 | 19 | 21 | 18 | 2 | 2 | 348 |
| 1919 | | 1 | | | | | | | | | | | 1 |
| Totals | 38 | 28 | 192 | 193 | 152 | 65 | 204 | 183 | 193 | 108 | 47 | 71 | 1474 |

# APPENDIX VI

# HONOURS AND AWARDS

Honours and Awards for the 2nd Battalion Royal Berkshire Regiment as announced in the *London Gazette* 1914 to 1920 (The date of announcement is given in brackets).

N.B. On occasions, the *London Gazette* indicates the Regiment only, not the battalions, in which the men were serving when the honour was approved. Some of the following who served in more than one battalion in the Royal Berkshire Regiment may have been serving in a different battalion at the time of the award. Others may have been omitted.

## Distinguished Service Order
Capt. Temp Maj. Edward Mortimer Allfrey, (4-6-1917)
Lt Acting Capt. Harold Thomas Forster, MC (26-9-1917 and 9-1-1918)
Lt-Col. J.A.A Griffin, 2nd Lincolnshire Regt attached to 2nd R. Berks (26-7-1918)
Capt., Arthur Ellis Fowke Harris, (23-6-1915 and 24-7-1915)
Maj., Thomas Edward Carew Hunt, (3-6-1916)
Capt., Btn. Maj., Acting Lt-Col. Auberon Godfrey Faulkner Isaac, MC (15-2-1919)
Maj., Arthur Gabell Macdonald, (3-6-1916)
Maj., Francis Hamilton Moore. (14-1-1916)
Acting Lt-Col. Guy Henry Sawyer , (3-6-1916)
Maj., Temp Lt-Col. C.R.H. Stirling. MC 2nd Scottish Rifles Attached 2nd R. Berks
    (24-11-1917 and 16-1-1918)
Maj., W.B. Thornton, (23-6-1915 and 24-7-1915)
2/Lt W.A. Upton, 2nd Wiltshire Regiment,
attached 2nd R. Berks., (4-2-1918 and 5-7-1918)

## Bar to Distinguished Service Order
Lt, Acting Maj., Harold Thomas Forster, DSO, 2nd R. Berks Attached Northampton
    Regiment, (16-9-1918)
Maj., Temp Lt-Col., Roland Haigh, DSO, Rifle Brigade, Attached 2nd R. Berks (15-6-
    1917) (N.B. He was awarded a 2nd Bar to the DSO, (26-7-1918)
Lt-Col. A.A. Hanbury-Sparrow, DSO MC (26-9-1917 and 9-1-1918)
Lt-Col. C.R.H. Stirling. DSO MC 2nd Battalion Scottish Rifles, attached, 2nd R. Berks.,
    (18-2-1918)

## Military Cross
2/Lt, Temp Capt., Harold Pearmine Allaway, North Staffordshire Regt, Attached 2nd R.
    Berks, (11-5-1917)
Lt AA Barrett., (May 1918)

2/Lt Norman David Bayley, (26-9-1917 and 9-1-1918)
2/Lt Cyril Brown, (3-6-1919)
Lt, Acting Capt., John Archibald Cahill, (11-5-1917)
Lt, Acting Capt., Alfred Douglas Clare, (16-9-1918).
Lt, Acting Capt., Henry Herbert Flint, 10th
Middlesex Regt T.F. attached 2nd R.Berks. (26-9-1917)
2/Lt Harold Thomas Forster. (19-8-1916)
Capt., Alex James Fraser, (14-1-1916)
Lt Oswald Spencer Francis, (18-10-1917 and 7-3-1918)
Capt. A.D. Gordon, (28-4-1915)
2/Lt Gilbert Lionel Gosling, (15-2-1919 and 30-7-1919)
Lt W McM. Guttman, (April 1918)
Lt Richard Haig, (1-1-1917)
Capt. Arthur Alan Hanbury Hanbury-Sparrow DSO (11-5-1917)
Lt D de V Hinde (18-6-1917)
2/Lt, Acting Capt., Oswald Montague James, (26-5-1917)
2/Lt Archibald Sherbrooke Knott. (26-7-1918)
Lt Frank Lawson, (15-2-1919 and 30-7-1919)
Lt, Temp Capt., Reginald Lewis, (3-6-1916)
2/Lt Gerald William Mant, (18-10-1917 and 7-3-1918)
2/Lt Ernest George Mason, (15-10-1918)
Lt Charles Mollett. (Awarded by G.O.C., 4th Army 16-8-1916)
2/Lt H.A. Mossman (25-4-1918)
Capt. Esdaile Addison Burkett Orr (14-1-1916)
2/Lt George Gordon Paine (14-1-1916)
Capt. Headley Thomas Wright Quick, (1-1-1918)
2/Lt Bernard Russell (2-10-1915)
2/Lt Frank James Smith, MM (4-2-1918 and 5-7-1918)
2/Lt Frank Allan Strange (30-7-1919)
Capt. Temp Maj., F.J.W. Weiss, (11-1-1917)
Lt Neville West, (24-7-1915)
2/Lt Wilfred Charles Weston, (4-6-1917)
2/Lt Arthur Whitfield, (4-2-1918 and 5-7-1918)
2/Lt Frederick Arthur Wilmott. (1-1-1918)
2/Lt James Barclay Murdoch Young, (17-9-1917)

**Bar to Military Cross**
Lt Harold Thomas Forster, DSO, MC (9-1-1918)
Lt Oswald Spencer Francis, MC (4-2-1918 and 5-7-1918)
2/Lt Archibald Sherbrook Knott, MC (16-9-1918)
Lt Acting Capt., Gerald William Mant MC (9-1-1918).
Lt Temp Capt., Charles Mollet, MC(2-12-1918)
2/Lt Acting Capt., James Barclay Murdoch Young, MC (9-1-1918).

**Distinguished Conduct Medal**
Sgt, 37353 Alfred R Albury, (3-9-1918)
Pte, 12400, Charles William Ashley, (4-3-1918)
Sgt, 201490, Harry L. Aust, (22-10-1917 and 26-1-1918)
Sgt, 7882, Ernest F Burrows, (23-6-1915 and 30-6-1915)
Pte Henry Burrows, (3-6-1916 and 21-6-1916)
Cpl 6259, Arthur Chivers, ( 4-3-1918)
Pte, 7620, John Christopher, (5-8-1915)

Sgt, 8511, Joshua Collins, (9-7-1917)
L/Sgt, 20230, William A. Connor, (22-10-1917 and 26-1-1918)
CSM, 5443, Richard Embling, (14-1-1916 and 11-3-1916)
Pte, 36329, Harry Gates, (4-3-1918)
L/Cpl, 7255, Sidney Grant, (22-10-1917 and 26-1-1918)
Pte, 36565, Charles W. Graves, (4-3-1918)
Sgt, 7901, John A. Gray, (5-8-1915)
L/Sgt, 6136, Thomas Hole, (11-5-1917)
CSM 220288, Arthur Howells, (4-3-1918)
Sgt, Acting CSM, 9132, Frederick J Huggins, (12-3-1919 and 2-12-1919)
Pte, 19216, Richard Ida. (22-10-1917)
Sgt, Acting CQMS, 5830, Frederick Leslie, (11-5-1917)
L/Cpl, 45278, Frederick C. Long, (18-2-1919)
Cpl, 45246, Charles Matthews, (3-6-1919)
Sgt, 7330, Arthur Maybury, (14-1-1916 and 11-3-1916)
Sgt, A/CQMS, 8022, Walter E Oakley, (11-5-1917)
A-Sgt, 6365 Frank E. Parker, (23-6-1915 and 30-6-1915)
Sgt, 7862, Bernard C. Shea, (5-8-1915)
Sgt, 8536, Albert Sturgess, (LG 17-9-1917)
Pte, 8162, Walter J. Taylor, (1-1-1919 and 3-9-1919)
Cpl, Acting Sgt, 9311, Jonah W. Trimmer, (3-6-1916 and 21-6-1916)
Pte, 8431, William Turner, (14-1-1916 and 11-3-1916)
Sgt, Acting CSM, 9332, George G. Turvey, MM, (3-9-1918)
Sgt, 7951, Henry (Harry) Venn, (23-6-1915 and 30-6-1915)

## Bar to DCM

CSM., 220288 Arthur Howells DCM, (LG 4-3-1918)
Sgt, 8536, Albert Sturgess, DCM, (4-3-1918)

## Military Medal

Pte, 37435, Edward Adams, (LG 17-9-1917)
Cpl, 15507, H. Alderman, (23-2-1918)
L/Sgt, 33357, John W Austin, (L G 28-9-1917)
L/Cpl, 16772, Daniel Ayres, (2-11-1917)
Sgt, 9717, Frederick Ballard, (19-2-1917)
Pte, 27442, A.E. Barke (17-9-1917)
L/Sgt, 9264, William Barnes, (19-2-1917)
Cpl 7454, Henry G. Bartlett, (LG 16-7-1918)
Pte, 12784, Francis Belcher (LG 6-1-1917)
L/Cpl, 19935, Arthur Berris, (13-3-1918)
Sgt, 220500, James Bestley, (14-5-1919)
Sgt, 27499, Frederick A. Branch, (16-7-1918)
Pte, 11726, William Breakspear, (14-9-1916)
Pte, 10963, A.T. Brion, (12-11-1917)
Pte, 15735, A. Brown, (6-1-1917)
Cpl 19444, W.H. Butler, (28-1-1918)
L/Cpl, 9502, David Byde, (21-12-1916)
Pte, 10663, J. Chalk, (28-9-1917)
Cpl, 11630, Thomas Charnick, (28-9-1917)
Pte, 8928, Robert Clarke, (6-1-1917)
Pte, 37466, Frederick C. Clipstone, (13-3-1918)
Pte, 11664, Edward Cocks, (13-3-1918)

Sgt, 10224, F. Coffey, (13-3-1918)
Pte, 203141, Raymond N. Coleman, (2-11-1917)
Pte, 10192, Edward E. Coles, (11-2-1919)
L/Cpl, 11670, Frank Collins, (2-11-1917)
L/Sgt, 8129, Joseph Cotterell, (2-11-1917)
Pte,22278, Francis J. Coxhead, (2-11- 1917)
Pte, 9270,Thomas Creffield, (2-11-1917)
Pte, 21985, Frederick Criddle, (2-11-1917)
Pte, 37230, George Curtis, (2-11-1917)
L/Cpl, 11715, Arthur G. Dance, (16-7-1918)
Pte, 8652, Edward Deffee, (2-11-1917)
Pte, 202694,Thomas E. Drinkwater, (3-3-1918)
L/Cpl, 37424, Fred Feaviour, (2-11-1917)
Pte, 37489, Walter L. Finch, (11-5-1917)
Pte, 17367, J.J. Fitzgerald, (2-11-1917)
Pte, 12037, T. Fletcher , (23-2-1918)
Pte, 17644, Albert J. George, (6-1-1917)
Sgt 7469, William A. Gillingham. (16-7-1918)
Pte, 17355, George Graham, (18-6-1917)
Pte, 38544, Henry W. Green, (13-3-1918).
Cpl, 37889, H. Grice, (17-9-1917)
Cpl, 7584, Bert A. Gurney, (10-8-1916)
L/Cpl, 17437, Albert J. Guttridge, (2-11-1917)
L/Cpl, 8003, Frederick C. Haines, (16-7-1918)
Acting Sgt, 7601, Ernest Harris, DCM, (21-9-1916)
Pte, 220481, E.J. Harris, (13-3-1919)
Pte, 17126,William H. Harry, (11-5-1917)
Cpl, 20071, C Hern, (13-3-1918)
Pte, 16929, Ralph Hogg, (21-10-1916)
Pte, 38551, Charles G Holder, (13-9-1918)
Pte, 201499 Ernest Hubbock, (16-7-1918)
Sgt, 8209,Thomas G. Huggins, (13-3-1918)
Pte, 9301, Harry Illsley, (11-11-1916)
Sgt, 8720,A. Johnson, (11-11-1916)
Pte, 37448, Alan Kilsby, (16-7-1918)
Pte, 17575,W.G. King, (2-11-1917)
Pte, 24529, A. Knight, (17-9-1917)
Pte, 11445, R.H. Langley, (1-9-1916)
Pte, 17560, G. Lawson, (23-2-1918)
Pte, 12721, G. London, (16-7-1918)
Pte, 9304, Arthur Long, (2-11-1917)
Pte, 15600, Henry C. Mace, (6-1-1917)
Pte, 19728, John T. Mannoch, (11-5-1917)
Cpl, 45196,Arthur Marsden, (14-5-1919)
L/Cpl, 9703,W.A. Marshall, (11-11-1916)
Cpl, 36399,Thomas Mead, (16-7-1918)
L/Sgt, 9335, E.P. Mitchell, (13-9-1918)
Cpl, 25265, Cornelious Moriarty, (14-5-1919)
L/Cpl, 12879, F. Neale, (2-11-1917)
Pte, 36836, Arthur Neate, (13-9-1918)
Pte, 9551, Albert J. Oakley, (6-1-1917)
Pte, 11995,W.J. Patrick, (16-7-1918)

Pte, 10655, C.H.W. Pearce, (2-11-1917)
Pte, 453483, R.J. Pitt, (14-5-1919)
Cpl, 10733, S. Prior, (11-5-1917)
Pte 8990, T. Ranscombe, (17-9-1917)
Pte, 453884, F Reading, (14-5-1919)
L/Cpl, 9388, William Rice, (11-11-1916)
Pte, 8253, S.A Rose, (21-12-1916)
Pte, 33036, William E. Russell, (13-3-1918)
Pte, 37825, Sydney A. Scott, (13-3-1918)
L/Cpl, 18313, A. Scriven, (11-11-1916)
Sgt, 15723, C. Sheppard, (16-7-1918)
Sgt, Acting CSM, 9802, G Skinner, (13-3-1918)
Sgt, 8454, Frank Smith, (22-1-1917)
Sgt, 7046, Samuel Smith, (11-11-1916)
Sgt, 8174, W. Smith, (11-5-1917)
Pte, 37488, W.P. Smith, (18-6-1917)
Sgt, 11732, Horace J. Stamp, (18-6-1917)
L/Sgt, 8708, Alfred Stark, (11-11-1916)
Cpl, 9610, William E. Stevens, (11-5-1917)
Pte, 9338, Harry Syrett, (11-11-1916)
Cpl, 27520, Arthur Taylor, (21-12-1916)
Pte, 27467, Joseph Tebbs, (13-3-1919)
Pte, 3/9355, Bertie Thorp, (6-1-1917)
Sgt, 9332, George G. Turvey, (13-3-1918)
Pte, 9595, George W. Tutty, (19-9-1916)
Pte, 9423, J. Twomey, (2-11-1917)
(Amended 13-9-1918 Tivomy to Twomey)
C.Q.M. S., 6323, Frederick Vockins, (11-11-1916) (Correction 9-12-1916)
Pte, 12271, Arthur Wale, (11-5-1917)
Pte, 34108, Frank Watling, (16-7-1918)
Pte, Acting Cpl, 19914, James W Wheeler, (17-9-1917)
Pte, 18090, F White, (11-5-1917)
Pte, 8092, W H Wicks, (28-9-1917)
Pte, 42431, Thomas Williams, (13-9-1918)

**Bar to Military Medal**
Pte, 12784, Francis Belcher, MM (17-9-1917)
Sgt, 8209, Thomas G. Huggins, MM, (13-9-1918)
Sgt, 36399. Thomas Mead, MM, (13-3-1919)
Sgt 10633, Frank Powell, MM, (2-11-1917)
Sgt, 9388, William Rice, MM, (6-1-1917)
Sgt, 9332, George G Turvey, MM, (16-7-1918)

**Mentioned in Dispatches**
CSM, 4661, Edward Addicott, (22-6-1915)
Capt. and Adj., Thomas Rupert Aldworth, (22-6-1915)
Capt., Temp Maj. E.M. Allfrey DSO, (7-1-1916 and 25-5-1917)
CSM, 5509, James Annetts, (9-7-1919)
2/Lt Edward Douglas D'Oyley Astley, (21-12-1917)
Lt, Acting Capt., A.A Barrett, MC, (9-7-1919)
Sgt, 12987, H.J. Bevan, (24-5-1918)
CQMS, 7813, W. Booker, (9-7-1919)

Sgt Acting WO Cl. 11, 5383, Bertie Boult,(21-12-1917)

Capt. Alan John Bowles, (15-6-1916)

Lt, Acting Capt., John Archibald Cahill. MC, (21-12-1917)

CSM, 5629, John Campbell, (15-6-1916)

Sgt, 37817, CG Corps, (28-12-1918)

Cpl, 8129, Joseph H. Cotterell, MM, (28-12-1918)

2/Lt, Acting Capt., H A Curtis, (24-5-1918)

CSM, 42210 (5443), Richard Embling, (22-6-1915)

Lt-Col., Temp Brigadier General, E. Feetham, (17-2-1915 and 22-6-1915)

Capt., A.J. Fraser. MC, (7-1-1916 and 4-1-1917)

Lt Harold T. Forster, DSOMC,(15-6-1916, 25-5-1917,21-12-1917 and 28-12-1918)

Sgt, 9213, John T. Garfield, (15-6-1916)

Lt A.D. Gordon, (22-6-1915)

Pte 13917, H.A.W. Goddard, (28-11-1917)

Lt A.D Gordon MC (22-6-1915)

Pte, 17355, George Graham, (25-5-1917)

Capt. Arthur H.H. Hanbury-Sparrow, DSO, MC (25-5-1917 and 21-12-1917)

Capt. Arthur Ellis Fowke Harris, (22-6-1915)

Lt H.H.R. Hilliard, (15-6-1916)

Lt-Col. Arthur Mervyn Holdsworth (4-1-1917)

2/Lt, Acting Capt., Howard Edward Howse, (21-12-1917)

Maj. G.P.S. Hunt, (7-1-1916)

Maj. Thomas Edward Carew Hunt, DSO, (21-12-1917)

Capt., Btn Major and Acting Lt-Col., Auberon

Godfrey Faulkner Isaac, DSO MC

(28-12-1918 and 9-7-1919)

Sgt, 5629, (8724), A Johnson, (15-6-1916).

Sgt, 37815, Arthur J Lawson, (9-7-1919)

Lt J.T. Leslie (23-6-1915)

Hon. Capt. and Q.M., H S Lickman, (22-6-1915 and 1-1-1916).

Maj., Temp Lt-Col. A G MacDonald, DSO (7-1-1916,15-6-1916, 21-12-1917 and 24-5-1918)

Lt, Temp. Capt., Donald Alistaire MacGregor, (22-6-1915)

2/Lt George Gordon Paine, (1-1-1916)

2/Lt J.W. Pavey, (28-12-1918)

Sgt, 8037, Fred Pearce, (1-1-1916)

2/Lt G.A. Pocock, (15-6-1916)

Lt, Acting Capt., H.E.W Prest (25-5-1917)

Pte, 8993, T. Ranscombe, MM (24-5-1918)

L/Cpl, 9388, William Rice, (22-6-1915)

Sgt, 26153, Philip H. Ruffles, (21-12-1917)

2/Lt Bernard Russell, (1-1-1916)

Capt., Maj, Acting Lt-Col. Guy Henry Sawyer, DSO, (1-1-1916, 4-1-1917 and 28-12-1918)

CSM, Acting R.S.M., WO Class 11, 7067, A. Shreeves, (25-5-1917)

CQMS, Acting CSM, 8454 Frank J. Smith, (21-12-1917)

Acting Sgt, 7046, Samuel Smith, (22-6-1915)

Pte, 9168, Albert Taylor (15-6-1916)

Capt., Lt-Col. W.B Thornton, DSO (22-6-1915, 4-1-1917 and 21-12-1917)

2/Lt L. Tremellen., (24-5-1918)

Sgt, Acting CSM, 6323, Frederick Vockins, (1-1-1916)

Lt Neville West, (1-1-1916)

CSM 6524, Wilfred Weston, (22-6-1915)
Pte, 8377, Albert Wheeler (4-1-1917)

**Meritorious Service Medal**
Sgt, 12987, Herbert J Bevan, (3-6-1919)
Sgt, 10487, Frederick Chapman, (17-6-1918)
Sgt, Acting Q.M.S., 9788, Herbert G. Child, (3-6-1919)
R.Q.M.S., 4737, Charles Godfrey, (17-6-1918)
Pte, 8426, Harry Paine, (18-1-1919)
9262, C Platt, (3-6-1919)
Sgt, 26153, Philip H. Ruffels, (17-6-1918)
Pte, 7770, Frederick Smith, (3-6-1919)
Sgt, 6243, Alfred E. Stannard, (18-1-1919)
CQMS, 5565, James Tapper, (3-6-1919)
Sgt, 8118, Charles Taylor, (3-6-1919)
CQMS, 4231, George Westbrook, (3-6-1919)

**Other**
Companion of the Order of St Michael and St George
Maj., Temp. Brigadier General G P S Hunt (14-1-1916)

**Foreign Decorations**
Croix de Guerre (France)
Acting Cpl, 20230, W. Connor, (22-5-1917)
Sgt 8037 F. Pearce, (24-2-1916)
Acting Capt., H.E.W. Prest, (22-5-1917)

The Cross of St George (Russian) – 4th Class
CSM., 5443, R. Embling, (24-8-1915)

The Medal of St George (Russian)
Pte, 9062, H. Fennell, Medal of St George, 3rd Class (24-8-1915)
Pte, 8251, T. Austin, Medal of St George, 4th Class (24-8-1915)

# THE ROLL OF HONOUR

The Roll includes the names of the Officers, Warrant Officers, Non-Commissioned Officers and Private Soldiers who lost their lives while serving with the 2nd Battalion, Royal Berkshire Regiment, from the outbreak of hostilities to the armistice.

It includes some Officers who, while still on the roll of the 2nd Battalion, were killed while serving with other units, such as Brigade or Divisional Headquarters, or were attached to other Regiments.

Disclaimer. This list has been compiled from the printed publications *Soldiers Died in the Great War* and *Officers Died in the Great War*, together with information provided by the Commonwealth War Graves Commission, the National Archive, and Regimental records. While every effort has been made to ensure accuracy and completeness, there are often discrepancies between the sources, and in these cases the most likely interpretation has been made. The authors would like to apologise for any omissions or errors, but cannot accept responsibility for any matters which may arise from them.

| Surname | Forenames | Rank | Number | Date | Residence |
|---|---|---|---|---|---|
| Abinger | Bernard Russell | 2/Lt | | 25-Sep-15 | |
| Abrahams | Edward James | Pte | 42265 | 27-May-18 | |
| Abrahams | Henry | Pte | 220451 | 14-Oct-18 | Limehouse |
| Adair | Charles William | L/Cpl | 8984 | 9-May-15 | |
| Adams | Albert E | Pte | 220095 | 2-Aug-18 | |
| Adams | Alexander Eli | Pte | 35354 | 22-Sep-18 | Faringdon |
| Adams | Charles Joseph | L/Cpl | 220501 | 7-Oct-18 | |
| Adey | Walter Edward | Pte | 12818 | 2-Apr-18 | |
| Adnams | Charles | Pte | 10301 | 4-Mar-17 | Donnington |
| Akers | Ernest | Pte | 8438 | 6-Oct-15 | Rousham |
| Alder | Alfred | A/Cpl | 9360 | 28-Oct-16 | Heathercroft |
| Alderman | William | A/Cpl | 16822 | 10-Apr-17 | Vernham Dean |
| Alexander | William | Pte | 16847 | 14-Mar-16 | |
| Allen | Charles | Pte | 24533 | 28-Oct-16 | Farley Hill |
| Allen | Frederick | Pte | 13023 | 5-Mar-17 | Shinfield |
| Allen | Frederick James | Pte | 7179 | 25-Sep-15 | Wallingford |
| Allen | John James | L/Cpl | 11579 | 1-Dec-17 | Silvertown |
| Allum | George | Pte | 10118 | 25-Sep-15 | |
| Allwood | Harry Baker | Pte | 20082 | 28-Oct-16 | Crookham |
| Anderson | Alexander | Pte | 10608 | 25-Sep-15 | Sandhurst |
| Anderson | David | Pte | 27503 | 5-Mar-17 | |
| Anderson | Frederick John | Pte | 33663 | 16-Aug-17 | Maidenhead |
| Anderson | George Thomas | Pte | 11555 | 25-Sep-15 | |

| | | | | | |
|---|---|---|---|---|---|
| Anderson | John Thomas | Pte | 6198 | 29-Jan-15 | Eaton Socon |
| Andrews | Frank | Pte | 9458 | 15-Mar-15 | Henley on Thames |
| Angell | Ernest | Pte | 8361 | 2-Dec-14 | Calne |
| Anger | Albert Edward | Pte | 9223 | 5-Aug-16 | Hanham Glos |
| Angier | Horace | Pte | 17410 | 1-Jul-16 | Streatham |
| Appleby | William Albert | Pte | 11404 | 16-Aug-17 | |
| Arnold | Bernard | Pte | 35966 | 11-Jun-18 | |
| Asbery | Bertie | Pte | 37441 | 16-Nov-16 | |
| Ashby | Thomas Alfred | Pte | 27452 | 1-Jul-16 | Kilburn |
| Ashley | Albert Victor | Pte | 38488 | 2-Dec-17 | |
| Atkinson | Lionel Edward Mapletoft | Lt | | 9-May-15 | |
| Aubrey | Richard | Pte | 16710 | 6-Mar-17 | Chieveley |
| Austin | Charles Edward | L/Cpl | 9274 | 18-Feb-15 | |
| Ayres | James Albert | Pte | 28103 | 18-Aug-17 | |
| Backway | Arthur Phillip | Pte | 38489 | 2-Dec-17 | Bideford |
| Bacon | William Alfred | Pte | 38490 | 11-Jun-18 | Twyford |
| Bailey | Albert John | Pte | 9523 | 25-Sep-15 | Mortimer |
| Bailey | Alfred Henry | Pte | 11936 | 18-Aug-16 | Camden Town |
| Bailey | Richard George | Pte | 17863 | 30-Aug-16 | North Shields |
| Baker | Alfred Herbert | Pte | 27468 | 1-Jul-16 | |
| Baker | Arthur James | Pte | 23726 | 1-Aug-17 | |
| Baker | Charles Reginald | Pte | 18955 | 16-Aug-17 | |
| Baker | Enoch George | Pte | 5304 | 15-Mar-15 | Bristol |
| Baker | George | Pte | 38668 | 29-Aug-18 | |
| Baker | Robert Henry | A/Cpl | 8510 | 15-Mar-15 | |
| Balchin | Arthur | Pte | 16792 | 8-Oct-15 | Windsor |
| Ball | John Henry | Pte | 35544 | 2-Apr-18 | |
| Ball | John Sidney | Pte | 10780 | 26-Oct-16 | |
| Ballard | Frederick | Sgt | 9717 | 26-Aug-16 | Abingdon |
| Banning | Thomas Henry | Pte | 8114 | 9-Mar-17 | |
| Barefoot | Albert Ernest | Pte | 15796 | 20-Jun-15 | Sandhurst |
| Barham | Henry | Pte | 9958 | 25-Sep-15 | London |
| Barker | Albert | Pte | 50538 | 20-May-18 | Redditch |
| Barker | Harold | Pte | 16997 | 1-Jul-16 | |
| Barker | John William | Pte | 8617 | 15-Mar-15 | Barnes |
| Barlow | Jesse | Pte | 26065 | 2-Dec-17 | Newbury |
| Barnard | Hubert | A/Cpl | 7511 | 4-Mar-17 | Ramsbury |
| Barnes | Arthur Moody | Cpl | 8825 | 25-Sep-15 | |
| Barnes | George | Pte | 9521 | 15-Mar-15 | Battersea |
| Barnes | Wilfred | Pte | 19797 | 23-Apr-18 | |
| Barnes | William | L/Sgt | 9264 | 17-Aug-16 | Fifield |
| Barnett | Henry John | Pte | 18343 | 1-Jul-16 | Abingdon |
| Barnicott | Frank Gunston | Pte | 50540 | 26-Apr-18 | Wallingford |
| Barrett | Edward Walter | Pte | 16338 | 25-Sep-15 | Kintbury |
| Barrett | Horace | Pte | 15793 | 13-May-15 | West Hanney |
| Barrett | William | Pte | 38666 | 2-Apr-18 | |
| Barrow | Thomas | Pte | 220259 | 27-Apr-18 | |
| Bartlett | Albert Victor | Pte | 33374 | 16-Aug-17 | Devonport |
| Baseden | Eric | Lt | | 26-Oct-16 | Caversham |
| Batchelor | Clement John Fell | Pte | 38493 | 25-Apr-18 | Napton |
| Bateman | Leslie | Pte | 27469 | 1-Jul-16 | |
| Bates | Lewis Arthur | Pte | 37589 | 4-Apr-17 | Epsom |
| Batty | Ernest Victor | Pte | 8467 | 15-Mar-15 | Pangbourne |
| Bawden | Herbert John | Pte | 19529 | 16-Aug-17 | |
| Bayley | Norman David | 2/Lt | | 20-Oct-18 | |
| Beacham | William Charles | Pte | 50545 | 27-Apr-18 | Allesley |
| Beales | Edward Ernest | Pte | 10259 | 25-Sep-15 | Spencers Wood |
| Bearley | William Henry | Pte | 42271 | 27-May-18 | Ettington |

| | | | | | |
|---|---|---|---|---|---|
| Beaver | William | Pte | 9707 | 27-Apr-15 | Binfield |
| Beck | Cecil Montague | Pte | 9991 | 1-Jul-16 | Ascott under Wychwood |
| Beck | George | Pte | 15992 | 16-Aug-17 | Didcot |
| Beckley | Arthur Ernest | Pte | 31136 | 27-Aug-18 | |
| Bedford | Seaton Hall | 2/Lt | | 1-Jul-16 | |
| Bedwell | John Herbert | Pte | 17402 | 1-Jul-16 | |
| Beech | Leonard | Pte | 19704 | 1-Jul-16 | Reading |
| Beeson | Alfred James | Sgt | 6482 | 1-Jul-16 | Wokingham |
| Belcher | Basil Henry | 2/Lt | | 1-Jul-16 | |
| Belcher | John | Pte | 22276 | 11-Jun-18 | Faringdon |
| Belcher | Thomas James | L/Cpl | 16001 | 29-Sep-15 | Binfield |
| Bellamy | William | Pte | 5285 | 9-May-15 | |
| Benfield | Lionel | Pte | 29552 | 7-Aug-17 | |
| Benn | George | Pte | 16182 | 28-Oct-16 | London |
| Benn | George | Sgt | 12729 | 2-Apr-18 | |
| Bennett | Albert Edward | Pte | 26869 | 11-Jun-18 | Shinfield |
| Bennett | Stanley William Joseph | Pte | 20065 | 31-Aug-17 | Staines |
| Bentley | Robert | Pte | 20186 | 31-Jul-17 | |
| Benwell | Charles | L/Cpl | 8076 | 4-Mar-17 | Watlington Oxon |
| Bernard | Albert Andrew | L/Cpl | 17966 | 27-Apr-18 | Beaconsfield |
| Berrisford | Arthur | Pte | 37877 | 16-Aug-17 | Lewisham |
| Berry | Edward | A-Sgt | 5410 | 9-May-15 | Fleet |
| Best | Frederick William | Pte | 38499 | 2-Dec-17 | Beaminster |
| Betteridge | Alexander | Pte | 42275 | 27-Apr-18 | Portsmouth |
| Bew | Harry | Pte | 10320 | 25-Sep-15 | Epsom |
| Bickerstaff | Bertram Percy | Pte | 38299 | 7-May-18 | Farnborough Hants |
| Biddle | Samuel Arthur | Pte | 11861 | 1-Jul-16 | Smethwick |
| Biggs | Herbert Frederick | Pte | 15386 | 18-Feb-18 | Clewer |
| Bill | Harry William | Pte | 16889 | 26-Sep-18 | |
| Binfield | Albert Edward | Cpl | 19672 | 16-Aug-17 | Camberley |
| Birbeck | Harold Joseph | Pte | 50540 | 9-Jun-18 | |
| Birchall | William Edmund | Pte | 10652 | 1-Jul-16 | |
| Bircham | Herbert | Pte | 37442 | 2-Mar-17 | Brampton |
| Bird | William George | Pte | 15759 | 2-Dec-17 | Oxford |
| Birmingham | Clement | Pte | 7461 | 15-Mar-15 | |
| Bishop | Charles William | Pte | 17675 | 4-Mar-17 | Hackney |
| Bishop | James Edmund | A/Cpl | 8715 | 15-Aug-15 | Edmonton |
| Bishop | Stanley | Pte | 16648 | 25-Sep-15 | Crookham Heath |
| Bishop | Walter | Pte | 14474 | 2-Dec-17 | Neath |
| Bitmead | Albert Arthur | Pte | 9631 | 25-Sep-15 | Islington |
| Bitten | Daniel | L/Cpl | 27457 | 28-Oct-16 | Cowling |
| Black | John | Pte | 8430 | 14-Jan-15 | Marlborough |
| Blackburn | John | Pte | 7287 | 2-Jun-15 | Southwark |
| Blackburn | Robert Henry | Pte | 9552 | 9-Apr-15 | Chiswick |
| Blake | Henry | Pte | 15835 | 1-Jul-16 | Faringdon |
| Bland | Charles Henry | Pte | 16936 | 1-Jul-16 | |
| Blatch | James | Pte | 8425 | 25-Sep-15 | Woodspeen |
| Blay | Ernest | Pte | 18987 | 10-Nov-16 | Bracknell |
| Blissett | Harry John | Pte | 11466 | 25-Sep-15 | |
| Bloomfield | Albert Victor | L/Cpl | 200924 | 16-Aug-17 | |
| Bloxham | Edward | Pte | 38507 | 11-Jun-18 | Southam Warks |
| Blundy | Leslie | Pte | 19724 | 30-Oct-16 | Chieveley |
| Board | Walter | Pte | 33364 | 23-Feb-17 | |
| Boden | Arthur James | Sgt | 12484 | 28-Oct-16 | |
| Bodie | James Robert | Pte | 9565 | 9-May-15 | Deptford |
| Boldini | William | Pte | 37948 | 27-Apr-18 | Plumstead |

| Bolton | Charles | Pte | 10230 | 9-May-15 | |
| Bolton | Oliver | Pte | 17571 | 28-Oct-16 | Marcham |
| Bolton | Victor Alma | Pte | 9007 | 25-Sep-15 | Marcham |
| Bone | Edmund George | Cpl | 8416 | 25-Sep-15 | Shaldon |
| Bonner | Bernard Henry | Pte | 10135 | 2-Apr-18 | Warborough |
| Bosher | Robert | Pte | 32935 | 7-Jul-18 | North Hagbourne |
| Bosley | William | Pte | 15800 | 2-Apr-18 | Didcot |
| Boucher | Harry | Pte | 42274 | 11-Jun-18 | |
| Boult | Bertie | Sgt | 5383 | 11-Jun-18 | Bracknell |
| Bourchier | Arthur George | 2/Lt | | 9-May-15 | |
| Bourne | Charles Alfred | Pte | 5990 | 25-Sep-15 | Oxford |
| Bowden | Frederick | Pte | 21986 | 31-Jul-17 | |
| Bowler | Francis Henry | Sgt | 6513 | 5-Jan-15 | |
| Bowler | Thomas | Pte | 15761 | 20-Oct-16 | Postcombe Oxon |
| Bowles | Alan John | Capt. | | 10-Apr-16 | Sittingbourne |
| Bowles | Harry | Pte | 9424 | 31-Jul-17 | |
| Bowley | Edward Charles | Pte | 9646 | 28-Oct-16 | Vernham |
| Bowyer | George | Pte | 19933 | 16-Jan-18 | Warfield |
| Bowyer | William Reginald | Pte | 203446 | 2-Apr-18 | |
| Boxall | Alfred | Pte | 9857 | 15-Mar-15 | |
| Boxell | James | Pte | 9871 | 9-May-15 | Yiewsley |
| Boyd | John | Pte | 37200 | 20-Mar-17 | |
| Boyd | William Daniel | Pte | 17920 | 2-Apr-18 | |
| Boyes | Frank Harold | Pte | 16937 | 1-Jul-16 | |
| Boyles | William Henry | Pte | 15668 | 7-Apr-15 | Donnington |
| Boyling | William John | Pte | 42277 | 27-Apr-18 | |
| Bracey | Richard Newton | Pte | 9425 | 1-May-15 | Winchcombe |
| Brackley | Charles | Sgt | 5144 | 15-Mar-15 | Wokingham |
| Bradford | Horace | Sgt | 45483 | 7-Oct-18 | Lutterworth |
| Bradley | Arthur Alfred | L/Cpl | 9219 | 25-Sep-15 | Twickenham |
| Bradley | William John | L/Cpl | 19948 | 1-Aug-17 | Wantage |
| Bradshaw | Reuben | Pte | 201123 | 19-Aug-17 | Wallingford |
| Bramley | Thomas | Pte | 11526 | 4-Mar-17 | |
| Branch | Frederick Albert | Sgt | 27499 | 27-Apr-18 | Raydon |
| Brandon | George | Pte | 12575 | 11-Jun-18 | |
| Branston | William | Pte | 50687 | 10-Oct-18 | |
| Brant | Charles | Pte | 8402 | 23-Oct-16 | |
| Brant | Charles Joshua | Pte | 16837 | 1-Jul-16 | Crowthorne |
| Breadman | Arthur | Pte | 34063 | 16-Aug-17 | Sunninghill |
| Breadmore | Percy George | Pte | 37641 | 28-Apr-17 | Wyke Hill |
| Breakspear | William | Pte | 11726 | 1-May-18 | West Hannay |
| Brean | Christopher George | Pte | 10025 | 10-Mar-15 | |
| Brent | Edward Henry Nelson | Pte | 37235 | 16-Aug-17 | |
| Brett | Frederick | Pte | 202494 | 27-Apr-18 | Hitcham |
| Brettell | Oliver | Sgt | 8371 | 9-May-15 | Oxford |
| Brewer | William George | Pte | 15703 | 1-Jul-16 | Upton |
| Bridge | Donald Gerald Clive | 2/Lt | | 23-May-15 | |
| Bristow | William | Pte | 21920 | 4-Apr-17 | |
| Britnell | Albert | Pte | 10105 | 25-Sep-15 | High Wycombe |
| Britton | Charles Eugene | Pte | 42286 | 11-Jun-18 | |
| Britton | Louis Webb | Pte | 43568 | 27-May-18 | |
| Broad | George Frederick | Pte | 19026 | 1-Aug-17 | |
| Brooker | Thomas | Pte | 9651 | 12-Jan-15 | Notting Hill |
| Brown | Charles | Pte | 202696 | 27-May-18 | |
| Brown | Edward Ernest | Pte | 38504 | 18-Nov-17 | |

| Brown | Francis | Pte | 220049 | 16-Aug-17 | Chalvey |
|---|---|---|---|---|---|
| Brown | Francis Jesse | Pte | 16759 | 19-Jun-15 | |
| Brown | George Charles | Pte | 24540 | 28-Oct-16 | |
| Brown | Harry | Pte | 20055 | 2-Jul-16 | |
| Brown | John George | Pte | 9809 | 13-Mar-15 | Stanford in the Vale |
| Brown | Leonard Wilfred | Cpl | 15754 | 4-Mar-17 | Barfield |
| Browning | Albert Anthony | Pte | 21934 | 28-Oct-16 | Thatcham |
| Bryant | Thomas Arthur | Pte | 9813 | 16-Nov-14 | Eton Wick |
| Buckingham | Sydney Walter | A/Cpl | 8728 | 1-Jul-16 | Maida Vale |
| Buckland | Francis | Pte | 10065 | 9-May-15 | |
| Budd | Ernest | Pte | 15515 | 17-May-15 | Swallowfield |
| Bulkeley | Thomas John | Pte | 11442 | 4-Mar-17 | Balham |
| Bull | Charles Edward Henry | Sgt | 8936 | 1-Jul-16 | Deptford |
| Bull | Sidney Frank | Pte | 8404 | 1-Jul-16 | Oxford |
| Bullock | James | Pte | 8616 | 9-May-15 | Devizes |
| Bullock | Rowland | Pte | 8959 | 11-Mar-15 | Oxford |
| Bunce | Arthur John | Cpl | 8072 | 31-Oct-18 | |
| Bunce | George | Pte | 9303 | 27-Jan-15 | Bagshot |
| Bunce | Henry | Pte | 10443 | 9-May-15 | |
| Burbridge | George | Cpl | 18302 | 10-Aug-17 | Christchurch |
| Burchell | Francis William | Pte | 38506 | 21-Sep-18 | Bleadon |
| Burchell | William | Pte | 17691 | 1-Jul-16 | Islington |
| Burgess | Stanley | Cpl | 17172 | 19-Aug-17 | Wargrave |
| Burke | John | L/Cpl | 17746 | 1-Jul-16 | |
| Burne | Thomas Oldbury | 2/Lt | | 25-Mar-18 | |
| Burrett | Albert Ernest | Pte | 8563 | 18-Dec-18 | Bermondsey |
| Burrett | Charles William | Pte | 9875 | 10-Mar-15 | Chiswick |
| Burrow | William | Sgt | 7385 | 12-Jan-15 | |
| Burrows | Ernest Frederick | CSM | 7882 | 16-Aug-17 | Farnham Common |
| Burt | Henry | Pte | 31408 | 2-Dec-17 | |
| Burton | Herbert William | Pte | 17154 | 4-Mar-17 | |
| Burton | Walter Albert | Pte | 28427 | 4-Mar-17 | |
| Burton | William Arthur | Pte | 15864 | 25-Sep-15 | Kintbury |
| Busby | John Henry | A/Sgt | 8456 | 9-May-15 | Kidlington |
| Bushnell | Henry George | L/Cpl | 9460 | 15-Mar-15 | Mortimer |
| Butcher | Arthur Algernon Lionel Hastings | 2/Lt | | 4-Mar-17 | |
| Butcher | John William | Pte | 27449 | 24-Sep-15 | Dover |
| Butler | Alfred | Pte | 8180 | 20-Sep-18 | Chertsey |
| Butler | Alfred | Pte | 31176 | 16-Aug-17 | Crowthorne |
| Butler | Frederick George | Pte | 31180 | 4-May-18 | |
| Butler | Harry | L/Sgt | 8951 | 22-Jun-16 | Windsor |
| Butler | Joseph Walter | Pte | 19929 | 10-Aug-17 | Easton |
| Butler | William | Pte | 33432 | 10-Aug-17 | Clewer |
| Butler | William Henry | Cpl | 19444 | 2-Apr-18 | |
| Buttle | Robert James | Pte | 17676 | 1-Jul-16 | London |
| Buxcey | Frederick | Cpl | 9733 | 25-Sep-15 | Drayton |
| Buxcey | Reginald | Pte | 10080 | 25-Sep-15 | Wallingford |
| Byde | David | L/Cpl | 9302 | 14-Nov-16 | Binfield |
| Bye | Walter Frank | Pte | 28722 | 15-Sep-18 | |
| Cahill | John Archibald | Capt. | | 16-Aug-17 | |
| Camfield | Charles Edwin | Pte | 37208 | 28-Oct-16 | |
| Campbell | John | RSM | 5929 | 15-Oct-17 | Southsea |
| Campbell | John | L/Cpl | 38220 | 27-Mar-18 | Ilford |
| Canning | Edward Charles | Pte | 9631 | 9-May-15 | |
| Cannon | Frederick Joseph | Pte | 24924 | 28-Oct-16 | |
| Carpenter | Frederick | Pte | 17580 | 13-Jul-16 | |

| Carpenter | James | Pte | 7029 | 14-Mar-15 | Watford |
| Carruthers | Alfred Edward | Pte | 6959 | 31-May-18 | Clerkenwell |
| Carswell | Malcolm Shanks | Lieut | | 17-Sep-17 | |
| Carter | Alfred William | Pte | 10238 | 31-Dec-15 | Abingdon |
| Carter | Charles | Pte | 9609 | 30-Nov-14 | |
| Carter | Francis Alfred | Pte | 9440 | 12-Sep-15 | Bucklebury |
| Carter | Frederick James | L/Cpl | 21873 | 24-Mar-18 | |
| Carter | Geoffrey Herbert | Lieut | | 12-Nov-16 | |
| Carter | William | Pte | 8439 | 9-May-15 | Newbury |
| Cartwright | Lewis Reginald | Pte | 42290 | 11-Jun-18 | Denham |
| Cashmore | John Arthur | Pte | 42279 | 6-Nov-18 | |
| Casson | James | Pte | 15698 | 9-May-15 | Lozells Warks |
| Catchpole | Frederick | Pte | 8751 | 18-Nov-18 | |
| Chadwick | William Allison | Pte | 27511 | 1-Jul-16 | |
| Challenor | Norman Bowen | Capt. | | 31-Jul-15 | |
| Challis | Ernest | Pte | 16339 | 23-Jul-16 | |
| Challis | Herbert | Pte | 50566 | 27-May-18 | |
| Chamberlain | Maurice David | Pte | 6976 | 25-Sep-15 | Bracknell |
| Chance | William George | L/Cpl | 10060 | 28-Oct-16 | Pimlico |
| Chandler | Frederick James | Pte | 10900 | 16-Aug-17 | |
| Chandler | Frederick William | Cpl | 8446 | 14-Mar-15 | |
| Chapman | Edward | A/Cpl | 37467 | 2-Apr-18 | |
| Charlton | Bert | Pte | 22148 | 4-Apr-17 | Stirchley |
| Charney | Thomas | Cpl | 11630 | 16-Aug-17 | Hackney |
| Chatfield | John | Pte | 18364 | 1-Jul-16 | Winshill |
| Cherrill | Harry | Pte | 5727 | 22-Mar-15 | Wallingford |
| Cheshire | Ralph William | Pte | 38510 | 14-May-18 | |
| Chesterton | Henry John | Pte | 10190 | 24-Jan-15 | Poplar |
| Childs | Charles Henry | Sgt | 7873 | 2-Dec-17 | North Holmwood |
| Chiles | William Frank | Pte | 9586 | 9-May-15 | Henley on Thames |
| Chivers | Arthur | Cpl | 6259 | 2-Apr-18 | Hove |
| Church | Walter George | Pte | 8642 | 1-Jul-16 | Maidenhead |
| Churchyard | John | Cpl | 227059 | 27-Apr-18 | |
| Clack | Robert Sidney | Pte | 39076 | 14-Oct-18 | Fareham |
| Clark | Charles Albert | Pte | 9113 | 31-Jul-17 | |
| Clark | Frederick William | Pte | 33350 | 2-Apr-18 | |
| Clark | William James | Pte | 17433 | 30-Sep-16 | Camberwell |
| Clarke | Albert Edward | Sgt | 12588 | 2-Apr-18 | |
| Clarke | Bertie James | Pte | 11054 | 11-Nov-16 | Boxford |
| Clarke | George | Pte | 18323 | 25-Sep-15 | Rugby |
| Clarke | George | Pte | 37447 | 29-Mar-17 | Farcet Hunts |
| Clarke | Maurice Edward | Pte | 38512 | 19-Nov-17 | |
| Clarke | Percy John | Pte | 37470 | 15-Mar-17 | Pattishall |
| Clarke | William | Pte | 16824 | 16-Oct-15 | Bucklebury |
| Claydon | John | Pte | 15736 | 9-May-15 | Haverhill |
| Clayton | George Edward | Pte | 15700 | 9-May-15 | |
| Clayton | Walter William | Pte | 35507 | 27-Apr-18 | |
| Cleeton | Ernest | Pte | 8993 | 14-Mar-15 | Ascot |
| Clements | Herbert George | Pte | 17356 | 1-Jul-16 | |
| Clements | Wilfred James | Pte | 19922 | 1-Aug-17 | |
| Clifton | William Henry | Pte | 9221 | 14-Mar-15 | Upper Brailes Warks |
| Clilverd | Edwin Albert | Pte | 8789 | 9-May-15 | Kensington |
| Coates | Frederick | Pte | 27301 | 2-Dec-17 | |
| Cobbett | Charles | Pte | 8196 | 14-Mar-15 | Brighton |
| Coe | George William Charles | Pte | 16930 | 7-Mar-16 | Camberley |
| Coggs | Henry John | Pte | 21800 | 2-Dec-17 | |

| | | | | | |
|---|---|---|---|---|---|
| Cole | Edward Henry | Pte | 11492 | 21-Jun-15 | Holloway |
| Coleman | John | Pte | 202141 | 16-Aug-17 | Grampound |
| Coleman | Raymond Noel | Pte | 203141 | 16-Aug-17 | Tewkesbury |
| Coles | Walter | Pte | 7962 | 1-Jul-16 | Watlington |
| Colhoun | Alick | Pte | 7573 | 9-May-15 | |
| Collett | John | Pte | 6017 | 9-May-15 | Maidenhead |
| Collins | Frank | L/Cpl | 11670 | 2-Dec-17 | Sandhurst |
| Collins | Frederick | Cpl | 9606 | 2-Apr-18 | Charlton |
| Collins | George | Pte | 11351 | 9-May-15 | Sandhurst |
| Collins | Joshua | Sgt | 8511 | 22-Aug-17 | Oxford |
| Collis | Charles John | Pte | 7215 | 25-Sep-15 | Lee |
| Collyer | Edward | Pte | 200178 | 16-Aug-17 | Chelmsford |
| Colyer | Edward Thomas Joseph | Cpl | 6262 | 1-Aug-17 | Leytonstone |
| Comley | William | Pte | 15855 | 1-Jul-16 | Marlow |
| Connell | Fred | Pte | 27480 | 2-Apr-18 | Shepherds Bush |
| Connell | James | Pte | 15712 | 10-Apr-16 | Westminster |
| Connor | William Albert | A/Sgt | 20230 | 15-Oct-17 | Tottenham |
| Conway | Louis Alfred | Pte | 20229 | 28-Jul-18 | Bristol |
| Cook | Albert | Pte | 21901 | 21-Sep-16 | Cholsey |
| Cook | Albert | Sgt | 8895 | 29-May-17 | Hungerford |
| Cook | Charles | Pte | 9623 | 25-Sep-15 | East Dulwich |
| Cook | Charles Henry | Pte | 42303 | 3-Jun-18 | |
| Cook | Ernest John | Pte | 15797 | 22-Jul-16 | Reading |
| Cook | Frederick Joseph | Pte | 44704 | 15-Sep-18 | |
| Cook | George Ernest | Pte | 9503 | 25-Sep-15 | Dockhead Surrey |
| Cook | James | Pte | 10111 | 1-Jul-16 | Wantage |
| Cook | John | Pte | 12249 | 27-May-18 | |
| Cooling | George John | A/Sgt | 8388 | 9-May-15 | |
| Cooper | Alfred James | Pte | 42304 | 27-May-18 | Edgbaston |
| Cooper | Ernest Edward | Pte | 22550 | 16-Aug-17 | |
| Cooper | Frank Robert | Pte | 44874 | 29-May-18 | |
| Cooper | John | Pte | 10070 | 25-Sep-15 | Ecchinswell |
| Cooper | Sidney | Pte | 10098 | 25-Sep-15 | Oxford |
| Cooper | Sidney | Pte | 15894 | 1-Jul-16 | |
| Cooper | William Edward | A/Sgt | 43581 | 27-May-18 | West Hampstead |
| Cordy | Victor Joseph | Pte | 21841 | 1-Aug-17 | |
| Cornick | Frederick George | Cpl | 18960 | 31-Jul-17 | Edgbaston |
| Cornish | Alfred Edward | Pte | 12741 | 25-Feb-18 | Highgate |
| Cottle | Frederick | Pte | 41544 | 22-Mar-18 | Lambeth |
| Cottrell | Alexander Joseph | Pte | 9278 | 13-Jul-15 | Englefield Green |
| Couldrey | Walter | Pte | 8767 | 25-Sep-15 | Oxford |
| Couling | Alfred Thomas | Pte | 26948 | 9-Apr-18 | |
| Coulson | Frank | Pte | 37421 | 15-Nov-16 | |
| Coutts | Alexander | Pte | 44865 | 27-May-18 | |
| Coveney | William | Pte | 10014 | 1-Oct-15 | Walworth |
| Cowdrey | Walter | Pte | 201966 | 15-Oct-18 | |
| Cox | Albert | Pte | 9472 | 25-Sep-15 | Farnham |
| Cox | Edwin Walter | Pte | 24656 | 6-Feb-17 | Wargrave |
| Cox | Frederick | Pte | 10231 | 25-Sep-15 | Mortimer |
| Cox | John George | Cpl | 8766 | 1-Jul-16 | |
| Cox | Martin Wilfred | Pte | 11562 | 12-May-15 | East Ham |
| Cox | Thomas | Pte | 17860 | 9-Mar-17 | London |
| Cox | William Charles | Pte | 8474 | 20-May-15 | Bucklebury |
| Crawford | Frederick Arthur | Pte | 38081 | 16-Aug-17 | Old Headington |
| Crawshaw | Thomas Henry | Pte | 37879 | 31-Jul-17 | |
| Crease | Alfred | Pte | 13693 | 3-Jul-16 | Bethnal Green |
| Cresswell | Arthur | Pte | 11685 | 25-Sep-15 | Basildon Berks |
| Cripps | Job | A/Cpl | 9112 | 14-Mar-15 | Bradfield |

| | | | | | |
|---|---|---|---|---|---|
| Crocker | George Ernest | Pte | 34058 | 16-Aug-17 | Inkpen |
| Crockford | Frederick Easter | Pte | 11840 | 25-Sep-15 | Plumstead |
| Crome | Robert Charles | Pte | 11489 | 9-May-15 | London |
| Crook | Edward | Pte | 8422 | 17-Jun-15 | |
| Crook | Sidney George | L/Cpl | 9419 | 24-Aug-16 | |
| Cross | Arthur Edwin | Cpl | 37266 | 16-Aug-17 | |
| Cross | Edward | Pte | 9002 | 16-Aug-17 | |
| Cross | George | Pte | 37636 | 4-Mar-17 | |
| Crosswell | Albert Ernest | Pte | 10154 | 12-Feb-16 | |
| Crowle | Edward John | Pte | 43634 | 27-Apr-18 | |
| Croxford | Leonard Henry | Pte | 42311 | 25-Apr-18 | |
| Crutchfield | Joseph | Drummer | 8287 | 23-Mar-15 | Finchampstead |
| Culley | George Thomas | Pte | 50576 | 11-Jun-18 | Westbury on Trym |
| Cunliffe | Robert Ellis | 2/Lt | | 9-May-15 | |
| Curley | Thomas | Pte | 27448 | 1-Jul-16 | |
| Curtis | Albert James | Pte | 8461 | 14-Mar-15 | |
| Curtis | Thomas | Pte | 5798 | 1-Jul-16 | Maidenhead |
| Dagley | Alfred James | Pte | 8969 | 19-Nov-15 | Battersea |
| Dallimore | Charles Edward | Pte | 42312 | 27-Apr-18 | Blackwater Hants |
| Dance | John Henry | Sgt | 10225 | 5-Mar-17 | Southall |
| Dando | Ernest James | Pte | 45152 | 22-Sep-18 | |
| Darch | Frederick | Pte | 21905 | 14-Sep-16 | |
| Darke | Ernest Victor | Pte | 37275 | 6-Aug-17 | Maidenhead |
| Dashwood | Percy William | Pte | 38519 | 18-Nov-17 | Lake |
| Davies | Cecil Lloyd | 2/Lt | | 25-Nov-16 | |
| Davies | Ernest Charles | L/Cpl | 8508 | 5-Dec-16 | Kumerhatti India |
| Davies | Harry | 2/Lt | | 10-Apr-16 | Ealing |
| Davies | Thomas Charles | Pte | 16297 | 10-Jun-15 | |
| Davis | Edward Stanley | Pte | 37297 | 4-Apr-17 | Maidenhead |
| Davis | Harry | Pte | 44864 | 27-May-18 | |
| Davis | Henry George | Pte | 11919 | 13-Mar-15 | |
| Davis | John | Pte | 6196 | 13-Sep-15 | Pewsey |
| Davis | John Thomas | L/Cpl | 10424 | 16-Aug-17 | South Ealing |
| Davis | Maurice James | Pte | 201763 | 16-Aug-17 | |
| Davis | Reginald | Pte | 17869 | 2-Apr-18 | Faringdon |
| Davy | Albert | L/Cpl | 203970 | 18-Feb-18 | Abingdon |
| Day | Albert William George | Pte | 18054 | 28-Oct-16 | Woolton Hill |
| Day | Arthur | Pte | 17182 | 1-Jul-16 | |
| Day | Leonard Albert | Pte | 20218 | 5-Mar-17 | |
| Day | Maurice | 2/Lt | | 9-May-15 | |
| Day | Percy James | Pte | 21988 | 4-Apr-17 | Bedminster |
| Day | William | Pte | 9401 | 9-May-15 | Bracknell |
| Deacon | Charles Mark | Pte | 38520 | 29-Aug-18 | |
| Dearlove | Frederick | Pte | 16654 | 25-Sep-15 | Steventon |
| Dell | George | Pte | 8829 | 13-Jan-15 | Langley |
| Denny | William Edwin | Pte | 220058 | 16-Aug-17 | |
| Denton | Arthur Edward | L/Cpl | 9848 | 1-Jul-16 | Wantage |
| Depear | Henry John | Pte | 37324 | 16-Aug-17 | |
| Derrick | Herbert | Pte | 37597 | 5-Mar-17 | |
| Devereux | Joseph | Pte | 37648 | 22-Mar-17 | Sandhurst Glos |
| Dew | George Edward | Pte | 7685 | 25-Sep-15 | Hungerford |
| Dicker | Charlie | Pte | 18732 | 2-Dec-17 | Faringdon |
| Dickson | George | Cpl | 11452 | 4-Mar-17 | Battersea |
| Dight | Arthur William | Pte | 11939 | 15-Nov-16 | Holloway |
| Dixon | Hugh Robert | Pte | 18962 | 18-Aug-17 | Didcot |
| Dodd | Albert | Pte | 8014 | 1-Jul-16 | Wallingford |
| Doe | Arthur | Cpl | 7924 | 1-Jan-15 | Wokingham |

| | | | | | |
|---|---|---|---|---|---|
| Dollin | Harold John | Pte | 38521 | 2-Dec-17 | |
| Dolphin | Walter John | Pte | 50582 | 11-Aug-18 | |
| Dore | Harold Young | Pte | 23935 | 28-Oct-16 | |
| Dormer | Joseph | Pte | 17423 | 30-Jan-16 | Bethnal Green |
| Dowling | Edward Seymour | Pte | 33314 | 27-Apr-18 | |
| Downes | Harry Albert | Pte | 27296 | 4-Apr-17 | |
| Dowse | William George | Pte | 9284 | 11-Nov-16 | |
| Drew | Wilfred James | Pte | 50583 | 26-Aug-18 | |
| Drewett | William | Pte | 16674 | 17-Nov-15 | Fosbury |
| Drinkwater | Horace | Pte | 18793 | 27-Apr-18 | Charlbury Oxon |
| Druitt | Joseph | 2/Lt | | 9-May-15 | |
| Duckles | William George | L/Cpl | 19017 | 16-Aug-17 | Devizes |
| Dudley | Herbert Charles | Pte | 45352 | 21-Sep-18 | Newport Pagnell |
| Duffield | Ernest | Pte | 8962 | 15-Mar-15 | Kentish Town |
| Dummer | Frederick | Pte | 37222 | 28-Oct-16 | |
| Dunbar | Alexander Bremmer | Pte | 46566 | 16-Oct-18 | |
| Dunford | Charles Churchill | L/Cpl | 16787 | 11-Jun-18 | Windsor |
| Dunley | Leonard | Pte | 37334 | 1-Nov-16 | London |
| Durbin | Walter John | L/Cpl | 33349 | 4-Mar-17 | Bedminster |
| Dyke | Walter Harry | Pte | 38524 | 5-Dec-17 | Parkstone |
| Eades | Frederick | Pte | 37326 | 9-Nov-16 | Dedworth |
| Eager | John Charles | Pte | 18632 | 1-Jul-16 | Tottenham |
| Eamer | Harry | Pte | 8532 | 1-Jul-16 | Twyford |
| Easdon | Herbert | Pte | 9220 | 25-Sep-15 | High Wycombe |
| Eaton | Frederick Joseph | Pte | 22459 | 27-Apr-18 | |
| Edmonds | Charles | A/Cpl | 16548 | 2-Apr-18 | |
| Edmonds | John James | Pte | 17279 | 1-Aug-17 | Walworth |
| Edmunds | Harry | Pte | 45261 | 29-Aug-18 | Newport Pagnell |
| Edwards | Edward | Pte | 9055 | 25-Sep-15 | Kintbury |
| Edwards | Edward | Pte | 15405 | 4-Mar-17 | Briton Ferry |
| Edwards | Frederick | L/Cpl | 12734 | 3-Mar-17 | Camden Town |
| Edwards | James | L/Sgt | 8132 | 18-Feb-15 | |
| Edwards | Owen Lawrence | Pte | 9093 | 1-Jul-16 | Marlow |
| Edwards | Sidney James | Pte | 9476 | 13-Mar-15 | Tilehurst |
| Eely | Charles | Pte | 9978 | 29-May-15 | Sydenham |
| Eldred | Edward | L/Cpl | 10525 | 25-Sep-15 | Marlow |
| Eley | Ernest | Pte | 35875 | 27-Apr-18 | |
| Ellins | James | Pte | 32831 | 26-Apr-18 | |
| Elliott | Albert Edward | Pte | 16171 | 27-Apr-18 | |
| Ellis | Alfred Herbert | Pte | 41709 | 1-May-18 | |
| Ellis | Frederick Jesse Harold | L/Cpl | 9783 | 25-Sep-16 | Camberley |
| Ellison | James | Pte | 15760 | 9-May-15 | Cippenham Green |
| Eltham | Ernest | L/Sgt | 5694 | 25-Sep-15 | Oxford |
| Emmens | Ernest George | Pte | 41537 | 27-May-18 | Kingswood Common |
| Englefield | Frederick Arthur Edward | Pte | 9982 | 18-Feb-15 | |
| Englefield | William John | Pte | 9806 | 25-Sep-15 | Eastney Hants |
| Etoe | George William | L/Cpl | 37674 | 19-Oct-17 | |
| Evans | Frederick Victor | L/Cpl | 15692 | 16-Nov-15 | Windsor |
| Evans | James | L/Sgt | 6005 | 1-Jul-16 | Stoke Poges |
| Evans | John William | L/Cpl | 9355 | 3-Jan-15 | Maidenhead |
| Eveleigh | Oliver James | A/Cpl | 22153 | 2-Apr-18 | |
| Everett | Frederick William | L/Cpl | 26333 | 18-Sep-17 | |
| Everitt | Douglas | Pte | 220061 | 9-Sep-17 | |
| Fairbrother | Frank Robert | Pte | 19939 | 1-Jul-16 | Cothill |
| Fairminer | Edward James | Sgt | 16615 | 25-Sep-15 | Farnham |

| Farley | Harry | Pte | 31324 | 27-Apr-18 | |
| Farnorth | William | Pte | 8122 | 25-Sep-15 | Nottingham |
| Farr | Gilbert Walter | L/Sgt | 7693 | 5-Mar-17 | Leicester |
| Farwell | Christopher John | Pte | 22122 | 5-Mar-17 | Bristol |
| Faulkner | William Frederick | L/Cpl | 8413 | 27-May-15 | Oxford |
| Feasey | Percy Walter | Pte | 36305 | 16-Aug-17 | Rickmansworth |
| Feeney | John | Cpl | 8546 | 20-Nov-15 | Bethnal Green |
| Fellows | Arthur | Pte | 27510 | 31-Jul-17 | |
| Feltham | Arthur Charles | Pte | 10163 | 15-Mar-15 | Battersea |
| Fennell | Albert | Pte | 26813 | 14-Nov-16 | |
| Fennell | Harold | Pte | 23769 | 11-Nov-17 | Windsor |
| Ferris | Charles Edward | Pte | 44872 | 27-Apr-18 | |
| Fidler | Harry Alfred | Pte | 9287 | 9-May-15 | Eton |
| Fielder | William | Pte | 28824 | 2-Apr-18 | Wokingham |
| Finch | Frank Marshall | 2/Lt | | 22-Sep-18 | |
| Finch | Herbert Marshall | Lt Col | | 9-May-15 | |
| Finchard | Allen Daniel | L/Cpl | 9754 | 1-Jul-16 | London |
| Finnes | William | L/Cpl | 5817 | 11-Mar-15 | |
| Fish | George | Pte | 24536 | 25-Oct-16 | Bracknell |
| Fisher | Charles | Pte | 6426 | 10-Mar-15 | Rotherhythe |
| Fisher | Ernest Edward | Pte | 38531 | 2-Dec-17 | Poole |
| Fitzgerald | Norman | Pte | 38214 | 2-Dec-17 | |
| Flack | Walter James | Pte | 200450 | 16-Aug-17 | Cobham |
| Fletcher | Thomas Alfred | Pte | 12037 | 2-Mar-18 | Islington |
| Fletcher | William Henry | Pte | 11949 | 4-Mar-17 | |
| Ford | Reginald William | Pte | 37338 | 12-Nov-16 | High Wycombe |
| Foren | Harry Michael | Pte | 38259 | 2-Apr-18 | Shepherds Bush |
| Foster | Frederick | Pte | 6565 | 6-Oct-16 | Notting Hill |
| Foster | William | L/Cpl | 11822 | 9-May-15 | Pebworth |
| Franklin | Thomas George | Pte | 9501 | 8-Jun-15 | Hounslow |
| Franklin | William | Pte | 9028 | 15-Dec-17 | |
| Frankum | George | A/Sgt | 8969 | 25-Sep-15 | |
| Freeman | Eli | Pte | 37443 | 15-Nov-16 | |
| French | Albert Edward | L/Cpl | 9769 | 27-Apr-15 | Hungerford |
| French | John | Pte | 5531 | 25-Sep-15 | Newbury |
| Frost | Frederick Thomas | Pte | 202213 | 26-Oct-17 | |
| Frost | Joseph | Pte | 201111 | 27-May-18 | Chelmsford |
| Fry | Leonard Alfred | Cpl | 37265 | 28-Oct-16 | |
| Fry | Thomas Henry | Pte | 50592 | 20-Apr-18 | Charlton Kings |
| Fryer | Francis William | L/Cpl | 7341 | 17-Jan-15 | Deptford |
| Fryer | George | Pte | 9708 | 11-Nov-16 | Maidenhead |
| Fuller | Albert Edward | Pte | 10341 | 2-Aug-16 | |
| Fuller | William Henry | Pte | 34084 | 27-May-18 | |
| Fumagalli | Charles | Pte | 17460 | 16-Aug-17 | West Bromwich |
| Fussell | Thomas Edward | Pte | 38256 | 25-Feb-18 | Tiverton |
| Fyfe | William George | Pte | 7263 | 25-Sep-15 | West Kensington |
| Fyfield | Albert Felix Gregory | Pte | 37223 | 16-Aug-17 | Thatcham |
| Gaden | John Percival | Pte | 50594 | 7-Oct-18 | Halesowen |
| Gadsby | David | Pte | 38533 | 2-Dec-17 | |
| Gaisford | Dudley | Drummer | 8257 | 25-Sep-15 | Bethnal Green |
| Gale | Arthur | Pte | 16373 | 3-Jul-17 | Thatcham |
| Gale | William George | Pte | 8397 | 12-Mar-17 | Slough |
| Galeford | John Harry | Pte | 42327 | 27-May-18 | |
| Gamble | George | Pte | 220108 | 16-Aug-17 | Quorn |
| Gardiner | John | Pte | 6439 | 30-May-15 | |
| Gardiner | William | A/Sgt | 8199 | 25-Sep-15 | Bethnal Green |
| Gardner | Albert | Pte | 9198 | 15-Mar-15 | Westbury on Severn |
| Gardner | Wilfred Harry | Pte | 10014 | 25-Sep-15 | London |

| Garlick | Albert Brice | Pte | 9765 | 25-Sep-15 | Shaw |
| Garlick | Gilbert George | Pte | 19732 | 1-Jul-16 | Gloucester |
| Garrett | Ernest | L/Cpl | 7432 | 4-Apr-17 | |
| Gash | William John | Pte | 17357 | 18-Oct-15 | |
| George | Samuel | Pte | 38535 | 11-Jun-18 | Redruth |
| Geraghty | Thomas | Pte | 38270 | 2-Dec-17 | |
| Gibbard | Frederick Charles | A/Sgt | 9453 | 15-Oct-17 | Camberwell |
| Gibbs | Albert Thomas | Pte | 8752 | 28-Apr-18 | Childrey |
| Giddings | Frank | 2/Lieut | 12872 | 2-Dec-17 | |
| Giddings | Frank | 2/Lt | 12872 | 2-Dec-17 | |
| Gilbert | Edward | Pte | 37232 | 28-Oct-16 | Westbury on Trym |
| Giles | A E | Pte | 15733 | 21-May-15 | |
| Giles | Albert Ernest | A/Cpl | 201759 | 11-Jul-17 | Southall |
| Giles | John Thomas | Pte | 8492 | 18-Nov-17 | Kidlington |
| Giles | Sydney Albert | Pte | 37335 | 27-Aug-18 | |
| Gilkerson | William | Pte | 11737 | 26-Apr-15 | Bracknell |
| Gill | Edwin Bateson | Pte | 18325 | 11-Jul-16 | Winscombe |
| Gill | James William | Pte | 13039 | 9-May-15 | |
| Gillespie | Edward George | Pte | 18305 | 1-Jul-16 | |
| Gillette | William Pilgrim | Pte | 220062 | 24-Mar-18 | |
| Gillingham | Rowland Cuthbert | Pte | 15648 | 4-Apr-17 | Abingdon |
| Gillingham | William Albert | Sgt | 7469 | 27-Apr-18 | |
| Gillmore | Henry Joseph | Pte | 9032 | 15-Mar-15 | |
| Gleed | Ernest | Pte | 9428 | 15-Mar-15 | Godalming |
| Goddard | Alec | Pte | 9053 | 16-Mar-15 | |
| Goddard | Bertram | Pte | 32856 | 16-Aug-17 | Donnington |
| Goddard | Charles | Pte | 10251 | 1-Jul-16 | Newbury |
| Goddard | George William | Cpl | 200475 | 2-Apr-18 | |
| Goddard | Stephen | Pte | 9485 | 9-May-15 | Windsor |
| Goddard | William John | Pte | 7436 | 29-Jan-15 | East Hendred |
| Godden | Frederick George | Pte | 9258 | 10-Mar-15 | Boxford |
| Godfrey | Charles | Pte | 37282 | 4-Mar-17 | Maidenhead |
| Godfrey | Hugh | 2/Lt | | 1-Jul-16 | |
| Godwin | William | Pte | 19831 | 13-Mar-17 | Cold Ash |
| Gold | George Rome | 2/Lt | | 27-May-18 | |
| Goodall | Albert James Gill | Lieut | | 1-Jul-16 | Reading |
| Goodall | Francis | Pte | 11739 | 1-Jul-16 | Wokingham |
| Goodchild | Charles John | L/Cpl | 9036 | 25-Oct-16 | Windsor |
| Goodchild | Walter John | Pte | 8589 | 25-Sep-15 | |
| Goodenough | Edward George | Pte | 27458 | 1-Jul-16 | Hemel Hempstead |
| Goodman | Joseph | Pte | 203462 | 2-Apr-18 | Nottingham |
| Goodwin | Frederick | Pte | 11953 | 1-Jul-16 | Tottenham |
| Gordon | Arthur George | Pte | 10097 | 10-Mar-15 | Maidenhead |
| Gordon | Norman | Pte | 37883 | 26-Apr-18 | Burton on Trent |
| Gordon | Robert | Pte | 9793 | 25-Sep-15 | Toronto Canada |
| Gore | Henry | Pte | 17412 | 18-Aug-17 | |
| Goring | Henry William | Pte | 17419 | 14-Sep-16 | Bethnal Green |
| Gosling | John | L/Cpl | 9524 | 9-May-15 | Mortimer |
| Gosling | William Stephen | Pte | 17574 | 25-Apr-16 | |
| Gould | George Penstone | L/Sgt | 17707 | 28-Oct-16 | Sonning |
| Gradden | William | Pte | 5646 | 15-Mar-15 | |
| Graham | George | Pte | 17355 | 27-Apr-18 | |
| Grainger | Charles Henry | Pte | 15805 | 1-Jul-16 | Sandhurst |
| Gray | Edward | L/Cpl | 11782 | 6-Mar-17 | Windsor |
| Gray | John Arthur | 2/Lt | | 4-Mar-17 | |
| Gray | William | Pte | 9787 | 3-Jun-15 | St Pancras |
| Green | Albert Oliver | Sgt | 9575 | 18-Aug-16 | Inkpen |
| Green | Ernest William | Sgt | 12811 | 2-Apr-18 | |

| | | | | | |
|---|---|---|---|---|---|
| Green | James | Pte | 15718 | 24-Jul-16 | Thatcham |
| Green | James Henry | Pte | 45423 | 29-Aug-18 | Banbury |
| Green | John Thomas | Pte | 14019 | 28-Sep-15 | Hackney |
| Green | Leonard | Pte | 16681 | 13-Aug-15 | |
| Green | Raymond | Pte | 17586 | 1-Jul-16 | Bucklebury |
| Greenaway | Herbert | L/Cpl | 17649 | 16-Aug-17 | |
| Greenbaum | Albert Edward | | | | |
| | Charles | Pte | 10032 | 16-Sep-15 | Leytonstone |
| Gregory | Edward Frederick | | | | |
| | John | Pte | 8723 | 1-Jul-16 | Chalvey |
| Gregory | Geoffrey Francis | Lieut | | 25-Sep-15 | |
| Griesbach | Claude Walter | 2/Lt | | 26-Oct-16 | |
| Gristock | John | Pte | 30879 | 28-May-18 | |
| Grove | John | Pte | 5993 | 9-May-15 | Maidenhead |
| Groves | Alfred Harry | Pte | 26854 | 4-Mar-17 | |
| Groves | Fred | Pte | 38667 | 2-Apr-18 | |
| Guest | George | Pte | 21888 | 4-Mar-17 | |
| Guest- | | | | | |
| Williams | Wynne Austin | Capt. | | 25-Sep-15 | |
| Gundry | William | Pte | 31348 | 2-Apr-18 | |
| Gunn | James Campbell | 2/Lt | | 27-May-18 | |
| Gunningham | Gilbert George | Pte | 42337 | 27-May-18 | Stogursey Som |
| Gurney | Bert Arthur | Sgt | 7584 | 28-Oct-16 | |
| Gurney | Stanley William | Pte | 19699 | 1-Jul-16 | Sheperds Bush |
| Gutteridge | William Alfred | Pte | 37053 | 4-Mar-17 | |
| Gylby | Leonard William | L/Cpl | 9532 | 25-Sep-15 | Lambourne |
| Hacker | George | Pte | 11007 | 20-Nov-17 | Newbury |
| Haines | Albert John | Pte | 37635 | 4-Mar-17 | Charney Berks |
| Hales | William Clifford | 2/Lt | | 23-Oct-16 | |
| Hall | Charles | Pte | 5412 | 21-Mar-15 | Guildford |
| Hall | Ernest James | Pte | 10110 | 14-Mar-17 | South Stoke |
| Hall | George | Pte | 9065 | 6-Feb-15 | Steventon |
| Hall | Percy | Pte | 15767 | 9-May-15 | Compton |
| Hall | William | Pte | 37845 | 15-Aug-17 | |
| Hallatt | Luther | Pte | 27297 | 16-Aug-17 | Sheffield |
| Hallett | Fred | Pte | 50604 | 11-Jun-15 | Portland |
| Hallett | Sidney Cyril | Pte | 24654 | 2-Apr-18 | Crowthorne |
| Hamer | Arthur | L/Cpl | 12535 | 16-Aug-17 | Walsall |
| Hamilton | Albert Charles | Pte | 8219 | 9-May-15 | |
| Hammersley | Ernest | Pte | 42338 | 28-May-18 | |
| Handley | James Edward | Pte | 27302 | 31-Dec-17 | |
| Handy | Arthur James | Pte | 203272 | 2-Apr-18 | Birmingham |
| Hanson | Thomas William | | | | |
| | Steadman | Pte | 27491 | 1-Jul-16 | |
| Harding | Henry | A/Sgt | 8876 | 14-Mar-15 | Westbury |
| Harding | John | Pte | 10533 | 26-Sep-15 | |
| Harley | Arthur | L/Cpl | 16379 | 1-Jul-16 | Oxford |
| Harman | Charles | RSM | 5671 | 10-Mar-16 | Plumstead |
| Harrington | Albert William | L/Cpl | 37215 | 4-Mar-17 | |
| Harris | Albert | Pte | 34364 | 27-Apr-18 | |
| Harris | Ernest | Sgt | 7621 | 3-Aug-16 | Burbage Wilts |
| Harris | Frederick | Pte | 5448 | 25-Sep-15 | Wallingford |
| Harris | Joseph | A/Cpl | 13507 | 2-Apr-18 | Shoreditch |
| Harris | Robert Henry | L/Cpl | 9363 | 1-Jul-16 | London |
| Harris | Stephen | L/Cpl | 23762 | 4-Mar-17 | |
| Harris | Thomas | Pte | 38546 | 26-Mar-18 | Walsall |
| Harrison | Arthur Edward | Pte | 16801 | 1-Jul-16 | Hungerford |
| Harrison | Joseph | Pte | 9015 | 28-Jan-15 | Hungerford |
| Harrison | Nathan | L/Cpl | 25987 | 27-Apr-18 | |
| Harrison | Thomas Philip | Pte | 42340 | 11-Jun-18 | |

| Harvey | John | Pte | 9519 | 15-Mar-15 | Stoke Newington |
| Harvey | Richard Prentice | Major | | 9-May-15 | |
| Harwood | Thomas John | Pte | 38549 | 2-Dec-17 | |
| Hatcher | Bernard Henry James | Pte | 10019 | 10-Mar-15 | |
| Hathaway | George | Pte | 18775 | 16-Aug-17 | Chobham |
| Hatherall | Charles Henry | Pte | 26823 | 25-Mar-17 | Tilehurst |
| Havell | Ernest Hubert | Pte | 43610 | 6-Oct-18 | Erdington |
| Hawes | Sidney | Pte | 7498 | 15-Nov-14 | High Wycombe |
| Hawketts | Wilfred | Pte | 42343 | 11-Jun-18 | |
| Hawkins | Arthur | Pte | 9398 | 17-Nov-14 | Hatfield |
| Hawkins | Robert | Pte | 9140 | 27-May-18 | |
| Hawkins | William Jesse | Pte | 16546 | 19-Aug-17 | |
| Hayne | Arthur Percy | Pte | 16958 | 1-Jul-16 | Holloway |
| Hayter | Clive | Sgt | 9329 | 11-Nov-16 | Upper Basildon |
| Hayward | George Henry | Sgt | 9782 | 2-Dec-17 | Charington Kings Glos |
| Hazell | George | Pte | 9170 | 15-Apr-15 | |
| Healey | John Michael | Pte | 10228 | 17-Jul-15 | Broadstairs |
| Heath | Albert George | Pte | 33882 | 18-Sep-17 | |
| Heath | Bartlett William | Pte | 9267 | 14-Mar-15 | Bracknell |
| Heather | John Joseph | Pte | 8064 | 4-Feb-15 | High Wycombe |
| Heaviside | Henry | L/Cpl | 17777 | 5-Aug-16 | Victoria Docks |
| Hedges | Frederick Mortimer | Pte | 8400 | 25-Sep-15 | |
| Hedges | Walter | Pte | 8646 | 23-Apr-15 | Maidenhead |
| Heming | Maurice Ivory | 2/Lt | | 1-Jul-16 | |
| Hemley | Alexander James | Pte | 9294 | 25-Sep-15 | Borough |
| Hemming | Albert | Pte | 15018 | 25-Sep-15 | Abingdon |
| Hemmings | Andrew Arthur | Pte | 41464 | 18-Mar-18 | |
| Herbert | Ernest | Pte | 9310 | 11-May-15 | Newbury |
| Herbert | George Henry | Pte | 7711 | 10-Mar-15 | Newbury |
| Herbert | William Thomas | Pte | 22047 | 4-Aug-17 | |
| Heredge | Frank | L/Cpl | 16656 | 4-Mar-17 | Culham |
| Hewett | Walter | Pte | 44832 | 27-May-18 | Chelston |
| Hewitt | Sidney | Pte | 16426 | 2-Dec-17 | Reading |
| Hey | George Leonard | Pte | 10069 | 25-Sep-15 | Walthamstow |
| Hicks | Frank | Pte | 15787 | 9-May-15 | Freemantle Hants |
| Hicks | James William | Pte | 37486 | 13-Aug-17 | |
| Hickson | Morris | Pte | 11520 | 25-Sep-15 | Nelson |
| Higginbotham | Harry | Cpl | 12322 | 1-Jul-16 | |
| Higgins | Harry | Pte | 10215 | 9-May-15 | Knowl Hill |
| Hill | Edwin Alfred | Pte | 32863 | 2-Dec-17 | |
| Hill | Henry | Pte | 43616 | 27-May-18 | Bampton Devon |
| Hill | Richard | Pte | 202804 | 16-Aug-17 | Highbury |
| Hillier | Bertie | Pte | 7038 | 9-May-15 | Hanwell |
| Hillier | James | Pte | 14027 | 9-May-15 | |
| Hillier | Reuben Ernest | Pte | 10626 | 25-Sep-15 | Kennington |
| Hills | Charles | Pte | 36344 | 2-Apr-18 | |
| Hinde | Cyril De Villiers | Lieut | | 11-Jul-17 | |
| Hine | Andrew | Pte | 203243 | 16-Aug-18 | Steventon |
| Hissey | Maurice Henry | Capt. | | 26-Oct-16 | |
| Hoare | Cecil | Pte | 27501 | 1-Jul-16 | Kensington |
| Hobbins | Howard | Pte | 44904 | 27-Apr-18 | Henley in Arden |
| Hobbs | Alfred | Pte | 15788 | 25-Sep-15 | Great Shefford |
| Hobbs | Herbert Matthew | Pte | 43609 | 31-May-18 | Nailsea |
| Hobbs | Jesse | L/Cpl | 8865 | 24-Sep-16 | Niagara Falls USA |

| | | | | | |
|---|---|---|---|---|---|
| Hobbs | William | Pte | 9454 | 25-Sep-15 | |
| Hocking | Edward Thomas | Pte | 33365 | 4-Mar-17 | |
| Hodder | George | Pte | 21994 | 28-Oct-16 | |
| Hodgson | George Graham | Lieut | | 9-May-15 | |
| Hodgson | George Wilfred | Pte | 10359 | 10-Dec-17 | Leytonstone |
| Hogan | Robert Garret Roche | 2/Lt | | 12-Mar-15 | |
| Holder | Charles George | Pte | 38551 | 11-Jun-18 | Hinton Amper |
| Holdsworth | Arthur Mervyn | Lt-Col. | | 7-Jul-16 | |
| Holland | John Henry | Pte | 37243 | 28-Oct-16 | |
| Hollington | George Edward | Pte | 36653 | 2-Aug-17 | Stourbridge |
| Holman | George Albert | Pte | 38552 | 1-Dec-17 | Devonport |
| Holmes | Charles Edward | Pte | 11965 | 25-Sep-15 | Battersea |
| Holmes | Ernest Andrew | Pte | 20039 | 1-Jul-16 | |
| Holton | James Freeman | Pte | 42346 | 31-May-18 | |
| Homer | Arthur Thomas | L/Sgt | 8130 | 25-Sep-15 | |
| Honhold | Charles Alfred | L/Cpl | 8894 | 22-Feb-15 | Acton |
| Hood | Percy Barron | L/Sgt | 11176 | 4-Mar-17 | Clapham Common |
| Hook | William | Pte | 10082 | 28-May-17 | Abingdon |
| Hooper | Robert | Pte | 20210 | 24-Oct-16 | Cheltenham |
| Hooper | Wallace Lionel | Pte | 44835 | 27-May-18 | Weston Supermare |
| Hope-Lumley | Reginald Lewis | Lieut | | 11-Oct-17 | |
| Hopper | Oswald Robert Lansdowne | Pte | 44842 | 11-Jun-18 | West Chilla Devon |
| Hopson | Edward | Cpl | 8688 | 5-Apr-15 | Dover |
| Horn | James | Pte | 8451 | 6-Mar-17 | Oxford |
| Horwood | Christopher Willie | Pte | 9228 | 25-Sep-15 | Wembley |
| Hough | Thomas Edward | Pte | 36342 | 2-Apr-18 | |
| Houldershaw | George Sanderson | Cpl | 36912 | 21-Nov-17 | |
| House | Ernest Charles | Pte | 202834 | 8-Sep-17 | Wycombe Marsh |
| House | Joseph Francis | 2/Lt | | 24-Mar-18 | |
| Housham | George Graham | Pte | 9373 | 25-Sep-15 | Bexhill on Sea |
| Howard | George | Pte | 20063 | 1-Jul-16 | East Hampstead |
| Howard | Walter | Pte | 8606 | 25-Sep-15 | Farnham |
| Howarth | Herbert | Pte | 37012 | 1-Dec-17 | |
| Howatson | Samuel David | Pte | 11954 | 31-Jul-16 | London |
| Howell | George Henry | Pte | 9167 | 4-Jul-15 | Dover |
| Howells | Arthur | CSM | 220288 | 11-Jun-18 | |
| Howes | Walter William | Pte | 21877 | 5-Mar-17 | |
| Howse | Harold Edward | A/Capt. | | 16-Aug-17 | |
| Hudson | Walter Richard | Pte | 50618 | 27-Apr-18 | |
| Hughes | Herbert | A/Cpl | 5922 | 27-May-18 | Exeter |
| Hugo | Stephen Hofmeyr | Capt. | | 21-Aug-16 | |
| Hulford | William Charles | Pte | 7313 | 27-Aug-16 | Hatfield |
| Humphrey | Henry George | Pte | 38555 | 6-Oct-18 | |
| Humphreys | Victor Richard | 2/Lt | | 24-Sep-16 | |
| Humphries | Henry | L/Cpl | 22990 | 2-Apr-18 | |
| Hunt | Frederick George | Pte | 50690 | 11-Jun-18 | |
| Hunt | James Henry | Pte | 20080 | 1-Jul-16 | |
| Hunt | Joseph Stanley | Pte | 15772 | 9-May-15 | Hungerford |
| Hunt | Norman Samuel | Pte | 220069 | 16-Aug-17 | |
| Hunt | Thomas George | Pte | 9222 | 3-Jul-16 | Padworth |
| Hunt | William | Pte | 16833 | 20-Oct-17 | Hungerford |
| Hunter | William Henry | Pte | 17579 | 21-Sep-16 | Little Coxwell |
| Hutchens | Stanley James | Pte | 42352 | 21-Sep-18 | Reading |
| Hutchins | Allan | Pte | 14011 | 25-Sep-15 | Steventon |

| Hyde | Albert John | Pte | 7074 | 9-May-15 | Newbury |
|---|---|---|---|---|---|
| Hyde | George William | Pte | 15465 | 25-Sep-15 | |
| Hyde | Kenneth Frederick | Pte | 44850 | 11-Jun-18 | |
| Ilsley | Francis Edward | Sgt | 7921 | 15-Mar-15 | |
| Infield | Albert George | Pte | 37463 | 3-Mar-17 | Wellingborough |
| Ingham | Ernest | Pte | 8986 | 25-Sep-15 | Slough |
| Ingram | Frank | Pte | 7772 | 11-Jun-18 | Fulham |
| Ingram | George Albert | Pte | 9307 | 25-Sep-15 | Fulham |
| Irwin | Alfred | Pte | 43594 | 21-Mar-18 | Ambleside |
| Izon | Andrew | Pte | 227056 | 27-May-18 | |
| Jackman | John | Pte | 14369 | 16-Aug-17 | Guildford |
| Jackson | Albert | Pte | 6498 | 16-Aug-17 | Sydenham |
| Jacob | Robert | Pte | 17248 | 1-Jul-16 | |
| Jacques | George Edward | L/Cpl | 9546 | 27-Aug-14 | Shepherds Bush |
| Jakeman | Thomas Richard | Pte | 44909 | 27-May-18 | Aylesbury |
| James | Ernest | L/Cpl | 8552 | 12-Jan-15 | Barry Glam |
| James | Frederick Herbert | Pte | 15815 | 25-Sep-15 | West Bromwich |
| James | George Edward | Pte | 16317 | 28-Oct-16 | |
| James | Harold Thomas | Pte | 42227 | 11-Jun-18 | |
| James | Joseph Henry | Pte | 201642 | 2-Apr-18 | |
| Jarrad | Charles William | Pte | 11826 | 25-Sep-15 | Oxley Staffs |
| Jeffries | Sidney | Pte | 36915 | 27-Apr-18 | |
| Jeffs | Albert | Pte | 9252 | 13-Mar-15 | Old Ford |
| Jelfs | John William | Pte | 33348 | 8-Apr-17 | Long Ashton |
| Jelfs | Joseph | Pte | 38217 | 31-Dec-17 | |
| Jenkins | Harry | Pte | 37850 | 2-Dec-17 | |
| Jenkins | Richard James | Pte | 15722 | 25-Sep-15 | Eccinswell |
| Jenkins | William Edward | Pte | 39136 | 20-Dec-18 | |
| Jennings | Charles | Pte | 50620 | 27-Apr-18 | Wheatley |
| Jennings | John | Pte | 16185 | 25-Sep-15 | Smethwick |
| Jepps | Charles | Pte | 23651 | 28-Oct-16 | Hitchin |
| Jesse | Frank | Pte | 44857 | 27-May-18 | East Knoyle Wilts |
| Jewell | George | Pte | 11791 | 9-May-15 | Barnstaple |
| Johnson | Albert | Sgt | 8056 | 10-Oct-15 | |
| Johnson | Jack | Pte | 27517 | 1-Jul-16 | |
| Johnson | John Alfred | Pte | 17024 | 1-Jul-16 | |
| Johnson | John William | Pte | 10672 | 14-Aug-16 | St Lukes Middx |
| Johnson | Jonathan | Pte | 27518 | 1-Jul-16 | Preston Lancs |
| Jones | Arthur | Pte | 17577 | 1-Jul-16 | Blackheath |
| Jones | Maiwand Alfred | A/Cpl | 8479 | 9-May-15 | |
| Jones | Thomas | Pte | 41751 | 19-Aug-18 | |
| Jones | William | Pte | 10174 | 25-Sep-15 | Wallingford |
| Jordan | Alec | Pte | 50622 | 17-Jun-18 | Bristol |
| Jose | Albert Richard | Pte | 10210 | 27-Apr-18 | Bromley by Bow |
| Joseph | William Franklin George | 2/Lt | | 27-May-18 | |
| Josey | John | Sgt | 5699 | 25-Sep-15 | Reading |
| Justice | George Henry | Pte | 37246 | 28-Oct-16 | Westbury on Trym |
| Kebby | Charles Arthur | Pte | 15339 | 1-Jul-16 | Smethwick |
| Keefe | William | Pte | 11778 | 16-Aug-17 | Bracknell |
| Keep | Harry | Pte | 6608 | 16-Dec-14 | Shinfield |
| Kelly | James Thomas | Pte | 45428 | 29-Aug-18 | |
| Kemp | Bert | Pte | 201901 | 8-Jul-17 | |
| Kemp | Frank Thomas | Pte | 42356 | 4-Oct-18 | |
| Kempton | Frank Henry | Pte | 36371 | 27-Apr-18 | Hoddesdon |
| Kendall | Albert | Pte | 9124 | 9-May-15 | Windsor |
| Kent | Charles | L/Cpl | 7421 | 31-Jul-17 | Cold Ash |
| Kernutt | William | Pte | 35158 | 27-Apr-18 | Ashford Hill |
| Key | Hugh | Pte | 227044 | 27-Apr-18 | |

| Kidby | Charles Henry | Pte | 42357 | 11-Jun-18 | Dartmouth |
| Kimber | William John | Pte | 8986 | 4-Aug-16 | Lambourne |
| King | Arthur Stanley | Pte | 38557 | 2-Dec-17 | Exeter |
| King | Charles Edward George | Pte | 16280 | 25-Sep-15 | Kintbury |
| King | Edward Thomas | Pte | 8358 | 19-Mar-15 | Oxford |
| King | Frederick | Pte | 8084 | 11-Apr-16 | Cowley |
| King | Frederick Albert | Pte | 20072 | 5-Mar-17 | |
| King | Herbert Edward | Pte | 17483 | 1-Dec-17 | Bray |
| King | John | Pte | 16341 | 25-Sep-15 | Kintbury |
| King | William George | Cpl | 9288 | 4-Apr-17 | Oxford |
| Kingham | James | Pte | 8696 | 9-Nov-14 | London |
| Kirkland | Tom Mackintosh | Pte | 37058 | 1-Dec-17 | Crumpsall Lancs |
| Kitchell | Timothy George | L/Cpl | 6633 | 25-Sep-15 | Pelworth |
| Kitchener | Arthur | L/Cpl | 11467 | 9-May-15 | |
| Knibbs | Henry George | Pte | 8280 | 21-Apr-15 | Twyford |
| Knight | Arthur | L/Cpl | 18797 | 4-Mar-17 | Ongar |
| Knight | Bertie | Drummer | 7868 | 25-Sep-15 | Portsmouth |
| Knight | Edward | Pte | 9498 | 27-Jan-15 | Lower Whitley |
| Knight | Edward Charles | Pte | 9764 | 24-Nov-14 | |
| Knight | Frank Thomas | Pte | 23785 | 27-Apr-18 | |
| Knight | Jack | Pte | 11565 | 24-Sep-16 | Bethnal Green |
| Knight | Stanley | Pte | 36373 | 2-Dec-17 | Walkern Herts |
| Knott | Archibald Sherbrook | 2/Lt | | 25-Apr-18 | |
| Knott | Frank | Pte | 17129 | 1-Dec-17 | |
| Knowles | Walford Vernon | 2/Lt | | 31-Dec-17 | |
| Lake | James | Pte | 50680 | 25-Apr-18 | |
| Lamb | Isaac | Pte | 9681 | 27-Nov-14 | Binfield |
| Lambourne | Alfred Edward | Pte | 8261 | 9-May-15 | |
| Land | Ernest George | Pte | 11574 | 10-Apr-16 | |
| Lane | Hamlyn Clifford | Pte | 50702 | 23-Jul-18 | |
| Lanfear | Sidney | Sgt | 9667 | 3-Aug-16 | Wantage |
| Langley | Albert Edward | Pte | 16273 | 2-Apr-18 | |
| Langley | Frank | Pte | 37290 | 5-Mar-17 | Crowthorne |
| Lanigan | William Joseph | Pte | 11639 | 25-Sep-15 | Custom House |
| Larner | William Henry | Pte | 9227 | 13-Jan-15 | |
| Lavery | John | Pte | 37855 | 31-Jul-17 | Minnigolf |
| Lawley | John Alfred | Pte | 43633 | 27-Apr-18 | Hednesford |
| Lawley | Rudolph | Pte | 33370 | 31-Jul-17 | |
| Lawrence | Arthur Henry | Pte | 9639 | 9-May-15 | Barking |
| Lawrence | Ernest Walter | Pte | 7392 | 25-Sep-15 | |
| Lawrence | Frederick George | Pte | 20090 | 1-Jul-16 | Crookham |
| Lawrence | Harry | Pte | 8545 | 10-Mar-15 | Durham |
| Lawrence | Horace | Pte | 37291 | 11-Jul-17 | Stoke Ferry Norfolk |
| Lawson | George | Sgt | 17560 | 2-Apr-18 | |
| Lee | Charles | Pte | 16326 | 3-Jul-16 | |
| Lee | Harry | Pte | 36381 | 27-Apr-18 | |
| Lee | James | Pte | 37185 | 18-Sep-17 | |
| Lee | James Clifford | 2/Lt | | 1-Aug-17 | |
| Lee | Joe | Sgt | 8696 | 25-Sep-15 | |
| Lees | George Leslie | Pte | 38117 | 27-Apr-18 | Saltley Warks |
| Legg | Reginald Campion | Pte | 38560 | 2-Apr-18 | |
| Leonard | George | Pte | 9194 | 25-Aug-15 | |
| Lester | Joseph Leighton | Pte | 19819 | 4-Mar-17 | |
| Levy | Hyman | Pte | 19751 | 1-Aug-16 | Whitechapel |
| Lewin | William Charles | Pte | 15737 | 9-May-15 | |
| Lewington | Frederick Francis | Pte | 20184 | 11-Nov-16 | Wallingford |
| Lewis | John Frederick | Sgt | 9980 | 17-Oct-17 | Reading |

| | | | | | |
|---|---|---|---|---|---|
| Lewis | Joseph Reginald | Pte | 44860 | 27-Apr-18 | |
| Lewis | Reginald Cameron | Capt. | | 1-Jul-16 | |
| Lewis | Thomas | | | | |
| | Frederick Hawkes | L/Cpl | 15374 | 25-Sep-15 | Faringdon |
| Light | Harry | Pte | 9816 | 25-Sep-15 | Henley on Thames |
| Lillington | Claude Clement | Pte | 220074 | 31-Jul-17 | Wallingford |
| Lipscombe | Eric Lancelot | Lieut | | 9-May-15 | |
| Litchfield | Thomas | Pte | 8292 | 25-Sep-15 | High Wycombe |
| Lloyd | Alfred William | Pte | 36786 | 27-Apr-18 | |
| Lloyd | James Ambrose | Pte | 9081 | 25-Sep-15 | |
| Loat | Horace John | Pte | 220075 | 16-Aug-17 | |
| Lock | Arthur | Pte | 19817 | 1-Jul-16 | Abingdon |
| Locke | John William | Pte | 7985 | 25-Sep-15 | Alresford |
| Locke | Nathan | Pte | 38274 | 2-Dec-17 | Bidford |
| Locke | William | Pte | 24669 | 16-Aug-17 | |
| Lockyer | Walter | Pte | 38100 | 27-Apr-18 | |
| Logan | William James | Pte | 9517 | 20-Mar-15 | London |
| Lomax | Gerald David | 2/Lt | | 11-May-15 | |
| Long | George | Pte | 21720 | 4-Mar-17 | |
| Looney | Joseph Henry | Pte | 10631 | 4-Apr-18 | |
| Lovegrove | William | Pte | 10165 | 31-Jul-17 | Steventon |
| Lovell | Francis William | Pte | 19953 | 28-Oct-16 | |
| Lovelock | Charles Henry | Pte | 37267 | 28-Oct-16 | Windsor |
| Lovelock | Thomas | L/Cpl | 8631 | 1-Jul-16 | |
| Lovelock | Thomas | A/Sgt | 10022 | 2-Apr-18 | Hungerford |
| | Harry James | | | | |
| Lovesey | Harry | Pte | 19737 | 1-Jul-16 | Swindon |
| Lovett | John Henry | Pte | 10468 | 25-May-15 | Limehouse |
| Lowther | Henry John Phillip | Pte | 9699 | 29-Mar-15 | Hammersmith |
| Lucas | Thomas | Pte | 37862 | 2-Dec-17 | |
| Luck | Arthur | Pte | 12009 | 16-Aug-17 | Brighton |
| Luff | Sidney Charles | Pte | 39414 | 2-Dec-17 | Eynesbury |
| Luing | Frederick John | Pte | 28821 | 2-Dec-17 | |
| Lunnon | Walter Ernest | Pte | 20074 | 1-Jul-16 | |
| Luty | Arthur | Sgt | 8393 | 11-Nov-16 | |
| Mabbitt | Alfred | Pte | 7114 | 15-Mar-15 | Baldock |
| Maccabee | Harry | L/Cpl | 7841 | 4-Mar-17 | |
| Mace | Gordon | Pte | 203215 | 4-Mar-18 | Wallingford |
| | Melville Thomas | | | | |
| Mace | Henry Charles | Pte | 15600 | 27-Apr-18 | |
| MacGregor | Donald Alistair | Capt. | | 15-Aug-15 | |
| Machen | Albert | Pte | 9290 | 9-May-15 | Bagshot |
| Macrow | George Joseph | Pte | 17350 | 1-Jul-16 | Islington |
| Malins | Harry | Pte | 10603 | 4-Mar-17 | Bracknell |
| Mann | Ernest | Pte | 36676 | 11-Jun-18 | |
| Manning | Ernest Albert | Pte | 42441 | 27-Apr-18 | |
| Mannooch | John Thomas | Pte | 19728 | 1-Aug-17 | London |
| Manns | William | Pte | 38564 | 11-Jun-18 | |
| | Edwin Vincent | | | | |
| Marks | Sidney | Pte | 201931 | 1-Aug-17 | |
| Marlow | Francis John | Sgt | 15411 | 3-Apr-18 | |
| Marriott | George | Pte | 45431 | 29-Aug-18 | Bicester |
| Marsh | Alfred Henry | L/Cpl | 12852 | 17-Aug-17 | |
| Marsh | Fred | Pte | 18554 | 26-Aug-16 | Marlborough |
| Marshall | Alfred David | Pte | 202624 | 16-Aug-17 | |
| Marshall | Walter | L/Cpl | 38566 | 16-Jan-18 | |
| Marshall | William | L/Cpl | 17184 | 1-Jul-16 | |
| Marston | William Frederick | Pte | 42369 | 27-Apr-18 | |
| Martin | John Henry | Pte | 17663 | 1-Jul-16 | Victoria Park |

| Maslin | Alfred | Pte | 6645 | 11-Jun-18 | Twyford |
|---|---|---|---|---|---|
| Mason | Albert Edward | L/Cpl | 16523 | 28-Oct-16 | Newbury |
| Mason | Edward Frank | Pte | 37292 | 18-Sep-17 | Kings Lynn |
| Mathews | Benjamin Ashway Conway | Pte | 5486 | 23-Dec-14 | Lambourne |
| Matthews | Colston Alfred | Pte | 38569 | 16-Jan-18 | |
| Matthews | George Henry | Pte | 9063 | 15-Mar-15 | |
| Matthews | Thomas William | Pte | 33362 | 31-Jul-17 | |
| Maunders | Charles | Pte | 5635 | 16-Jul-15 | Sheffield |
| Maurice | John Capel | 2/Lt | | 7-Oct-18 | |
| Mawer | Herbert William | Pte | 20088 | 1-Jul-16 | Romford |
| May | Frank | Pte | 16769 | 25-Sep-15 | Battersea |
| May | Thomas Henry Alfred | Pte | 33272 | 7-Feb-17 | |
| May | William | Pte | 16628 | 1-Jul-16 | |
| Mayfield | Charles Henry George | Pte | 18222 | 4-Apr-17 | Cheltenham |
| Mayho | Ernest Archibald | Pte | 8737 | 25-Sep-15 | Reading |
| McArdle | Hugh | Pte | 11501 | 9-May-15 | Glasgow |
| McDonald | Donald | Pte | 42438 | 27-May-18 | |
| McGrath | William Richard | Pte | 15476 | 9-May-15 | London |
| McLoughlin | John | Pte | 17669 | 1-Jul-16 | |
| McMillan | Matthew | Pte | 35021 | 2-Apr-18 | |
| McMurdie | John Edward | Pte | 27493 | 4-Mar-17 | Islington |
| Meacock | Arthur | Pte | 37638 | 16-Aug-17 | Harmondsworth |
| Meanley | William Albert | Pte | 44895 | 27-Apr-18 | |
| Medlicott | Edward Morley | Lieut | | 11-Apr-16 | |
| Meek | Frederick Charles | Pte | 43617 | 14-Jun-18 | Cambourne |
| Menhenitt | William James | Pte | 21714 | 4-Mar-17 | Plymouth |
| Merrick | Herbert Frederick Rivers | Lieut | | 3-May-17 | |
| Merritt | Albert Edward | Pte | 9260 | 11-Jan-15 | Oxford |
| Merritt | John George Thomas | Pte | 17986 | 28-Oct-16 | |
| Mesher | George | Pte | 16139 | 25-Sep-15 | Great Marlow |
| Mickman | Charles Collier | Pte | 18966 | 5-Apr-17 | Farnborough Hants |
| Middleton | David | L/Cpl | 8913 | 9-May-15 | |
| Miles | Gordon Stanley | Pte | 38663 | 26-Feb-18 | Eastleigh |
| Millard | Arthur | Pte | 202504 | 20-Aug-17 | |
| Miller | Charles Henry | Pte | 17444 | 1-Jul-16 | |
| Miller | Frank Henry | 2/Lt | | 27-May-18 | |
| Miller | Richard | Pte | 10532 | 28-Sep-15 | Windsor |
| Miller | William | Pte | 6484 | 1-Jun-15 | Chieveley |
| Mills | Albert Edward | 2/Lt | | 16-Aug-17 | |
| Mills | Edward George | Pte | 8983 | 29-Jul-15 | East Ilsley |
| Mills | George William | Pte | 27509 | 1-Jul-16 | |
| Mills | William Charles | Pte | 8504 | 3-Dec-14 | |
| Mills | William John | Pte | 9868 | 1-Jul-16 | Acton |
| Miners | Bernard Francis | Pte | 44724 | 29-Aug-18 | |
| Mines | John | Pte | 11629 | 16-Aug-17 | Haggerstown |
| Mitchell | Jesse Reuben | Pte | 8851 | 9-May-15 | Wokingham |
| Mitchell | John | Pte | 8539 | 24-Jan-15 | Witney |
| Money | Leonard Charles | Pte | 19757 | 1-Jul-16 | Reading |
| Monk | Vincent | Pte | 8791 | 28-Oct-16 | |
| Mood | Percy | L/Cpl | 19719 | 18-Nov-17 | Masham |
| Moody-Ward | Richard Guy Torrington | Capt. | | 9-May-15 | |
| Moore | Howard Frederick | Pte | 42371 | 27-Apr-18 | |
| Moore | Walter | Pte | 21908 | 3-Mar-17 | |

| Moorman | Arthur | Pte | 220450 | 6-Oct-18 | |
| Morgan | Charles | Pte | 11455 | 1-Jul-16 | Hoxton |
| Morgan | Frederick Charles | Pte | 38573 | 2-Apr-18 | |
| Morgan | James | Pte | 45194 | 21-Sep-18 | |
| Morris | Henry Francis | Pte | 16902 | 1-Jul-16 | Kentish Town |
| Morris | John | Pte | 9568 | 11-Dec-14 | |
| Morse | Tom | Pte | 16629 | 25-Sep-15 | Port Tennant Glam |
| Moses | Louis | Pte | 20204 | 1-Jul-16 | Princetown |
| Mosey | Johnathan | Pte | 37892 | 16-Aug-17 | |
| Mossman | Harold Alexander | 2/Lt | | 25-Apr-18 | |
| Mott | Ernest Richard | Pte | 220277 | 2-Apr-18 | |
| Mott | Frederick Charles | Pte | 9390 | 28-Oct-16 | Wantage |
| Mott | Frederick Charles | Pte | 38574 | 17-Jan-18 | |
| Mott | Frederick James | Pte | 15281 | 5-Jul-16 | Lambourne |
| Mowbray | Edwin Hilton | Pte | 203373 | 2-Apr-18 | |
| Musgrave | John Charles | Pte | 202024 | 27-Apr-18 | |
| Nailer | Edward John | Pte | 15777 | 1-Jul-16 | |
| Nailor | Henry | Pte | 15717 | 4-Mar-17 | |
| Nailor | Maurice Henry | Pte | 16754 | 2-Jul-16 | |
| Nash | Austin Percival | Pte | 37293 | 5-Mar-17 | |
| Nash | William Henry | Pte | 10001 | 1-Jul-16 | |
| Neale | Sidney Joseph | A/Cpl | 9232 | 15-Mar-15 | Abingdon |
| Neighbour | Alfred William | Pte | 19956 | 1-Jul-16 | Wantage |
| Neighbour | Sidney Hubert | Pte | 37534 | 27-Apr-18 | Maidenhead |
| Neil | Frederick | Pte | 220078 | 21-Aug-17 | Cirencester |
| Newbold | Harry Buckley | Pte | 202495 | 12-Jul-17 | Ashby de la Zouch |
| Newcombe | Stanley John | Pte | 37843 | 16-Aug-17 | Enfield |
| Newell | William | Pte | 17731 | 1-Jul-16 | High Wycombe |
| Newman | Albert | Pte | 16313 | 17-Aug-16 | |
| Newman | Ernest William | L/Cpl | 8644 | 9-May-15 | Wantage |
| Newman | George | Pte | 17137 | 24-Oct-17 | |
| Newman | Thomas | A/Cpl | 8080 | 3-Aug-16 | |
| Newstead | Arthur James | Pte | 17744 | 10-Apr-16 | Manor Park |
| Newstead | Ernest | Pte | 37475 | 4-Apr-17 | Boston Lincs |
| Nicholls | Harry Edward Earls | L/Cpl | 20219 | 18-Mar-17 | |
| Nicholls | Harry George | 2/Lt | 10375 | 27-May-18 | |
| Nicholson | Donald Walter | Pte | 22128 | 16-Aug-17 | Harrow |
| Nightingale | George Frank | Pte | 9199 | 25-Sep-15 | Walthamstow |
| Nipper | Arthur Frank | Pte | 42263 | 13-Sep-18 | Wrington |
| Nisbett | Fred Albert | Pte | 18245 | 28-Oct-16 | Forest Gate Essex |
| Norman | Charles | Pte | 8705 | 21-Dec-14 | Poplar |
| Norman | Ernest | Pte | 37812 | 20-Aug-17 | Deptford |
| Norris | Alfred William | L/Cpl | 15944 | 1-Jul-16 | Sunninghill |
| Norris | Ernest Archibald | Pte | 10212 | 1-Jul-16 | Slough |
| Norris | Harry James | Pte | 11287 | 2-Apr-18 | |
| Norris | William Charles | Pte | 9186 | 10-Mar-15 | |
| Northover | William Fred | Pte | 18342 | 23-Oct-16 | Preston |
| Norton | Ernest Leslie | Pte | 220079 | 19-Oct-17 | |
| Norton | Sidney | Pte | 10078 | 9-May-15 | Faringdon |
| Norvall | Charles George Hughes | Pte | 10464 | 25-Sep-15 | Boscombe |
| Nugent | Charles | Capt. | | 19-Nov-18 | |
| Nunn | Charles Herbert | Pte | 9691 | 23-Dec-14 | Hoxton |
| Nunn | Frederick | Pte | 13312 | 16-Aug-17 | |
| O'Leary | John | Pte | 9812 | 17-Aug-17 | |
| O'Lieff | John | Pte | 220080 | 16-Aug-17 | |
| O'Regan | James | Pte | 9818 | 25-Sep-15 | Upper Holloway |

| Oakley | Albert Edward | Pte | 19827 | 1-Jul-16 | |
| Oakley | Albert James | Pte | 9551 | 16-Aug-17 | Cheam |
| Oke | Robert William Leslie | A/Capt. | | 25-Sep-15 | |
| Oliver | Ernest Charles | Pte | 9389 | 4-Feb-15 | |
| Oliver | Lionel Bernard | CSM | 27472 | 2-Apr-18 | |
| Oliver | Sidney James | L/Cpl | 15621 | 9-May-15 | |
| Ollington | Harry George | Cpl | 27450 | 1-Jul-16 | Mayfair |
| Orchard | William | Pte | 16547 | 4-Apr-17 | |
| Osborn | Albert Walter | Pte | 10204 | 27-Apr-18 | Peckham |
| Osborn | Tom | Pte | 9731 | 4-Feb-15 | |
| Osborne | Stanley | Pte | 42380 | 27-May-18 | St Stephens Cornwall |
| Osman | Ernest | Pte | 18655 | 18-Feb-18 | Woodcote |
| Owen | Thomas | Pte | 8521 | 17-Feb-15 | Aldbourne |
| Page | George Harry Frampton | Pte | 10983 | 1-Jul-16 | London |
| Page | Walter Percy | Pte | 20065 | 29-Oct-16 | Edgbaston |
| Paget | Arthur Wilmot | Pte | 37552 | 1-Dec-17 | |
| Paice | Harry Charles | L/Cpl | 18047 | 1-Apr-18 | |
| Paice | Henry | Pte | 201905 | 16-Aug-17 | |
| Painter | Arthur Herbert | Pte | 21876 | 26-Aug-16 | |
| Painter | Thomas | Pte | 8896 | 16-Aug-17 | Cowes IoW |
| Palfrey | Frederick Arthur | Pte | 37204 | 28-Oct-16 | |
| Palfreyman | Charles | L/Cpl | 9705 | 25-Sep-15 | Chivers Coton Warks |
| Palmer | Charles Henry | Pte | 17342 | 27-Apr-18 | |
| Palmer | William | Pte | 18091 | 5-Mar-17 | Twyford |
| Pardoe | Arthur John | Pte | 42383 | 11-Jun-18 | Preston Lancs |
| Pargeter | Ronald Leonard | Pte | 42384 | 27-Apr-18 | |
| Parker | Frank Edward | A/Sgt | 6265 | 24-Mar-15 | Kennington |
| Parker | Henry John | Pte | 8326 | 25-Sep-15 | |
| Parker | Herbert Albert | Pte | 33302 | 2-Apr-18 | |
| Parker | William James | Pte | 16900 | 22-Aug-16 | Islington |
| Parkes | Charles William | Pte | 44908 | 11-Jun-18 | |
| Parkin | Joseph | L/Cpl | 9892 | 1-Jul-16 | Great Missenden |
| Parrett | William | Pte | 11757 | 9-May-15 | |
| Parsons | Henry James | Pte | 37295 | 4-Mar-17 | |
| Partridge | Joseph | Pte | 11447 | 25-Sep-15 | Camden Town |
| Patston | Charles George | L/Cpl | 6388 | 28-Oct-16 | Egham |
| Pattison | Sidney | Pte | 37864 | 1-Aug-17 | Crewe |
| Paxton | Wilfred | L/Cpl | 220081 | 15-Feb-18 | Finmere |
| Payne | Herbert | Pte | 6342 | 25-Sep-15 | Marlow |
| Payne | Osmond Guy | Lieut | | 1-Jul-16 | |
| Peacock | William James | Pte | 36426 | 2-Apr-18 | |
| Pearce | Albert Thomas | Pte | 8529 | 16-Aug-17 | Chaddleworth |
| Pearce | Fred | Sgt | 8037 | 1-Jul-16 | West Hampstead |
| Pearce | Frederick | Pte | 16533 | 24-Jan-17 | |
| Pearce | Henry | Pte | 7857 | 26-Aug-16 | Newbury |
| Pearce | Herbert Joseph | Pte | 17753 | 1-Jul-16 | Faringdon |
| Pearce | Horace John | Pte | 10918 | 10-Mar-15 | Oxford |
| Pearsall | William | Pte | 38580 | 27-Apr-18 | |
| Pearse | Frederick Samuel | Pte | 43573 | 27-Apr-18 | Plymouth |
| Peck | Frederick William | Pte | 10021 | 15-Mar-15 | Wokingham |
| Pedder | Robert | Pte | 36420 | 21-Jul-18 | |
| Peedle | Rupert | Pte | 220083 | 16-Aug-17 | Great Missenden |
| Penfold | William Frederick | Pte | 17247 | 16-Jan-16 | Canning Town |
| Penney | Lionel John | Pte | 7265 | 17-May-15 | Peckham |
| Perris | Albert | Pte | 37296 | 30-Jan-17 | |
| Perry | Charles William | Pte | 7398 | 30-Oct-16 | Ash Vale |

| Perry | Thomas Edward | Pte | 16832 | 25-Sep-15 | Pewsey |
| Peters | Ralph Charles | Pte | 9879 | 9-May-15 | Teddington |
| Pharo | Arthur Thomas | L/Cpl | 20061 | 1-Jul-16 | |
| Phillips | Albert | Sgt | 8477 | 9-May-15 | Yattendon |
| Phillips | Walter Fitzgerald | Pte | 6019 | 9-May-15 | Luton |
| Phipps | Arthur Sydney | Pte | 33931 | 27-Apr-18 | |
| Piercy | Arthur Leonard | Pte | 17151 | 4-Mar-17 | Twyford |
| Pink | Charles William | Pte | 9234 | 9-May-15 | Poplar |
| Pinney | Charles Clifford | Pte | 42386 | 27-Apr-18 | Crewkerne |
| Pirie | George | Pte | 46624 | 7-Oct-18 | |
| Pizzey | James Thomas | Pte | 8355 | 14-Mar-15 | Shepperton Green |
| Pleasant | Harold George | A/Sgt | 8885 | 1-Jul-16 | Thame Oxon |
| Plester | William Robert | Cpl | 9656 | 29-Aug-18 | Basingstoke |
| Plowman | Joseph | Pte | 10243 | 27-Oct-16 | Abingdon |
| Plumridge | Frederick Ernest | Pte | 9820 | 25-Jan-15 | |
| Pocock | Frederick | Pte | 11721 | 15-Mar-15 | Bracknell |
| Pointer | William | Pte | 17728 | 30-Oct-16 | Drayton |
| Polack | Lipman | L/Cpl | 9116 | 20-Jul-15 | Mile End |
| Pollard | William John | Pte | 33938 | 16-Aug-17 | Rugby |
| Pollard | William Joseph | Pte | 37339 | 26-Jan-17 | Tingewick |
| Poole | George | Pte | 9722 | 25-Sep-15 | Bampton |
| Poole | Herbert | Pte | 31331 | 11-Jun-18 | |
| Poole | Joseph Ronald | Pte | 37224 | 23-Oct-16 | |
| Pope | James William | Pte | 41748 | 27-Apr-18 | |
| Porter | Robert Henry | Pte | 9726 | 10-May-15 | Maidenhead |
| Poulton | Arthur | L/Cpl | 37863 | 16-Aug-17 | Merton |
| Povey | Henry | Pte | 30110 | 9-Apr-17 | Steventon |
| Powell | William | Pte | 37218 | 25-Oct-16 | |
| Pratt | Ernest | L/Cpl | 9509 | 30-Sep-15 | Swindon |
| Preen | Arthur | Pte | 15813 | 28-Oct-16 | Shrewsbury |
| Prescott | Henry | Pte | 41798 | 11-Jun-18 | Bolton |
| Preston | Jesse | Pte | 5731 | 11-Jun-18 | Faringdon |
| Price | Philip Joshua | Pte | 37298 | 3-Feb-17 | |
| Price | Reuben | Pte | 42391 | 27-Jun-18 | Droitwich |
| Price | Thomas John | Sgt | 6638 | 9-May-15 | Portsmouth |
| Prince | Charles | Pte | 9129 | 12-Jan-15 | Hanwell |
| Prince | Henry | L/Cpl | 5827 | 11-Mar-15 | |
| Prior | Albert | Pte | 15978 | 1-Jul-16 | Newbury |
| Prior | John Thomas | Pte | 9847 | 15-Mar-15 | |
| Prior | Stephen | Sgt | 10733 | 12-Apr-17 | Streatley |
| Privett | Arthur William | A/Cpl | 9645 | 9-May-15 | Peckham |
| Pudney | Benjamin Harry | Pte | 17396 | 23-Aug-16 | East Ham |
| Pulley | Lionel Jack | Pte | 42392 | 27-Apr-18 | Redditch |
| Purchell | William John | L/Cpl | 17060 | 2-Apr-18 | Reading |
| Purland | Harry | Pte | 11614 | 9-May-15 | Blackfriars |
| Pusey | Harry | A/Cpl | 7577 | 25-Sep-15 | Wooburn Common |
| Quarterman | Evelyn Stewart | Pte | 17733 | 1-Jul-16 | High Wycombe |
| Quarterman | Harry | Pte | 7570 | 30-Oct-18 | Hanwell |
| Quelch | Charles James | Pte | 200942 | 2-Apr-18 | Midgham |
| Quinney | Frank Wilbert | Pte | 50710 | 27-May-18 | |
| Rackley | Edward Andrew | Pte | 201419 | 6-Sep-17 | Maidenhead |
| Radcliffe | Arthur Holman | Sgt | 45178 | 21-Sep-18 | Birmingham |
| Raisey | Ernest | Pte | 200919 | 2-Apr-18 | |
| Raisey | Frederick | Pte | 37513 | 4-Mar-17 | Brockenhurst |
| Rance | Arthur | Pte | 38795 | 3-Apr-18 | Denham |
| Randall | Frank Clifford | Pte | 37611 | 31-Jul-17 | Bradford-on-Avon |
| Rathband | Hubert | L/Cpl | 220280 | 18-Sep-18 | |
| Ravenor | Alexander | Pte | 10402 | 11-Mar-15 | Battersea |

| | Michelson | | | | |
|---|---|---|---|---|---|
| Rawlings | Frederick George Reginald | Pte | 43638 | 27-Apr-18 | Guildford |
| Rawlings | William | Pte | 9081 | 25-Sep-15 | Oxford |
| Rawson | John George | Pte | 37476 | 16-Aug-17 | Kettering |
| Ray | Clifford Edgar | Pte | 38281 | 2-Dec-17 | |
| Raynes | Albert Brainerd | 2/Lt | | 10-Mar-15 | |
| Redding | Albert | Pte | 42397 | 27-Apr-18 | Amersham |
| Reeley | William Francis | L/Sgt | 8592 | 29-Mar-17 | West Hendred |
| Reid | Robert | Pte | 27508 | 5-Mar-17 | Kirknewton Midlothian |
| Reynolds | Arthur | Pte | 43892 | 16-Oct-18 | Upton Snodsbury |
| Richards | Alfred | Pte | 12574 | 25-Sep-15 | |
| Richardson | Arthur | Pte | 28945 | 2-Apr-18 | |
| Richardson | Cecil | Pte | 36872 | 9-Sep-17 | Corsham |
| Richardson | Clifford Ernest | Pte | 34144 | 16-Aug-17 | Maidenhead |
| Richardson | Ernest William | Pte | 10134 | 16-Aug-17 | Andover |
| Richardson | William Frederick | Pte | 9271 | 9-May-15 | Ottowa Canada |
| Ridgeway | George Albert | Pte | 17672 | 1-Jul-16 | Bow |
| Ridgley | Charles Henry John | Pte | 10065 | 10-May-15 | |
| Ridpath | John William | Pte | 9748 | 23-Oct-16 | Brixton |
| Ritchie | John | Cpl | 27453 | 1-Jul-16 | Ilford |
| Rivers | Ernest Francis | Pte | 23951 | 31-Mar-18 | Newbury |
| Rixon | Edwin James | Pte | 19295 | 4-Apr-17 | Henley on Thames |
| Roberts | Albert George | Pte | 9648 | 9-May-15 | |
| Robertson | Alexander | L/Cpl | 19726 | 1-Jul-16 | Wellingborough |
| Robinson | Alfred | Pte | 37629 | 16-Aug-17 | |
| Robinson | Benjamin Stanley | 2/Lt | | 1-Jul-16 | |
| Robinson | Sidney John | Pte | 202418 | 11-Jun-18 | Gloucester |
| Roddy | Edward Charles | Pte | 50712 | 28-May-18 | Coventry |
| Rogers | Frederick | Pte | 16308 | 4-Dec-17 | Camberley |
| Rogers | Frederick | Pte | 9980 | 26-Jan-15 | Little Marlow |
| Rogers | George Charles | L/Cpl | 16310 | 25-Sep-15 | Thatcham |
| Rogers | Isaac | Pte | 43620 | 27-Apr-18 | Salisbury |
| Rolfe | Frederick | A/Sgt | 15891 | 1-Jul-16 | Hungerford |
| Rolfe | Herbert Dennis | Pte | 220084 | 16-Aug-17 | Aylesbury |
| Rolingson | George Edward | Pte | 9168 | 16-Aug-17 | Diss Norfolk |
| Rose | Mark | Cpl | 12396 | 27-Apr-18 | |
| Round | Frank | Pte | 17006 | 16-Aug-17 | Walsall |
| Rouse | Albert Edward | Pte | 21987 | 2-Oct-16 | Bristol |
| Rowe | Gilbert James Burbery | 2/Lt | | 17-Apr-18 | |
| Rowlands | Francis Joseph | L/Cpl | 9796 | 25-Sep-15 | Maidenhead |
| Rowley | Hugh Travers | Capt. | | 1-Jul-16 | |
| Roy | Charles Herbert | Pte | 37726 | 27-May-18 | Birmingham |
| Rudkin | Ernest Harry | Pte | 37867 | 2-Dec-17 | Bourne Lincs |
| Rumble | Joseph William | Cpl | 7743 | 2-Dec-17 | Newport Mon |
| Russell | Bernard | 2/Lt | | 25-Sep-15 | |
| Russell | George William | Pte | 17594 | 1-Jul-16 | Grian Kent |
| Sabey | Albert John | Pte | 17461 | 31-Oct-16 | South Hackney |
| Sage | William Henry | Pte | 42400 | 26-Apr-18 | Bristol |
| Salt | Archibald Newton John | Pte | 203208 | 25-Apr-18 | Hungerford |
| Salt | Richard Henry Gordon | Pte | 37302 | 17-Jan-18 | |
| Samuels | Arthur | Pte | 6309 | 18-Nov-14 | Paddington |
| Sangster | Fergus | L/Cpl | 8171 | 31-Jul-17 | Feltham |
| Sapsford | Arthur Richard | Pte | 10237 | 7-Jul-15 | Bow |

| | | | | | |
|---|---|---|---|---|---|
| Saville | Alfred William | Pte | 8495 | 15-Mar-15 | Ball Common Essex |
| Sayer | Stephen | Pte | 10514 | 14-Sep-16 | Wantage |
| Schneider | Stewart Spearing | 2/Lt | | 1-Jul-16 | |
| Scoles | John | Pte | 33371 | 4-Apr-17 | Plymouth |
| Scott | John William | L/Cpl | 13528 | 17-Aug-17 | Dalston Middx |
| Scouse | Charles | Pte | 8571 | 17-Oct-17 | |
| Searing | Amos Thomas | Pte | 33662 | 2-Apr-18 | Rickmansworth |
| Searle | Arthur | Pte | 27494 | 4-Mar-17 | West Kilburn |
| Sears | Arthur | Pte | 43622 | 25-Apr-18 | Birmingham |
| Searson | Wilfred | Pte | 37428 | 25-Aug-17 | |
| Seed | Walter | Pte | 37768 | 2-Apr-18 | |
| Self | George Thomas | Pte | 17365 | 22-Mar-18 | New Cross |
| Sere | William | Pte | 39250 | 6-Apr-17 | Wood Newton Yorks |
| Sewell | Alfred | Pte | 8453 | 5-Mar-17 | Marlow |
| Sexton | Hugh | Pte | 11996 | 10-Mar-15 | St Albans |
| Seymour | Thomas John | Pte | 19741 | 1-Jul-16 | |
| Seymour | William | Pte | 11472 | 15-Mar-15 | Theale |
| Sharp | John Robert | A/Cpl | 17446 | 16-Aug-17 | |
| Shaw | John Horace | Pte | 9192 | 12-Oct-15 | |
| Sheffield | Roger Edward | Pte | 19723 | 1-Jul-16 | |
| Shepherd | Henry Arthur | Pte | 17690 | 1-Jul-16 | Lambeth |
| Shepherd | Joseph | Cpl | 8350 | 13-Mar-15 | Newbury |
| Shield | John | Pte | 37893 | 11-Jul-17 | Leadgate |
| Shirreff | Francis Gordon | 2/Lt | | 1-Jul-16 | |
| Shirvill | Thomas Henry | Pte | 200220 | 16-Aug-17 | Highbury |
| Sibley | William George | Pte | 9158 | 10-Mar-15 | Cowley |
| Sibun | Edward Charles | Pte | 10240 | 29-May-15 | Borough |
| Silcock | Gerald | Pte | 12984 | 16-Aug-17 | Putney |
| Silver | Albert Hercombe | Pte | 9001 | 22-Mar-15 | |
| Silver | Jack | Pte | 18383 | 17-Jun-16 | Cookham Dean |
| Simmons | Albert | Pte | 12962 | 15-Nov-16 | Kennington |
| Simmons | Frederick Mahone | Cpl | 9829 | 30-Oct-16 | Stonehouse |
| Simmons | Percy John | Pte | 8462 | 1-Jul-16 | East Challow |
| Simmons | Russell Louis Harry | 2/Lt | | 25-Sep-15 | |
| Simpson | Bertie | Pte | 10038 | 29-Jan-15 | Faringdon |
| Simpson | Frederick | Pte | 37460 | 7-Apr-17 | |
| Simpson | Richard | Pte | 38597 | 2-Dec-17 | Alton Hants |
| Sims | Arthur Alfred | Pte | 37257 | 16-Aug-17 | |
| Singers | Frederick Charles | Cpl | 9805 | 2-Apr-18 | Peckham |
| Skelts | Edward William | Pte | 10049 | 10-Jun-15 | Shadwell |
| Skipp | Alfred | Pte | 16789 | 30-Sep-15 | |
| Skippers | Henry Percival | Pte | 9477 | 15-Mar-15 | Buksar India |
| Skitrall | William Lewis | Pte | 203041 | 2-Apr-18 | |
| Slade | Wilfred John | Pte | 19813 | 1-Jul-16 | Twyford |
| Slatter | Victor John | L/Cpl | 9147 | 25-Sep-15 | Abingdon |
| Slaughter | Charles David | Pte | 11805 | 30-Jul-16 | Binfield |
| Sly | Harry | Pte | 9769 | 4-May-15 | Hackney Wick |
| Small | Alfred | Pte | 10153 | 10-Mar-15 | Pangbourne |
| Smewing | Joseph James | Pte | 9145 | 17-Jun-15 | Abingdon |
| Smith | Alfred Edwin | L/Cpl | 8557 | 15-Mar-15 | Wheatley Oxon |
| Smith | Alfred George | Pte | 200175 | 16-Aug-16 | |
| Smith | Arthur Richard | Pte | 9068 | 7-Apr-15 | Hungerford |
| Smith | Francis William | Pte | 9525 | 15-Mar-15 | |
| Smith | Frank | Pte | 10119 | 8-Oct-15 | Newbury |
| Smith | Frederick | Pte | 9903 | 1-Jul-16 | Teddington |
| Smith | George | Pte | 9407 | 12-Mar-15 | |
| Smith | George Ernest | A/Sgt | 17406 | 2-Apr-18 | |

| Smith | George Thomas | Pte | 15810 | 9-May-15 | Reading |
|---|---|---|---|---|---|
| Smith | Halford Charles | A/Cpl | 14038 | 16-Aug-17 | Clapton |
| Smith | Harold | Pte | 34158 | 27-Apr-18 | |
| Smith | Harry | Pte | 220087 | 2-Apr-18 | Long Eaton Derbyshire |
| Smith | Harry Robert | L/Cpl | 8659 | 24-May-15 | Oxford |
| Smith | Herbert William | A/Sgt | 7973 | 24-Jul-16 | Dover |
| Smith | James Edward | L/Cpl | 13838 | 1-Jul-16 | Stoke Newington |
| Smith | James Henry | Pte | 38603 | 29-Apr-18 | Leamington |
| Smith | Louis | Pte | 8538 | 30-Oct-16 | Ramsbury |
| Smith | Richard George | Pte | 50676 | 8-Sep-18 | |
| Smith | Sidney Walter | Pte | 23662 | 5-Mar-17 | |
| Smith | Victor Robert | Pte | 11775 | 25-Sep-15 | Crowthorne |
| Smith | William | L/Cpl | 9774 | 15-Mar-15 | Holloway |
| Smith | William George | Sgt | 7784 | 15-Mar-15 | |
| Snell | Alfred James | Pte | 11546 | 9-May-15 | Peckham |
| Snooks | Richard Charles | Pte | 11554 | 12-May-15 | East Dulwich |
| Soans | Augustus Frederick | L/Cpl | 10805 | 5-Mar-17 | Enfield |
| Somerville | Ernest George | L/Cpl | 37268 | 23-Oct-16 | Maidenhead |
| Somner | Ernest | Pte | 15859 | 9-May-15 | Welwyn Garden City |
| Southern | Phillip | Pte | 12030 | 2-Apr-18 | |
| Southgate | George | Pte | 8634 | 25-Sep-15 | Leyton Essex |
| Spake | Richard Henry | Pte | 19785 | 11-Apr-17 | Itchin Hants |
| Sparkes | Frederick William James | Pte | 202790 | 1-Aug-17 | |
| Sparkes | Victor | L/Cpl | 9812 | 25-Sep-15 | Camberley |
| Speller | James | Pte | 9862 | 25-Sep-15 | Ealing |
| Spicer | Edward | Pte | 36453 | 16-Aug-17 | Welwyn |
| Spriggs | Augustus Henry | Pte | 11982 | 10-Mar-15 | Winchester |
| Stacey | Gilbert Rexworthy | Pte | 21902 | 18-Sep-18 | Bristol |
| Stacey | William | L/Cpl | 10877 | 22-May-16 | Hungerford |
| Stagg | James Henry | Pte | 37307 | 4-Feb-17 | Woolhampton |
| Staley | Frederick James | Pte | 37617 | 27-Apr-18 | |
| Staley | George Henry | Pte | 37616 | 4-Mar-17 | Hillesden |
| Staniland | Arthur Ernest | Pte | 37618 | 2-Apr-18 | |
| Stark | Alfred | Sgt | 8708 | 28-Oct-16 | Southgate |
| Starmer | Frederick | Pte | 9550 | 27-Nov-15 | Southwark |
| Steel | Albert Henry | Pte | 10030 | 15-Mar-15 | Ardington |
| Steele | Albert | Pte | 10262 | 25-Sep-15 | Stratfield Turgis |
| Stephens | George Charles | Pte | 201834 | 14-Jun-18 | Horfield |
| Stephens | William | L/Cpl | 45288 | 23-Sep-18 | |
| Stephenson | Arthur | Pte | 11438 | 4-Apr-17 | Shepherds Bush |
| Stephenson | James | Pte | 16222 | 1-Jul-16 | Preston |
| Stevens | Joseph William | Pte | 18826 | 24-Mar-18 | |
| Stevens | William | Pte | 38609 | 3-Jan-18 | Bethnal Green |
| Stimpson | Thomas Henry | L/Cpl | 8403 | 1-Jul-16 | Sutton Courtenay |
| Stirling | Colin Robert Hoste | Lt-Col. | | 29-May-18 | |
| Stirrat | Quintin | Pte | 37869 | 1-Aug-17 | Glasgow |
| Stocking | George | Pte | 17436 | 14-Mar-16 | Bermondsey |
| Stokes | Henry Jesse | Pte | 37465 | 16-Aug-17 | Dundee |
| Stokes | John Hill | Capt. | | 22-Mar-15 | |
| Stone | Owen | Pte | 8535 | 15-Oct-15 | Hackney |
| Stott | Arthur | L/Cpl | 19700 | 1-Jul-16 | Highbury |
| Strange | Frank | Pte | 44906 | 27-May-18 | Yate |
| Strangeward | Sidney George | Pte | 27465 | 1-Jul-16 | Huntingdon |
| Streak | Howard William | Pte | 41470 | 11-Jun-18 | |

| | | | | | |
|---|---|---|---|---|---|
| Street | William John | Pte | 16835 | 25-Sep-15 | Newbury |
| Stroud | Leonard | Pte | 16342 | 25-Sep-15 | Kintbury |
| Stroud | Thomas | Pte | 9759 | 10-Dec-14 | Marlow |
| Stubbs | Frank | CSM | 8204 | 1-Jul-16 | Lavant |
| Styche | Walter | L/Cpl | 12043 | 25-Mar-18 | Paddington |
| Styles | Arthur Bertram | L/Cpl | 11922 | 2-Apr-18 | |
| Sumpster | William John | Pte | 203227 | 22-Mar-18 | Sandhurst |
| Sutton | Richard Charles | Pte | 38610 | 13-Aug-18 | Seaton |
| Swain | Albert | Pte | 9727 | 25-Sep-15 | |
| Swain | Arthur | Pte | 18365 | 25-Sep-15 | Walsall |
| Swain | Edward George | Pte | 15719 | 1-Jul-16 | Newbury |
| Syrett | Harry | L/Cpl | 9338 | 16-Aug-17 | Swindon |
| Tabb | Leonard Stanley | Pte | 43577 | 21-Mar-18 | St Colomb |
| Tame | Alfred | L/Cpl | 9054 | 9-May-15 | |
| Tame | John | Pte | 12793 | 16-Aug-17 | Windsor |
| Tame | William George | A/Cpl | 8265 | 9-May-15 | Windsor |
| Tanner | Ewart William | L/Cpl | 34765 | 11-Jun-18 | |
| Tarry | William Ernest | Pte | 9877 | 14-Mar-15 | Twyford |
| Taunton | George | L/Cpl | 17065 | 11-Jun-18 | Vauxhall |
| Taylor | Albert Edward | Pte | 8277 | 10-Mar-15 | |
| Taylor | Albert Howard | Pte | 22144 | 12-Mar-17 | |
| Taylor | Albert Victor | L/Cpl | 5805 | 9-May-15 | East Dulwich |
| Taylor | Alfred James | Sgt | 8996 | 2-Aug-16 | Ufton |
| Taylor | Charles Cecil | Pte | 8147 | 9-May-15 | High Wycombe |
| Taylor | Charles David | Pte | 8712 | 14-Mar-15 | North Kensington |
| Taylor | Ernest | Pte | 27455 | 16-Aug-17 | West Gorton Lancs |
| Taylor | Ernest Henry | Pte | 11849 | 1-Jul-16 | |
| Taylor | Francis | Pte | 36797 | 2-Dec-17 | |
| Taylor | Robert | Pte | 37309 | 11-Nov-16 | Newbury |
| Taylor | Victor George | Cpl | 27498 | 28-Aug-16 | Fareham |
| Taylor | William | Pte | 19497 | 31-Jul-17 | Ashampstead |
| Taylor | William George | A/Cpl | 16026 | 1-Jul-16 | Theale |
| Tebbutt | Henry Edward | Pte | 38662 | 27-Apr-18 | |
| Tedder | Ernest | Pte | 8687 | 15-Jul-16 | Feltham |
| Tedder | Matthew | L/Cpl | 9567 | 25-Sep-15 | Feltham |
| Terrett | Henry | Pte | 45444 | 29-Aug-18 | |
| Thatcher | Hubert Archibald | Pte | 37310 | 28-Oct-16 | Newbury |
| Thatcher | Walter | Cpl | 37644 | 16-Aug-17 | Maidenhead |
| Thomas | Albert Edward | Cpl | 6547 | 25-Sep-15 | Battersea |
| Thomas | Alfred Benjamin | Pte | 46626 | 14-Oct-18 | |
| Thomas | Richard Francis | Pte | 37639 | 16-Aug-17 | |
| Thompson | Arthur Gerald | Pte | 37819 | 16-Aug-17 | Blackheath Kent |
| Thompson | William Edward | Pte | 36861 | 31-May-18 | |
| Thorn | George | Pte | 25888 | 4-Apr-17 | |
| Thorne | George Frederick | L/Cpl | 8874 | 1-Jul-16 | Edmonton |
| Thorne | John | Pte | 36481 | 16-Aug-17 | |
| Thurmer | Ernest Thomas | Pte | 9566 | 9-May-15 | Winkfield |
| Tigwell | Thomas | Pte | 8394 | 25-Oct-14 | Burghfield |
| Titchener | Edward William | Pte | 17037 | 28-Mar-17 | Faringdon |
| Toates | Alfred John | Pte | 19771 | 1-Jul-16 | Impington Cambs |
| Todd | Ralph | Pte | 11316 | 4-Feb-15 | Bracknell |
| Toms | William Locke | L/Cpl | 9904 | 10-Mar-15 | London |
| Townley | Arnold | Pte | 33344 | 4-Mar-17 | Edgbaston |
| Townsend | Arthur | Pte | 8892 | 25-Sep-15 | Highclere |
| Townsend | William Joseph | Pte | 11980 | 9-May-15 | Highbury |
| Townson | Alfred | L/Cpl | 38226 | 11-Jun-18 | Eastbourne |
| Trenfield | Cecil | Pte | 11512 | 2-Jun-15 | Newick Sussex |

| Trim | Frank | L/Cpl | 9349 | 25-Sep-15 | Aberkenfig Glam |
|---|---|---|---|---|---|
| Trimmer | Jonah William | Sgt | 9311 | 1-Jul-16 | Gimshall |
| Trolove | Gerald Egrament | Pte | 37884 | 31-Jul-17 | Leicester |
| Trotter | Ronald Herbert Gillet | Lieut | | 25-Sep-15 | |
| Troup | Stewart Houghton | Lieut | | 2-Dec-17 | |
| Truckle | Thomas Frederick | Pte | 38269 | 2-Dec-17 | East Grinstead |
| Trulock | George Edward | Pte | 6230 | 30-Oct-16 | Canning Town |
| Tucker | Alfred Arthur | Pte | 42414 | 11-Jun-18 | |
| Turner | George | Pte | 5638 | 9-May-15 | Maidenhead |
| Turner | Horace | Pte | 5586 | 25-Sep-15 | Newbury |
| Turner | Michael Henry | Cpl | 10303 | 30-Jan-17 | Uckfield |
| Tustain | Harold John | L/Cpl | 12285 | 10-Apr-18 | |
| Tuttle | Edward John | Pte | 10350 | 31-Jul-17 | Sulhampstead |
| Twiddy | Ernest Edward | Pte | 19687 | 1-Jul-16 | Narborough |
| Upstone | George Frederick | Pte | 202386 | 16-Aug-17 | Mortimer |
| Varnell | Samuel George | Pte | 22274 | 4-Mar-17 | Maidenhead |
| Venn | Henry | Sgt | 7951 | 17-Mar-15 | Bagshot |
| Vesey | James | Lieut | | 25-Sep-15 | |
| Vince | Frank | Pte | 9697 | 7-Apr-15 | Bracknell |
| Vipan | Charles | Pte | 37451 | 17-Oct-17 | Barnett |
| Vockins | Albert Edward | Pte | 8458 | 6-Jan-15 | Hungerford |
| Wade | Ernest Alfred | L/Cpl | 11070 | 16-Aug-17 | |
| Wadhams | Phillip Douglas | Pte | 21917 | 2-Aug-17 | |
| Wagstaff | Walter | Pte | 39260 | 27-Apr-18 | |
| Wait | Herbert Alfred Vincent | 2/Lt | | 2-Dec-17 | |
| Waite | Albert Edward | Pte | 37312 | 4-Apr-17 | |
| Waite | Ernest Steven | Pte | 16372 | 25-Sep-15 | Fawley Bucks |
| Waite | Frederick Charles | L/Cpl | 6510 | 25-Sep-15 | Henley on Thames |
| Wakely | Frederick John | Pte | 38243 | 1-Dec-17 | Wimbledon |
| Walder | Percy Louis | L/Cpl | 20652 | 17-Oct-17 | Shepherds Bush |
| Walker | Cyril Francis Stanley | Pte | 45493 | 21-Sep-18 | Witney |
| Walker | Ernest | L/Cpl | 8471 | 1-Jul-16 | Oxford |
| Walker | George James | Pte | 9675 | 12-Jun-15 | |
| Walker | Henry George | Pte | 17422 | 1-Jul-16 | |
| Walker | Henry Scott | L/Cpl | 8503 | 26-Dec-16 | |
| Wall | Leslie | Pte | 14673 | 15-Aug-15 | West Bromwich |
| Wallen | James | Pte | 22549 | 5-Mar-17 | |
| Walley | Arthur | Pte | 33424 | 2-Apr-18 | |
| Walley | Henry | L/Cpl | 9048 | 10-Mar-15 | |
| Walley | Thomas Charles | Pte | 42418 | 27-May-18 | St Gluvias |
| Wallin | George | Pte | 9344 | 17-Mar-15 | Cookham |
| Walters | Royland Henry | Pte | 13016 | 2-May-18 | |
| Ward | Dudley Beaumont | Pte | 37314 | 5-Mar-17 | Windsor |
| Ward | Harry James | Pte | 10005 | 27-Sep-15 | Fulham |
| Ward | Walter | Pte | 19110 | 16-Aug-17 | |
| Ware | William Henry | Pte | 203634 | 16-Aug-17 | |
| Wareham | John Arthur | Pte | 33408 | 27-May-18 | Custom House Essex |
| Warman | Alfred George | L/Cpl | 8778 | 25-Sep-15 | Acton |
| Warmington | Abel Frederick | Pte | 50673 | 4-Jul-18 | Wolvercote |
| Warner | William | Sgt | 7427 | 15-Mar-15 | Faringdon |
| Warren | Frederick James | Pte | 19014 | 1-Jul-16 | Twyford |
| Warrwick | Stanley | Pte | 7247 | 5-Mar-17 | Penge |
| Washington | Sidney James | Pte | 9536 | 9-May-15 | Hammersmith |
| Waters | Arthur George | CSM | 5575 | 24-Jul-16 | North Moreton |
| Watkins | Thomas | 2/Lt | | 9-May-15 | |

| | | | | | |
|---|---|---|---|---|---|
| Watkinson | Herbert | Pte | 33734 | 18-Mar-18 | Cranleigh Surrey |
| Watmough | Ernest | Pte | 36942 | 11-Jun-18 | |
| Watson | Cedric Gordon | Lieut | | 9-May-15 | |
| Watson | Frederick William | Pte | 19378 | 1-Jul-16 | Kentish Town |
| Watts | Charles Clifford | Pte | 37882 | 31-Jul-17 | Wednesbury |
| Watts | Fred | A/Sgt | 8341 | 9-May-15 | Baulking |
| Watts | Leonard | Pte | 16356 | 1-Jul-16 | Inkpen |
| Watts | Richard Horace | Pte | 19820 | 1-Jul-16 | |
| Wayman | George Thomas | Pte | 11548 | 11-May-15 | Dulwich |
| Wayman | Walter Andrew | Pte | 12790 | 17-Oct-17 | |
| Wear | Ernest | Pte | 37646 | 1-Aug-17 | Stroud |
| Webb | Albert William | Cpl | 8999 | 1-Jul-16 | Blewbury |
| Webb | Bertie Thomas | Pte | 10053 | 25-Sep-15 | Cippenham |
| Webb | Edgar George | Pte | 8637 | 1-Jul-16 | Blewbury |
| Webb | Frederick Jacob | Pte | 9162 | 1-Jul-16 | Troveyrhew Glam |
| Webb | Harold Claude | L/Cpl | 38134 | 22-Feb-19 | |
| Webb | Harry | L/Cpl | 8364 | 25-Oct-16 | Binfield |
| Webb | Sidney | Pte | 45471 | 29-Sep-18 | Redditch |
| Webb | Sidney Ernest | L/Cpl | 15744 | 2-Dec-17 | Clewer |
| Webber | Albert Frank | Pte | 20225 | 1-Jul-16 | Ilford |
| Webber | Charles | L/Cpl | 10838 | 25-Apr-18 | |
| Webber | Ernest George Claude | Pte | 38621 | 16-May-18 | |
| Webber | William Henry | Pte | 42423 | 27-Apr-18 | |
| Webster | Edward Mackay | 2/Lt | | 1-Aug-16 | |
| Weddle | Thomas Henry | L/Cpl | 8083 | 15-Mar-15 | |
| Welch | John William | L/Cpl | 37349 | 1-Aug-17 | |
| Welch | William James | Pte | 9768 | 17-Nov-14 | Wantage |
| Weller | James William | Pte | 9791 | 28-Feb-15 | Worcester Park |
| Wells | Alfred | Pte | 37621 | 3-Mar-17 | Bradford Yorks |
| Wells | Frederick James | A/Sgt | 6590 | 27-Oct-16 | Barton Lancs |
| Wells | Louis Conrad | 2/Lt | | 31-Mar-18 | |
| Wender | William Cuthbert | Sgt | 9747 | 18-Feb-18 | Victoria |
| West | Alfred Henry | Pte | 27488 | 4-Jul-16 | Woolston Hants |
| West | Arthur | L/Cpl | 8472 | 1-Jul-16 | Hull |
| West | Gilbert | Pte | 9225 | 9-May-15 | Pamber |
| West | Henry | Pte | 37316 | 30-Jan-17 | Maidenhead |
| Westall | Jesse James | Pte | 30008 | 17-Oct-17 | Shinfield |
| Westall | William | Pte | 19911 | 1-Jul-16 | Newbury |
| Whale | Frederick Walter | Cpl | 23561 | 4-Mar-17 | |
| Wharton | Percival Charles | Sgt | 8120 | 9-May-15 | Haseley |
| Wheadon | Charles | Pte | 38262 | 3-Jun-18 | |
| Wheeler | Albert | Pte | 8300 | 10-Mar-15 | Thatcham |
| Wheeler | Albert | Sgt | 8377 | 26-Feb-18 | Bagshot |
| Wheeler | Alfred John | Pte | 42426 | 21-Sep-18 | |
| Wheeler | Frederick | Pte | 17724 | 7-Aug-16 | |
| Wheeler | Thomas Alfred | L/Cpl | 9330 | 24-Nov-14 | Abingdon |
| Wheeler | William James | A/Cpl | 8029 | 25-Sep-15 | Sunninghill |
| Whichello | Edgar | Pte | 11738 | 4-Apr-17 | Wallingford |
| White | Charles | Pte | 11592 | 25-Sep-15 | Bethnal Green |
| White | Charles Alfred | Pte | 38626 | 2-Dec-17 | Hackney |
| White | Edward | Sgt | 6972 | 16-Aug-17 | Southsea |
| White | Henry Richard | Cpl | 9620 | 17-Nov-15 | Charlton |
| White | Percy | Pte | 9172 | 27-Apr-15 | Feltham |
| White | Reginald Ernest | Pte | 42427 | 27-May-18 | Chalvey |
| White | William Frederick | Pte | 203048 | 16-Aug-17 | |
| Whitehead | Sydney | Pte | 18363 | 1-Jul-16 | |
| Whitmarsh | Walter | Pte | 203265 | 16-Aug-17 | |
| Whittaker | Alfred | Pte | 7018 | 2-Apr-18 | Durham |

| Whittle | Stanley John | Pte | 37885 | 16-Aug-17 | |
| Whitty | John Henry | L/Cpl | 37878 | 16-Aug-17 | Saitney Ches |
| Wiblin | Harry | L/Cpl | 200314 | 13-Dec-17 | |
| Wickens | Henry George | Pte | 22150 | 5-Mar-17 | Tilehurst |
| Wickens | John | Pte | 16435 | 28-Sep-17 | Shiplake |
| Wickens | Stephen | L/Cpl | 9912 | 25-Sep-15 | Tilehurst |
| Wickens | William | Pte | 16027 | 23-Oct-16 | |
| Wickens | William | Pte | 16680 | 1-Jul-16 | Hounslow |
| Wicks | Charles John | Pte | 17859 | 1-Jul-16 | |
| Wicks | Edward | Pte | 200194 | 20-Aug-17 | |
| Wicks | Edwin | Pte | 37220 | 2-Apr-18 | |
| Wicks | Harry | Pte | 22115 | 31-Jan-17 | |
| Wiggins | Joseph Thomas | Cpl | 17782 | 14-Oct-18 | Harefield |
| Wilde | Ernest William | Pte | 31161 | 2-Apr-18 | |
| Wilkins | Frederick | Pte | 9618 | 20-Sep-14 | Charlton |
| Wilkinson | Arthur James | L/Cpl | 8670 | 28-Oct-16 | Southall |
| Wilkinson | Frederick | Pte | 10061 | 25-Sep-15 | Romford |
| Wilkinson | Leonard Castleton | L/Cpl | 12062 | 2-Dec-16 | Lambeth |
| Wilks | Albert | Pte | 9493 | 25-Sep-15 | |
| Williams | Albert | L/Cpl | 8968 | 25-Sep-15 | East Ilsley |
| Williams | Edward Howard | Pte | 36820 | 2-Apr-18 | Birmingham |
| Williams | Francis James | Pte | 36167 | 18-Sep-18 | |
| Williams | Frederick | Pte | 9101 | 16-Aug-17 | Mortlake |
| Williams | Herbert | Pte | 220092 | 16-Jan-18 | Birkenhead |
| Williams | James | Pte | 11631 | 1-Jul-16 | Hoxton |
| Williams | Roden Noel | Pte | 45239 | 29-Aug-18 | |
| Williams | Thomas | Pte | 42431 | 27-May-18 | |
| Williams | Walter Charles | Pte | 21995 | 24-Oct-16 | |
| Williams | William John | L/Cpl | 5748 | 25-Sep-15 | Burnham |
| Williams | William John | Pte | 42430 | 26-Apr-18 | Bere Alston |
| Willis | Edward Joseph | Pte | 10115 | 15-Mar-15 | Newbury |
| Willis | Frederick | Pte | 9896 | 25-Sep-15 | Binfield |
| Wilson | Arthur | Pte | 11877 | 25-Sep-15 | Binfield |
| Wilson | Cecil William | Pte | 37318 | 4-Mar-17 | Wallingford |
| Wilson | Joseph | Pte | 42433 | 27-May-18 | |
| Wiltshire | Edward | Pte | 38631 | 29-Dec-17 | |
| Wiltshire | Thomas | Pte | 37634 | 8-Mar-17 | |
| Winney | George | L/Cpl | 9570 | 7-Jul-16 | |
| Winsor | Caleb George | L/Cpl | 8252 | 1-Jul-16 | |
| Winter | Albert John | Pte | 43580 | 11-Jun-18 | Bridgewater |
| Winter | William Henry | Pte | 203013 | 19-Feb-18 | |
| Winters | Samuel James | Pte | 27471 | 1-Jul-16 | Portsdown |
| Witham | Joseph Edward | Pte | 17597 | 10-Nov-16 | |
| Witherell | Thomas Edward | Pte | 10173 | 25-Sep-15 | |
| Wolfe | Douglas Robert | Pte | 15876 | 5-Mar-17 | Bracknell |
| Wood | Allen | Pte | 45240 | 23-Sep-18 | Ross |
| Wood | Harry | Pte | 37483 | 2-Dec-17 | Braunston |
| Wood | Herbert Frederick Charles | Pte | 33056 | 2-Dec-17 | Stantonbury |
| Wood | James | Pte | 9108 | 16-Mar-15 | Ealing |
| Woodbridge | Arthur | Pte | 15840 | 25-Sep-15 | |
| Woodland | Oliver Alfred | Pte | 8905 | 9-May-15 | Cove |
| Woodley | Charlie | Pte | 203209 | 19-Jun-18 | Steventon |
| Woodley | Ernest | Pte | 203961 | 9-Aug-18 | Steventon |
| Woodruff | Charles Herbert | L/Cpl | 30646 | 27-Apr-18 | |
| Woods | Alan | Pte | 8447 | 11-Dec-14 | Australia |
| Woods | Charles William | Pte | 8216 | 1-Oct-16 | Clandon |
| Woodward | Joseph | Pte | 9212 | 25-Sep-15 | Birmingham |
| Woodwards | Edward | Pte | 19810 | 15-Sep-16 | Bracknell |
| Wooff | Alfred | Pte | 9762 | 25-Apr-18 | Bethnal Green |

| | | | | | |
|---|---|---|---|---|---|
| Wooster | Edward John | L/Cpl | 6091 | 1-Jul-16 | West Hampstead |
| Wootton | Edward John | L/Cpl | 16384 | 9-Jun-18 | |
| Workman | Thomas Oswell | Pte | 220093 | 30-Jul-17 | Dursley |
| Wright | Edwin George | Pte | 10658 | 1-Jul-16 | Kintbury |
| Wright | Ernest William | Pte | 42434 | 11-Jun-18 | Bedworth |
| Wright | Frederick Stephen | L/Cpl | 37461 | 14-Nov-16 | Beccles |
| Wright | George Edward | Pte | 9405 | 1-Jul-16 | Tiverton Som |
| Wright | Joseph | Pte | 27439 | 16-Aug-17 | |
| Wright | Thomas | 2/Lt | | 1-May-15 | |
| Wyre | Percy | Sgt | 5408 | 25-Sep-15 | |
| Yates | Thomas | Pte | 37485 | 4-Apr-17 | Stretford |
| Yerkiss | Foster | Pte | 37887 | 11-Sep-17 | Colne Yorks |
| York | John Mornington Otto | Pte | 44863 | 27-May-18 | |
| Young | Owen | Pte | 37431 | 15-Nov-16 | Northampton |
| Youngman | Harry | Pte | 37430 | 30-Oct-16 | Mundesley |

# APPENDIX VIII

# THE DELHI DURBAR MEDAL RECIPIENTS

The men of the 2nd Battalion, Royal Berkshire Regiment, who were listed as recipients of the Delhi Durbar Medal in 1911, with their subsequent history, where this is known.

| Surname | Initials | Serial No. | Rank | Note |
|---------|----------|-----------|------|------|
| Addicott | E | 4661 | Sgt | discharged 7/5/19 at end of 2nd period |
| Akers | W | 8111 | Pte | discharged 15 /6/16 unfit |
| Aldworth | C | 9026 | Pte | Allocated Army Number 5328178 |
| Aldworth | T R | | Lt | kia 11/3/15 |
| Aldworth | W | 4693 | QMS | commissioned in Essex Regt 21/2/14, died 21/1/68 |
| Arbuthnot | G H | | Major | served with 5th Btn – appointed town major of Noeux les Mines, died 26/1/52 |
| Baigent | E | 7949 | Pte | kia France 15/9/14 |
| Baigent | M | 7940 | Cpl | discharged 31/3/20 end of 1st period |
| Bailey | A | 8123 | Pte | transferred to MGC 1/1/16 as 16042 |
| Barratt | EA | 8437 | Bandmaster | discharged 9/9/14 after claim for 3 months |
| Barratt | T | 9462 | Bandsman | allocated Army Number 5328251 |
| Beasley | W | 7852 | Pte | discharged 2/6/15 unfit |
| Bedwell | C | 8158 | Pte | transferred to Labour Corps on 30/6/17 as 324198 discharged unfit 12/9/18 |
| Bennett | E | 4638 | Pte | discharged 20/3/19 at end of second period |
| Betteridge | E | 8338 | L/Cpl | transferred to R Warwicks 9/8/15 as 14123 |
| Bevan | W | 7761 | Pte | discharged 31/3/20 end of 1st period |
| Blackford | E | 8181 | Pte | kia France 9/1/15 |
| Blanchard | W | 4009 | Pte | transferred to Labour Corps as 298391 11/7/17 |
| Booker | W | 7813 | L/Sgt | allocated Army Number 5328118 |
| Booth | W | 7399 | Pte | allotted Army Number 5328106 |
| Boult | B | 5383 | Pte | presumed dead 27/5/18 |
| Bretrell | O | 8371 | L/Cpl | kia at Fromelles 9/5/15 |
| Brown | T | 8442 | Pte | Discharged 21/12/14 unfit |
| Buckingham | P | 8627 | Pte | discharged – 26/11/19 end of 1st period |
| Burgess | E | 8070 | Pte | Allocated Army Number – 5328126 |
| Burrows | E | 7882 | Cpl | kia France 16/8/17 |
| Busby | J | 8456 | Pte | kia at Fromelles 9/5/15 |
| Butler | F | 7843 | Pte | kia at Zonnebeke 26/10/14 |
| Cannon | T | 7853 | Pte | discharged – 3/3/20 end of 1st period |

| | | | | |
|---|---|---|---|---|
| Carpenter | J | 7029 | L/Cpl | kia 10/3/15 |
| Cherrill | W | 7830 | Pte | discharged 9/10/18 unfit |
| Childs | C | 7873 | Pte | kia 2/12/17 in France – occupation policemen |
| Christopher | J | 7620 | Bandsman | transferred to Labour Corps on 24/1/18 as 511683 |
| Coles | A | 7936 | Drummer | discharged 31/3/20 end of 1st period |
| Cook | A | 8895 | Pte | dow at Cheltenham 29/5/17 |
| Cook | F | 7506 | Pte | allotted army number 5328108 |
| Cooling | C | 8388 | Pte | kia at Fromelles 9/5/15 |
| Cotton | A | 7083 | Pte | allotted Army Number 5328097 |
| Crombleholme | H | 5927 | Cpl | discharged 14/10/12 at end of engagement |
| Daysh | R | 6378 | Pte | allotted Army Number 5328087 |
| Dewe | M | 5469 | Pte | discharged 5/3/14 recalled and discharged again 28/2/20 at end of 2nd period |
| Dipper | H | 7800 | Pte | discharged – 8/12/14 unfit |
| Drewits | T | 7637 | Pte | discharged 31/3/20 end of 1st period |
| Edwards | J | 8132 | L/Cpl | dow 18/2/15 in France |
| Evans | T | 8513 | Pte | discharged 7/8/16 unfit |
| Farmer | SB | 5117 | Clr Sgt | kia 13/10/15 with 5th Royal Berks |
| Fawcett | C | 7698 | Pte | discharged 26/4/16 unfit |
| Feetham | B | | Lt-Col. | kia 29/3/18 with rank of Major General |
| Fishbourne | M | 7984 | Pte | discharged 31/3/20 end of 1st period |
| Fraser | AJ | | Capt. & Adjt | won MC |
| Goddard | W | 7436 | Pte | kia 29/1/15 |
| Godfrey | C | 4737 | QMS | discharged 24/10/19 end of 2nd engagement |
| Goodenough | W | 8320 | L/Cpl | Allocated Army Number 5328134 |
| Gough | F | 8175 | Pte | kia France 24/8/14 |
| Gough | R | 5423 | Sgt | transferred to R Warwicks as 14122 9/8/15 died 11/12/57 |
| Hackett | T | 8348 | Pte | transferred to RDF 3/3/17 as 29461 |
| Hamilton | A | 8219 | Pte | kia France 9/5/15 |
| Hammond | W | 7493 | Pte | kia 27/4/17 |
| Hancock | A | 7144 | Pte | discharged 31/3/20 at end of 1st period |
| Harding | H | 8876 | L/Cpl | kia at Neuve Chapelle 10/3/15 |
| Harding | M | 7651 | L/Cpl | discharged 31/3/20 end of 1st period |
| Harvey | F | 9035 | L/Cpl | discharged 30/4/16 unfit |
| Hawkins | W | 8041 | Pte | transferred to Devon Regt 12/2/17 |
| Heath | C | 7872 | L/Cpl | kia at Zonnebeke 15/11/14 |
| Heather | J | 8064 | Pte | kia France 4/2/15 |
| Hewitt | G | 8694 | L/Cpl | transferred to 4th Bn 27/10/16 |
| Higgs | L | 6644 | L/Cpl | discharged 10/11/15 end of engagement |
| Hodges | W | 7922 | L/Cpl | Allocated Army Number 5328121 |
| Holmes | E | 8152 | Pte | discharged 31/3/20 end of 1st period |
| Holmes | W | 7913 | L/Cpl | discharged 20/12/16 unfit |
| Horwood | E | 7482 | Pte | discharged 31/3/20 at end of 1st period |
| Huggins | G | 8197 | Pte | discharged 7/10/15 unfit |
| Huggins | T | 8209 | L/Cpl | discharged 31/3/20 end of 1st period |
| Ilsley | F | 7921 | L/Cpl | kia France 10/3/15 |
| Ingram | H | 8285 | Pte | discharged 31/10/17 unfit |
| Inman | G | 7551 | Pte | allotted Army Number 5328111 |
| Jones | M | 8479 | Pte | kia at Fromelles 9/5/15 |
| Keep | W | 7887 | Pte | dow in France 29/5/16 |
| Kelly | G | 7052 | Pte | discharged 12/2/16 rejoined R Berks as 31159 |
| Kew | D | 7931 | Pte | transferred to 4th Bn 29/10/16 as 203021 |

| Kirk | H | 8155 | Pte | discharged 31/3/20 end of 1st period |
|------|---|------|-----|--------------------------------------|
| Laing | S | 5789 | L/Sgt | taken PoW, transferred to 16th Londons as L19594 15/11/19 |
| Lawes | S | 7636 | Pte | discharged 6/2/16 unfit |
| Lawrence | J | 7950 | Pte | kia 9/5/17 |
| Leigh | H | 8912 | Pte | discharged 5/7/16 unfit |
| Lickman | HS | 2431 | Lt QM | commissioned as quartermaster 12/06 |
| Lloyd | A | 6643 | Pte | discharged on 19/11/15 end of engagement reenlisted in Hampshires as D/13620 |
| Lovelock | T | 8631 | Pte | kia at Ovillers 1/7/16 |
| Luker | D | 8325 | Pte | kia France 16/5/15 |
| Luty | A | 8393 | Pioneer Sgt | kia France 4/4/16 |
| Macy | WC | 5460 | Sgt | discharged 5/1/20 at end of 2nd period |
| Matthews | H | 7896 | Pte | discharged 20/4/16 unfit |
| Mills | E | 8983 | Pte | kia France 29/7/15 |
| Morgan | F | 6104 | Pte | discharged 21/3/13 end of engagement |
| Newman | H | 7387 | Drummer | discharged 2/1/15 unfit |
| Oakley | W | 8022 | Pte | discharged 31/3/20 end of 1st period |
| Painter | T | 7851 | Pte | kia at Cuinchy 15/4/15 |
| Parker | F | 6365 | Pte | died of tetanus at Leicester 24/3/15 |
| Pash | T | 8322 | Pte | transferred to RGA 1/1/14 as 40430 |
| Pearce | F | 8037 | Pte | kia at Ovillers 1/7/16 |
| Phillips | A | 8477 | L/Cpl | kia at Fromelles 9/5/15 |
| Platt | C | 9262 | L/Cpl | Allocated Army Number 5328218 |
| Price | P | 8336 | L/Cpl | discharged 3/7/16 unfit |
| Quick | HT | 2769 | Sgt Maj | commissioned as 2/Lt 5/11/14, died 1961 |
| Reeley | H | 8576 | L/Cpl | Allocated Army Number 5328147 |
| Robinson | E | 8214 | L/Cpl | discharged 15/4/13 unfit |
| Rose | C | 7958 | Pte | transferred to Rifle Brigade 12/12/16 |
| Rose | T | 7559 | L/Cpl | allotted Army Number 5328112 |
| Samuels | A | 6309 | Pte | kia 18/11/14 |
| Saunders | A | 7861 | Pte | discharged 31/3/20 end of 1st period |
| Savidge | A | 5436 | Pte | transferred to RE 27/4/16 as 35666 |
| Sheppard | J | 8350 | L/Cpl | dow in France 13/3/16 |
| Sherwood | F | 8424 | Pte | discharged 31/3/20 end of 1st period |
| Shilton | W | 7930 | L/Cpl | discharged 28/4/20 unfit |
| Sibley | W | 9158 | Pte | kia at Neuve Chapelle 10/3/15 |
| Siney | F | 9277 | Pte | Allocated Army Number 5328223 |
| Smith | G | 7087 | Pte | purchased discharge for £18 on 17/7/13 |
| Smith | P | 8068 | Pte | kia at Gheluveldt 1/11/14 |
| Smith | S | 7894 | Pte | discharged on 31/3/20 end of 1st period |
| Smith | V | 8406 | Cpl | Allocated Army Number 5328141, PoW |
| Spencer | A | 6016 | Pte | discharged 23/3/16 unfit |
| Stallwood | D | 7928 | Pte | kia at Zonnebeke 26/10/14 |
| Stannard | A | 6243 | Pte | discharged 5/8/20 unfit |
| Steele | O | | Capt. | kia 25/10/14 |
| Sturgess | T | 8097 | Pte | kia at Salonika 25/9/16 |
| Sturgess | W | 7946 | Pte | discharged on 21/8/20 end of 1st period |
| Talbot | A | 8489 | Pte | discharged on 5/10/16 unfit |
| Taylor | C | 8118 | L/Cpl | Allocated Army Number 5328127 |
| Taylor | W | 3597 | Sgt Drummer | discharged on 9/2/20 as surplus to requirement |
| Thorpe | C | 3768 | Pte | discharged unfit on 26/7/16 |
| Townsend | A | 8892 | Pte | kia at Loos 25/9/15 |
| Turner | W | 8431 | Pte | discharged on 22/4/16 unfit |
| Walters | W | 8685 | Pte | transferred to Labour Corps on 16/10/17 as 413448 |

| Waring | G | 7897 | Pte | kia at Festubert 9/1/15 |
| Warner | C | 9011 | Pte | discharged on 30/6/16 unfit |
| Warner | R | 5276 | Band Sgt | transferred to Labour Corps as 413456 29/1/18 |
| Watts | F | 8341 | L/Cpl | kia at Fromelles 9/5/15 |
| Webb | A | 8999 | L/Cpl | kia at Ovillers 1/7/16 |
| Wells | T | 3977 | Sgt Cook | discharged on 18/1/19 end of engagement, died 12/3/58 |
| Woodage | F | 8230 | L/Cpl | transferred to Labour Corps 29/10/17 as 456894 |
| Woodland | O | 8905 | L/Cpl | kia at Fromelles 9/5/15 |
| Woodley | A | 6548 | Pte | discharged 17/6/15 end of engagement |

# PRINCIPAL SOURCES

*Official History of the Great War* (France and Belgium), J.E. Edmunds (1928)

*The Eighth Division in War 1914-1918*, J H Boraston and C.E. Bax (1926)

*The Royal Berkshire Regiment Vol.2*, F. Loraine Petrie (1922)

*Old Soldier Sahib*, Frank Richards

War Diaries (2nd Royal Berks, 25th Brigade, 8th Division), together with associated operational orders

Cabinet Papers at National Archives (CAB45/132-138)

Medal Rolls at National Archives (WO329)

*The Land-locked Lake*, A.A. Hanbury-Sparrow (1932)

*The Last of the Ebb*, S. Rogerson (1937).

*No Man's Land*, J. Toland (1980)

*General Jack's Diary*, edited by J. Terraine (1964)

*The First Day of the Somme*, M. Middlebrook (1971)

*Somme*, Lyn MacDonald

*Passchendaele – The Day by Day Account*, C. McCarthy (1995)

*British Regiments 1914-18*, E. James (1974)

*Berkshire and the War*

*The Times History of the War*

*War Illustrated News*

*China Dragon (The Journal of the Royal Berkshire Regiment)*

*The Regimental Journal of the Duke of Edinburgh's Royal Regiment*

*Berkshire Chronicle*

*Maidenhead Advertiser*

*Newbury Weekly News*

*Reading Mercury*

*Reading Standard*

*Oxford Journal*

*North Berkshire Herald*

Michelin Maps of France

Various personal papers and diaries

# INDEX

Note that certain entries are grouped - see Battles, Books, Cemeteries and Memorials, Diseases, Pastimes, Royal Family, Ships, Weapons. The forces of individual nations are grouped under the nation in the sequence Higher formations, Corps, Divisions, Regiments, other units We have not indexed either the Roll of Honour or the Delhi Durbar Medal Roll

Place-name spelling in official and unofficial documentation of the period is very variable. We have taken spellings from Michelin's touring and motorist atlas which covers the whole of France and a good bit of Belgian Flanders. For technical reasons, French accents are not included within the index although they are within the main body of text.

If you are interested in purchasing other books published by Tempus, or in case you have difficulty finding any Tempus books in your local bookshop, you can also place orders directly through our website

www.tempus-publishing.com